THE MILITIA
OF
WASHINGTON COUNTY
VIRGINIA

1777–1835

Officers 1777–1835

Militia Men 1798–1835

Gerald H. Clark

Heritage Books
2023

HERITAGE BOOKS
AN IMPRINT OF HERITAGE BOOKS, INC.

Books, CDs, and more—Worldwide

For our listing of thousands of titles see our website
at
www.HeritageBooks.com

A Facsimile Reprint
Published 2023 by
HERITAGE BOOKS, INC.
Publishing Division
5810 Ruatan Street
Berwyn Heights, MD 20740

Originally published 1979

International Standard Book Number
Paperbound: 978-0-7884-7793-5

INTRODUCTION

The militia system, the concept of a militarily armed and trained citizenry, existed in Virginia for over 250 years. During that period, all free, white males, except millers, ministers and a few other specified persons, were required to be enrolled for most of their adult lives in the militia company in the bounds of which they resided, and were required to provide themselves with a serviceable gun and other accouterments.

The two indices that follow are a part of a broader study of the militia of Washington County, Virginia, over the period, 1785-1835. Because of the convenient access to the L.P. Summers publication of Washington Coudnty Court Minute Book No. 1 in his <u>ANNALS OF SOUTHWEST VIRGINIA</u>, the militia information therein is included here, giving these indices a span of the years 1777-1835, inclusive. These indices are intended as a summary view of the militia service of all officers and militia men of the county during this period, to the extent that a record of such service is preserved. These indices are also intended as a guide to the sources of the manuscript material from which they have been compiled.

MILITIA OFFICERS SOURCES

1. WASHINGTON COUNTY, VIRGINIA COURT MINUTE BOOK NO. 1, spanning the period 28 January 1777 through 17 August 1784. Dates prior to 1785, appearing in the index, are from the Summer's book, excepting only the 1784 references to Aaron Lewis and William Edmiston, "about removing to North Carolina", which references are from the Executive Papers - Militia.

2. THE EXECUTIVE PAPERS - MILITIA FOR WASHINGTON COUNTY, VIRGINIA 1785-1835, inclusive, filed by year in the Archives Department, Virginia State Library, in Richmond. These papers are the principal source of the information contained in this index, and they consist of:

a. Copies of Washington County court orders recommending officers of the militia line, to the year 1830 when the court ceased to have any authority in naming militia officers. (Except for Court Minute Book No. 2, spanning the period 19 Jan 1819 through 19 Jul 1821, the originals of these court orders were lost, if the tradition is true, when the courthouse was burned in 1864.) "Recommendations" appearing in the index are from these court orders unless otherwise indicated.

b. Correspondence and reports originating in Washington County and addressed to the Governor, Council of State or Adjutant General of Virginia.

c. Certifications of elections of officers in the so-called volunteer companies that proliferated after the year 1799. After the year 1829, all militia officers were elected by the men of the unit involved. (The court made a final recommendation of Officers on 18 May 1830, but it is doubted that these recommendations were sustained.)

d. Muster Rolls and Officer lists, to the extent that these are preserved.

3. THE UNFILED MILITIA FINES LISTS FOR WASHINGTON COUNTY, identified in the Archives Department, Virgini State Library, as Auditor's Item No. 159. The peritinenet preserved lists are as follows:

70th Regiment - The years 1798 through 1835, except for the years 1808 and 1828.

105th Regiment - From its formation in 1799 through the year 1835.

In general, only "muster fines" assessed while the individual was an officer are shown here. Muster fines assessed against militiamen, including men who had been or later became officers, is the principal basis of the Militia Men Index of Washington County.

MILITIA MEN INDEX

The principal purpose of this index of militia men is to identify to the extent permited by the preserved record, the militia unit or units in which the named persons served. It is estimated that about 60% of the militia men who served during the period, 1798-1835, are so identified.

Under the militia laws of Virginia, during most of the years encompassed by this index, it was required that all militia men attend four company musters, one battalion muster and one regimental muster in each year. Failure to attend any one of these musters without a valid excuse resulted in the assessment of a seventy -five cent fine, levied by the regimental court of enquiry that sat in November of each year. Lists of these fines were given to the county sheriff for collection the following year. On the orders of the same courts of enquiry, the sheriff made disbursements from the funds arrising from these fines to meet the prescribed operating expenses of the county militia. The sheriff was required by law to make an exact accounting to the state auditor of public accounts of both his collection and disbursement of these funds. Thus it is that the annual lists of militia fines for Washington and the other counties of Virginia are preserved in the Virginia State Archives.

Unfiled, these lists and related papers are identified in the Archives Department of the Virginia STate Library as Auditor's Item No. 159. For Washington County, the pertinent preserved lists are as follows:

70th Regiment - the years 1798-1835, except for the years 1808 and 1828, which appear to be lost.

105th Regiment - From its formation in 1799 through the year 1835. (Legibility of the year 1831 is very poor.)

Additionally, among the filed Executive Papers - Militia, in the Archives Department of the Virginia State Library, there are preserved six muster rolls of "volunteer" companies that were a part of the Washington County Militia at different times. The men appearing on these rolls are included in this index. The rolls are listed as follows:

A New Rifle Company, 1st Batt., 70th Reg. 1807.

Troop of Cavalry, 1st Batt., 105th Reg., 1809.

Light Infantry Company, 1st Batt., 105th Reg., 1809.

Rifle Company, 2nd Batt., 105th Reg., 1809.

Artillery Company, 105th Reg., 1815.

Rifle Company, 1st Batt., 105th Reg., 1829.

The data presented here reflects the constant interplay of the changing militia laws and changes in the county population and boundaries. Also reflected is the very uncertain movement of communications between Washington County and the State Capitol in Richmond over the many years.

The most frequently used spelling of names is used here without regard for what might now be the preferred spelling. The use of the expression "not seen" signifies a missing earlier document, of which there are many, particularly during the earlier years and during the War of 1812.

Gerald H. Clark
Bristol, Tennessee
1979

DIVISION OF MILITIA

In the beginning there was Augusta County that was formed from Orange County in 1738 and comprised all of the territory from the Blue Ridge Mountain to Wisconsin and the Mississippi River. This county was broken into several other counties, i.e. Botetourt in 1769, Montgomery in 1776 and Washington in 1776. From Washington County territory other areas were established:

Russell 1785
Grayson 1792-1793
Lee 1792-1793
Tazewell 1799
Scott 1814

As the counties were established, the 70th was broken into the 78th for Grayson, 72nd for Russell, 105th Washington, 112th for Tazewell and the 124th for Scott. During the earlier period, the names found in Washington County will be found later in these other counties.

In 1798, the militia of Washington County had increased sufficiently to justify the division of the 70th Regiment to create a second regiment in the county, designated the 105th Regiment. In compliance with the request of Governor James Wood, the county court convened on 20 March 1799, for the purpose of dividing the 70th Regiment, which was done in this way:

The First Battalion of the 70th Regiment would be composed of the companies of William Rowan, Sabeus Main, John Edmondson and Patrick Campbell. The Second Battalion of the 70th Regiment would be composed of the companies of Charles Tate, Francis Preston, Berry Caywood, Abram Hayter, Jr. and Samuel Meek.

The First Battalion of the newly formed 105th Regiment would be composed of the companies of James Keys, Alexander Doran and James Vance. The Second Battalion of the 105th Regiment would be composed of the Companies of Matthew Willoughby, Robert Hensley, Elijah Gillenwaters and Samuel Hensley.

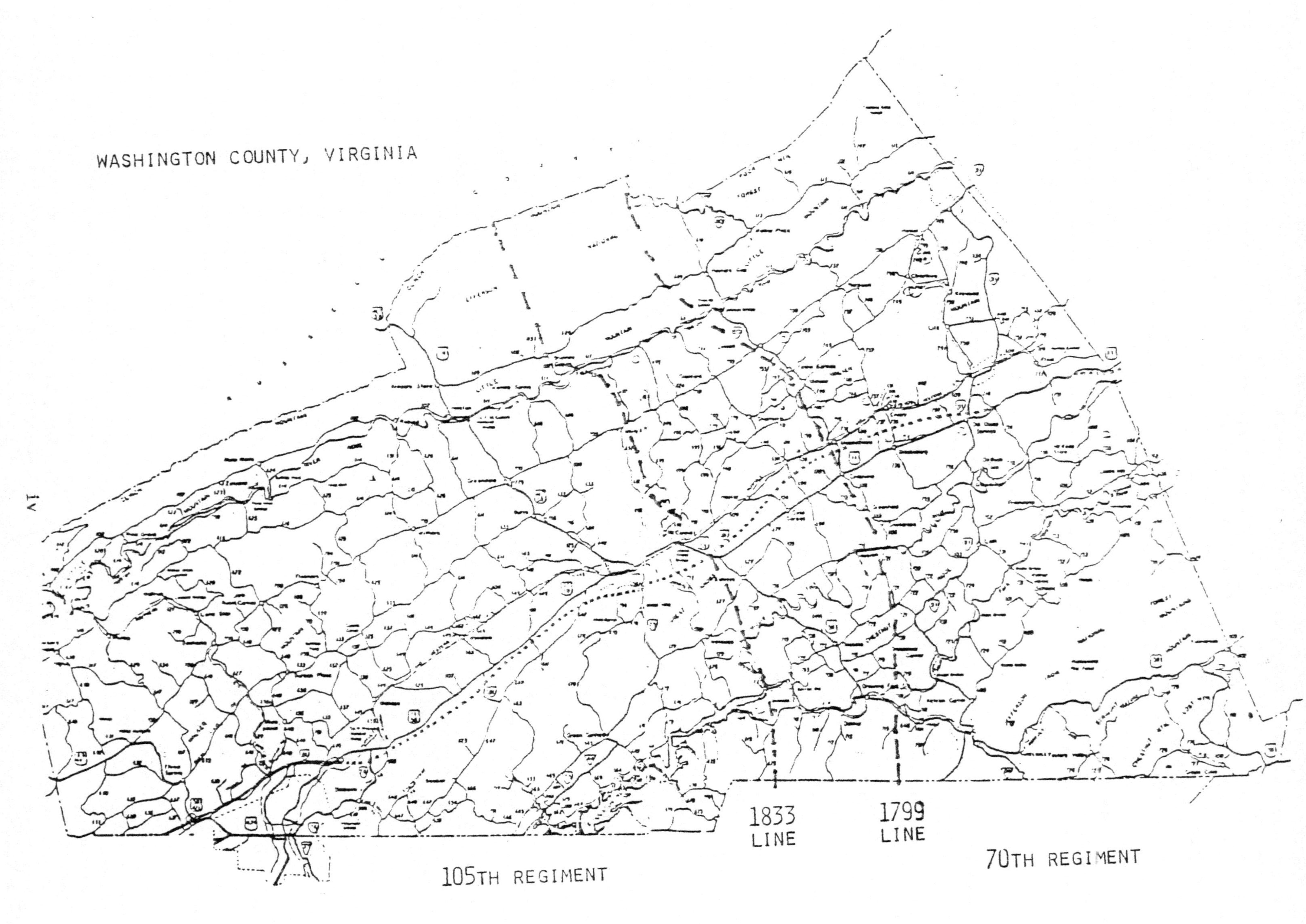
WASHINGTON COUNTY, VIRGINIA
1833
LINE
1799
LINE
105TH REGIMENT
70TH REGIMENT

****

ACKLIN, JAMES V.
- Selected 2nd Lieut., Volunteer Company of Rifleman, 1st Batt., 105th Reg., 15 Sep 1807.
- Commission as 2nd Lieut. of Riflemen 5 Oct 1807, per Officer Roll, 105th Reg., 1808.
- Muster fine, "2nd Lieut." - 105th Reg.,1809, $2.00.
- Muster fine, "Lieut.", 105th Reg., 1811, $3.00.

ACKLIN, JOHN R.
- Recommended Ensign in Capt. Robert Craig's Company of Infantry, 1st Batt., 105th Reg., in the room of James Redpath, removed, 17 Jun 1800.
- Removed; replaced as Ensign by James Bailey, 19 Jun 1804.
- Selected 1st Lieut., Volunteer Company of Riflemen, 1st Batt., 105th Reg., 15 Sep 1807.
- Commissioned as 1st Lieut. of Riflemen 5 Oct 1807, per Officer Roll, 105th Reg.,1808.
- Muster fines (2), "1st Lieut.",105th Reg., 1809, $5.00.
- Muster fine "Lieut.", 105th Reg., 1811, $4.00.

ADAMS, GEORGE
- Recommended Captain, Washington County Militia, 26 Feb 1777.
- Commissioned 12 May 1777.
- Took Oath of Office 19 Aug 1778.

ADAMS, JOE
- Elected 2nd Lieut., 70th Reg., 18 Apr 1835.

ADAMS, JOSHUA
- Recommended Ensign, 70th Reg., in the room of John Anderson, resigned 17 May 1803.
- Resigned; replaced as Ensign by Robinson Gannaway, 20 May 1806.

ALLEN, JAMES
- Recommended Ensign, Company of Riflemen, 70th Reg., in the room of Andrew Patterson promoted, 21 May 1811.
- Earlier recommendation not seen but because he resigned, replaced as Lieut. by James Meek, Jr., 16 May 1815.

ALLEN, JOHN
- Elected Ensign, Rifle Company, 70th Reg., 1 Jan 1821.

ALLEN, WILLIAM
- Elected 3rd Lieut., Company of Artillery, 70th Reg., in the room of Solomon Ruggles who omitted to qualify, 10 Oct 1835.

ALLISON, CHARLES
- Recommended Lieut., Washington Co. Militia, 26 Feb 1777.

ANDERS (ANDRES, ANDIS), WILLIAM
- Recommended Ensign, 2nd Batt., 105th Reg., in the room of James Gray, promoted, 21 Jun 1825.
- Recommended Lieut. in the room of James Gray, resigned, (Replaced as Ensign by James L. Davis), 20 May 1828.
- Resigned; replaced as Lieut. by William Gray. Election certified by Capt. James L. Davis, 14 May 1833.
- Elected Lieut., Troop of Cavalry, 105th Reg., 24 May 1834.
- Commissioned as Lieut. of Cavalry, 30 Jul 1834, per Officer Roll, 105th Reg., Oct, 1834.

ANDERSON, AUDLEY (ADLEY)
- Recommended Ensign, 105th Reg., in the room of James Larkey, promoted Captain, 17 May 1803.
- Removed; replaced as Ensign by Joseph Hickam, 19 Nov 1805.

ANDERSON, ISAAC
- Recommended Ensign, 2nd Batt., 105th Reg., in the room of Joseph Hickam, promoted, 19 Jul 1808.
- Commission as Ensign not yet issued because "lately nominated", per Officer Roll, 105th Reg., 1808.
- Recommended Captain of a new company, 2nd Batt., 105th Reg., 15 Nov 1808.
- (Appears as Major, South Battalion, 124th Reg., in Scott County, VA, 15 Feb 1815.)

ANDERSON, JACOB
- Recommended Lieut., 70th Reg., in the room of John Thomas, Sr., promoted 16 Jun 1829.

ANDERSON, JOHN
- Recommended Captain Washington County Militia, 26 Feb 1777.
- Commissioned as Captain 16 May 1777.
- Took oath of Office 16 Feb 1779.

ANDERSON, JOHN
- Recommended Lieut., Washington County Militia, 26 Feb 1777.

****

ANDERSON, JOHN
- Recommended Ensign, 5th Company, 2nd Batt., 70th Reg., 21 Jun 1793.
- Recommended Lieut. in the room of Patrick Campbell, 1st Batt., 70th Reg., 19 Jun 1794.
- Resigned; replaced as Lieut. by Arthur Campbell, Jr., 18 Oct 1798.
- Recommended Lieut., 2nd Batt., 105th Reg., in the room of William Anderson, removed, 15 Oct 1799.

ANDERSON, JOHN
- Earlier recommendation not seen, but because he resigned, replaced as Ensign in the 70th Reg. by Joshua Adams, 17 May 1803.

ANDERSON, WILLIAM
- Recommended Ensign, 2nd Batt., 70th Reg., 19 Feb 1793.
- Recommended Lieut. in the room of John Skillern, promoted, 19 Jun 1794.
- Recommended Lieut., 2nd Batt., 70th Reg., 21 May 1799.
- Removed; replaced as Lieut. in 2nd Batt, 105th (sic) Reg., by John Anderson, 15 Oct 1799.

ANDERSON, WILLIAM
- Recommended Ensign, Capt. Rowan's Comp., 1st Batt., 70th Reg., in the room of James Buchanan who is under age, 19 Jun 1794.
-Resigned; replaced as Ensign by John Dungans, 16 Aug 1796.

APPERSON, FRANCIS
- Recommended Captain, 2nd Batt., 70th Reg., in the room of John Apperson, resigned, 16 May 1820.
- Resigned; replaced as Capt. by John Fudge, 21 Jun 1825.

APPERSON, GABRIEL
- Recommended Ensign, 1st Batt., 105th Reg., in the room of William T. Duff, promoted, 18 Jul 1826.

APPERSON (EPPERSON), JOHN
- Recommended Ensign, 1st Batt., 70th Reg., in the room of William Poston, promoted, 17 Jan 1798.
- Recommended Lieut. in the room of William Apperson, promoted, 16 May 1815.
- Earlier recommendation not seen, but because he resigned, replaced as Capt. by Francis Apperson, 16 May 1820.

APPERSON (EPPERSON), WILLIAM
- Recommended Lieut., 70th Reg., in the room of (Samuel) McReynolds, who refuses to accept, 20 Feb 1810.
- Recommended Capt., 2nd Batt., 70th Reg., in the room of William S. Logan, resigned, 16 May 1815.

ARMSTRONG, BAKER
- Recommended Ensign of a new company, 2nd Batt., 105th Reg., 15 Nov 1808.

ARNETT (ARNITT), ANDREW
-Recommended Lieut., 70th Reg., 16 Jun 1829.
- Commissioned as Lieut., 17 Jul 1829, per Officer Rolls, May and Oct, 1834.
- Muster fine, 70th Reg., 1835, $5.00.
- Date of Commission 17 Jul 1829, confirmed by Col. James Edmondson, Jr., 21 Jun 1835.

ARNETT, THOMAS
- Elected 2nd Lieut., Company of Light Infantry, 70th Reg., 22 May 1835.

BAILEY, JAMES
- Recommended Ensign, Company of Light Infantry, 1st Batt., 105th Reg., in the room of John Acklin, removed, 19 Jun 1804.
- Recommended Lieut., in the room of Michael Shaver, resigned, 16 Jul 1805.
- Resigned; replaced as Lieut., by William Berryhill, 20 May 1806.

BAILEY, ROBERT
- Elected Lieut., 1st Batt., 105th Reg., in the room of Nicholas H. Ruley, resigned, 13 May 1831.
- Resigned; replaced as Lieut. by Andrew Gibson, 14 Apr 1832.

BAKER, (EVAN)
- Mentioned as former "quartermaster", Apr 1784.

BAKER, JACOB
- Recommended Cornet, Troop of Cavalry, 105th Reg., in the room of Abram Bradley, promoted. (Mentioned by Claiborne Watkins as "a merchant in the town of Abingdon".) 1 Feb 1800.
- Recommended 1st Lieut., in the Troop of Cavalry, 3rd Reg., 3rd Division, assigned to the 105th Reg., 15 Sep 1801.
- Recommended Captain of Cavalry, 105th Reg., in the room of Abraham Bradley, promoted, 20 Nov 1804.
- Resigned; replaced as Captain by Robert Houston, 18 Aug 1807.

****

BALFOUR, ANDREW
- Recommended Ensign, 2nd Batt., 105th Reg., in the room of John Gray, Jr., promoted, 19 May 1818.
- Did not accept; replaced as Ensign by Samuel Snoddy, 21 Dec 1819.

BARB, ABRAHAM
- Recommended Ensign, Capt. Fulkerson's Company, 2nd Batt., 105th Reg., 18 Feb 1812.
- "Removed" - scratched out on the manuscript; Abraham Nordyke recommended to replace him as Ensign 16 May 1815.
- Removed; replaced as Ensign in Capt. (Abraham) Fulkerson's Rifle Company, 105th Reg., by Abraham Nordyke, 19 Mar 1816.
- John Miller recommended Ensign to fill Barb's vacancy, 19 May 1818.

BARKER, JOEL
- Muster fine, 105th Reg., 1827, $15.00.
- Elected Lieut., Company of Riflemen, 2nd Batt., 105th Reg. Election certified by Col. Abraham Fulkerson, 4 Oct 1829.
- Resigned; replaced as Capt. by Peter S. Hanby, 7 Apr 1832.

BARKER, JOSEPH
- Elected Ensign, Rifle Company, 2nd Batt., 105th Reg., by unanimous vote to the men of the company. Election certified by Captain Nathan Smith, 15 Jun 1824.

BARKER, WILLIAM
- Elected Ensign, Rifle Company, 2nd Batt., 105th Reg. Election certified by Abraham Fulkerson, Colonel, 105th Reg., 3 Oct 1829.
- Elected Lieut., in the room of Peter S. Hanby, promoted, 7 Apr 1832.
- Commission as Lieut., dated 9 Apr 1832, per Officer Rolls, 105th Reg., 1833 and Oct 1834.

BARNETT, ALEXANDER
- Recommended Ensign, Washington County Militia, 26 Feb 1777.
- Recommended Captain, 19 Apr 1780.
- Mention of his "late company", Company No. 8, 1st Batt., 1785.
- Served as Major on the Board that designated Clinch Mountain to be the dividing line between the 1st and 2nd Batt., 30 Jul 1785.
- (Appears as County Lieut. of the Russell County, Virginia Militia in 1786)

BARTLET, WILLIAM
- Recommended Lieut., Washington County Militia, 19 Apr 1780.

BEATIE, ABSOLOM
- Appointed Quartermaster, 70th Reg., per Officer Roll, 70th Reg., May 1834.
- Appointed Adjutant 70th Reg., per Officer Roll, 70th Reg., Oct 1834.

BEATIE, ARMSTRONG
- Recommended Ensign, 70th Reg., in the room of William Smith, who does not accept, 21 May 1811.
- Did not accept; replaced as Ensign by David Richason, 18 Feb 1812.
- Recommended 2nd Lieut., Troop of Cavalry, 70th Reg., in the room of John Clark, promoted, 19 May 1818.

BEATIE, DAVID
- Recommended Lieut., Washington County Militia, 26 Feb 1777.
- Recommended Captain, 19 Apr 1780.
- Commission as Captain, 9 May 1780.
- Took oath of office, 16 Aug 1780.

BEATY, DAVID (Son of William)
- Recommended Cornet, Troop of Cavalry 70th Reg., in the room of Tobias Smith, removed, 16 May 1815.
- Resigned; replaced as Cornet by Matthew Ryburn, 19 May 1818.

BEATIE, JAMES
- Recommended Cornet, Troop of Cavalry, 70th Reg., in the room of James Orr, promoted, 19 May 1807.
- Recommended 2nd Lieut., Troop of Cavalry, in the room of John Orr, resigned, 21 May 1811.
- Recommended 1st Lieut., Troop of Cavalry in the room of James Orr, promoted, 20 Dec 1814.
- Recommended Capt., Troop of Cavalry, 70th Reg., in the room of James Orr, resigned, 19 May 1818.
- Resigned; replaced as Capt. by John Clark, 16 May 1820.

BEATIE, JAMES
- Recommended Lieut., 1st Batt., 70th Reg., in the room of Andrew Edmiston, promoted, 20 Aug 1822.
- Resigned; replaced as Lieut., by Robert Todd, 21 Jun 1825.

BEATIE, JAMES M.
- His election not seen, but his commission as Cornet, Troop of Cavalry, 70th Reg., dated 5 Jan 1833, per Officer Roll,

****

70th Reg., May 1834.

BEATIE, JOHN
- Recommended Ensign, Washington County Militia, 20 May 1779.

BEATIE, JOHN
- Recommended Ensign, 2nd Batt., 70th Reg., in the room of John Duffey, promoted, 19 May 1807.
- Recommended Lieut., in the room of John Duffey, removed, 19 Jan 1808.
- Recommended Capt., 2nd Batt., 70th Reg., in the room of Andrew Edmiston, removed, 20 Feb 1810.
- Removed; replaced as Captain by James Scott, 21 May 1811.

BEATY, JOSIAH N.
- Recommended Ensign, 70th Reg., in the room of Joseph Thomas, promoted, 16 May 1820.
- Resigned; replaced as Ensign by Leonidas Love, 21 May 1822.

BEATIE, MADISON
- Elected Cornet, Troop of Cavalry, 70th Reg., Sep 1832.
- Elected 1st Lieut., Troop of Cavalry, in the room of David R. Smith, promoted, 23 May 1834.
- Commission as Lieut. dated 7 Jul 1834 per Officer Roll, 70th Reg., Oct 1834.

BEATIE, ROBERT
- Recommended Ensign, 1st Batt, 70th Reg., in the room of James Kincannon, removed, 18 Feb 1812.
- Recommended Capt., in the room of George Byars, resigned, 16 May 1815.
- Muster fine, "Capt.", 70th Reg., 1820 $5.00.
- Recommended Major, 2nd Batt., 70th Reg., in the room of Thomas Tate, resigned, 16 May 1820.
- Resigned over contested court recommendation of Joseph C. Trigg to be Lieut. Col. of the 70th Reg., replaced as Major by Robert Stewart, 20 May 1823.

BEATY, SAMUEL
- Recommended Ensign, 70th Reg., in the room of John Smith, resigned, 16 May 1815.
- Removed; replaced as Ensign by John Martin, 18 May 1819.

BEATTIE, WILLIAM
- Recommended Ensign, 1st Batt., 70th Reg., 19 Feb 1793.
- Recommended Ensign, 4th Company, 1st Batt, 70th Reg., 21 Jun 1793.
- Recommended Lieut., in the room of Matthew Kincannon, resigned, 15 Aug 1797.
- Recommended Capt., 2nd Batt, 70th Reg., in the room of Samuel Meek promoted, 6 Jul 1799.
- Resigned; replaced as Captain by Andrew Edmistion, 19 Jan 1808.

BERRY, HUGH
- Recommended Ensign, Capt. Alexander Doran's Company, 2nd Batt., 70th Reg., in the room of William Berry, promoted, 19 Jun 1794.
- Recommended Lieut., in the room of Alexander Doran, promoted, 16 Aug 1796.
- Recommended Captain, 1st Batt., 105th Reg., in the room of Alexander Doran removed, 15 Sep 1801.
- Commission as Captain dated 29 Sep 1801, per Officer Roll, 105th Reg., 1808.
- Appears as Captain, list of Muster Fines, 105th Reg., 1810, possibly 1812.

BERRY, JOHN
- Recommended Lieut., Washington County Militia, 26 Feb 1777.

BERRY, JOHN
- Recommended Ensign, 1st Batt., 105th Reg., in the room of Nathan M. Laughlin, removed, 19 May 1818.
- Did not accept; replaced as Ensign by John W. Woods, 21 Sep 1819.

BERRY, THOMAS
- Recommended Ensign, Washington County Militia, 23 Nov 1780.
- Recommended Lieut., 8 May 1787.

BERRY, WILLIAM
- Recommended Ensign, 2nd Batt., 70th Reg., 19 Feb 1793.
- Recommended Ensign, 4th Company, 2nd Batt., 70th Reg., 21 Jun 1793.
- Recommended Lieut., Capt. Alexander Doran's Company 2nd Batt., 70th Reg., in the room of Doran promoted, 19 Jun 1794.
- Resigned; replaced as Ensign (sic) by John McCauley, 16 Aug 1796.

BERRY, WILLIAM
- Recommended Ensign, 105th Reg., in the room of Bartholomew Neel, resigned 19 Aug 1804.
- Resigned; replaced as Ensign by John Trimble, 17 Feb 1807.

BERRYHILL, WILLIAM
- Recommended Lieut., 105th Reg., in the

****

room of James Bailey, resigned, 20 May 1806.
- Did not accept; replaced as Lieut. by Lewis Toncray, 19 May 1807.

BICKLEY, CHARLES
- Nominated Ensign, Washington County Militia, 17 Apr 1782.
- (Appears as Captain, Russell Co. VA, 1786.)

BIRCH, JOHN
- Elected Lieut., new Company of Artillery, 70th Reg. Election certified by Col. R. B. Edmondson, 19 Jul 1834.
- (Company not approved; new elections required)
- Elected 1st Lieut., Company of Artillery, 70th Reg., 11 Apr 1835.

BISHOP, LEVI
- Recommended Ensign, Captain Aaron Lewis' Company, Washington County Militia, 22 Apr 1778.
- Recommended Lieut., 20 Nov 1778.
- Recommended Lieut., 20 May 1779.

BISHOP, LEVI
- Recommended Ensign, 1st Batt., 70th Reg., in the room of Levi Lester, promoted, 19 Jun 1804.
- Recommended Lieut., in the room of Levi Lester, promoted, 18 Aug 1807.
- Recommended Captain, in the room of Levi Lester who refuses to accept, 19 Jan 1808.
- Resigned; replaced as Capt. by William Houston, 16 May 1815.

BLACK, JAMES C.
- Recommended Ensign, 2nd Batt., 70th Reg., in the room of William B. Logan, removed, 20 May 1828.
- (Appears as a private, Roll of a new Rifle Company, 1st Batt., 105th Reg., 6 Jun 1829.)

BLACK, JOSEPH
- Recommended Lieut., Washington County Militia, 26 Feb 1777.
- Recommended Captain, 16 May 1781.
- Mention of his "late company", Company No. 8, 2nd Batt., 1785.

BLACKAMORE, WILLIAM
- Recommended Ensign, Washington County Militia, 19 Apr 1780.
- Recommended Lieut., 20 Mar 1782.

BLACKBURN, WILLIAM
- Recommended Lieut., Washington County Militia, 26 Feb 1777.
- Recommended 1st Lieut., 20 Nov 1778.

BLACKWELL, JOSEPH
- Elected 2nd Lieut., Company of Artlillery, 105th Reg. Election certified by John Preston, Colonel, 105th Reg., 13 Oct 1821.
- Resigned; replaced as 2nd Lieut. by Isaac Debusk, 12 Apr 1823.

BLAIR, JAMES
- Recommended Lieut. of Cavalry, Washington County Militia, 11 Apr 1788.

BONHAM, JOHN
- Recommended Ensign, 2nd Batt., 70th Reg., 19 Feb 1793.
- Recommended Ensign, 2nd Company, 2nd Batt., 70th Reg., 21 Jun 1793.

BORAR, BAZIL
- Recommended Lieut., Washington County Militia, 20 Nov 1782.

BOWEN, ARTHUR
- Recommended Ensign, Washington County Militia, 26 Feb 1777.
- Recommended Captain, 22 Mar 1781.
- Mentioned as Captain, Company No. 2, 2nd Batt. 1785.
- Mentioned as Major on board that designated Clinch Mountain the dividing line between the 1st and 2nd Batt., 30 Jul 1785.
- Recommended Captain, 8 May 1787.
- Recommended Captain, 1st Batt., 70th Reg., 19 Feb 1793.
- Recommended Captain, 2nd Company, 1st Batt., 70th Reg., 20 Jun 1793.
- Resigned; replaced as Captain by Patrick Campbell, 19 Jun 1794.

BOWEN, ARTHUR, JR.
- Recommended Lieut., 70th Reg., in the room of William Love, resigned, 16 May 1815.
- Muster fine, 70th Reg., 1819, $5.00.
- (Arthur M. Bowen) resigned; replaced as Lieut. by John Thomas, 16 May 1820.

BOWEN, CHARLES
- Recommended Captain, Washington County Militia, by ballot, 1785.

BOWEN, REES (RIECE)
- Recommended Ensign, Washington County Militia, 26 Feb 1777.
- Recommended Ensign, 19 Aug 1778.

****

BOWEN, WILLIAM
- Recommended Captain, Washington County Militia, 26 Feb 1777.

BOWERS, WILLIAM
- Elected 3rd Lieut., 70th Reg., 28 Feb 1835.

BOWLES, JOHN
- Recommended Ensign, Washington County Militia, 13 Oct 1789.

BRADLEY, ABRAHAM
- Recommended Ensign, 70th Reg., in the room of James Craig, promoted, 19 Oct 1794.
- Recommended by Capt. Claiborne Watkins to be Cornet, Troop of Cavalry, 3rd Reg., 3rd Division of the Militia of Virginia. (Replaced as Ensign by Robert Kincaid.) 1 Jul 1797.
- Recommended 2nd Lieut, Troop of Cavalry, attached to the 105th Reg., in the room of John Crockett, promoted in Wythe County, 1 Feb 1800.
- Recommended Captain, Troop of Cavalry, 3rd Reg., 3rd Division, in the room of Claiborne Watkins, resigned, 15 Sep 1801
- Recommended Major, 2nd Batt., 105th Reg., in the room of John Preston, Jr. promoted, 20 Nov 1804.
- Commission as Major dated 31 Dec 1804, per Officer Roll, 105th Reg., 1808.
- "Over 45 years of age and declines to act"; replaced as Major by Abrah Fulkerson, 16 Apr 1817.

BRADLEY, JAMES
- Recommended Ensign, Washington County Militia, 14 Oct 1788.
- Court order not seen, but recommended Major, 1st Batt., 105th Reg., Aug 1799.
- The County Court was asked by the Executive to reconsider their recommendation of Bradley to be Major; the Court declined to reconsider, with Robert Campbell, Gent., dissenting, 21 Jan 1800.
- Resigned; replaced as Major, 1st Batt., 105th Reg., by James White, 19 Jun 1804.

BRADLEY, JOHN
- Recommended Captain, Artillery Company 105th Reg., in the room of Samuel Glen, removed, 16 Jul 1805.
- Refused to accept: replaced as Captain by James Withroe, 20 May 1806.

BRADLEY, REUBEN
- Recommended Lieut, 105th Reg., in the room of James Whitehill Craig, promoted, 16 Sep 1800.
- Recommended Captain, 1st Batt., 105th Reg., in the room of James Craig, resigned, 17 Nov 1801.
- Commission as Captain dated 8 Dec 1801, per Officer Roll, 105th Reg., 1808.
- Colonel John Preston, Commandant of the 105th Reg. states, "Reuben Bradley is over 45 years... ceases to sit...refuses to surrender his commission" 16 Jun 1812.
- Replaced as Captain by John Moffett, 16 Jun 1812.

BRADLEY, ROBERT E.
- Elected 1st Lieut, Company of Artillery, 105th Reg., in the room of John Woodsides, resigned, 27 Apr 1832.
- Commission as Lieut. dated 18 May 1832, per Officer Roll, 105th Reg., 1833.
- Commission as Lieut. dated 20 Jun 1832, per Officer Roll, 105th Reg., Oct, 1834.

BRADLEY, WILLIAM
- Recommended Ensign, Light Infantry Company, 14 Feb 1787.
- Recommended Lieut., 13 Oct 1789.
- Recommended Lieut, Company of Grenadiers, 2nd Batt., 70th Reg., 19 Feb 1793.
- Removed out of the state; replaced as Lieut. by John Fulkerson, 19 Jun 1794.

BROWN, MATTHEW
- Recommended Ensign, 2nd Batt., 70th Reg., in the room of Robert Rhea, promoted, 18 Oct 1798.

BROWN, SAMUEL
- Recommended 2nd Lieut, Troop of Cavalry 105th Reg., in the room of John Montgomery, promoted, 15 Nov 1808.
- Appears as private on the Muster Roll, Troop of Cavalry, 1st Batt., 105th Reg., 9 Apr 1809.
- Muster fine, "Lieut.", 105th Reg., 1811, 1812.

BROWNLOW, JOSEPH A.
- Elected 4th Lieut., 105th Reg., 6 Jun 1835.

BUCHANAN, JAMES
- Recommended Ensign, Capt. Rowan's Company, 1st Batt., 70th Reg., 16 Apr 1794.
- Under age, declined to serve; replaced as Ensign by Willliam Anderson, 19 Jun 1794.

BUCHANAN, JOHN
- Recommended 2nd Lieut., Capt. George

Adams' Company, Washington County Militia, 22 Apr 1778.

BUCHANAN, JOHN
- Elected Ensign, Capt. John S. Caldwell's Company, 70th Reg., in the room of James Hand, resigned, 16 Nov 1833.
- Commission as Ensign dated 16 Nov 1833, per Officer Roll, 70th Reg., Oct, 1834.
- Elected 1st Lieut., 14 Feb 1835.

BUCHANAN, MATTHEW
- Recommended Ensign, 70th Reg., in the room of Enoch Smith, resigned, 15 Sep 1801.

BUCHANAN, ROBERTS, SR.
- Recommended Captain, Washington County Militia, 26 Feb 1777.

BUCHANAN, ROBERTS
- Recommended Lieut., Washington County Militia, 19 Nov 1783.
- Recommended Lieut., 8 May 1787.
- Recommended Lieut, 1st Batt., 70th Reg., 19 Feb 1793.
- (Recommendation not resubmitted 20 Jun 1793).

BUCHANAN, SAMUEL
- Recommended Ensign, Washington County Militia, 23 Nov 1780.
- Recommended Lieut., Capt. Keys' Company 1st Batt., 70th Reg., in the room of Samuel Gilliland, removed, 19 Nov 1795.
- Removed(?); replaced as Lieut. (1st Batt., 105th Reg.) by Robert Edmiston, 21 Jan 1801.

BUCHANAN, SOLON
- Elected Captain, Company of Light Infantry, 70th Reg., in the room of Samuel Chastain, resigned, 22 May 1835.

BUCHANAN, WILLIAM
- Recommended Lieut., 105th Reg., in the room of Samuel McGinnis, who does not accept, 19 May 1807.
- Commission as Lieut. dated 6 Jun 1807, per Officer Roll, 105th Reg., 1808.
- Recommended Captain, 1st Batt., 105th Reg., in the room of Welcome Martin, removed, 18 Feb 1812.
- Resigned; replaced as Captain by William E. Buchanan, 15 Jul 1817.

BUCHANAN, WILLIAM
- Earlier recommendation not seen, but because he did not accept, replaced as Ensign by John M. Tate, 21 May 1821.

BUCHANAN, WILLIAM E.
- Earlier recommendation not seen, but because of his promotion, replaced as Ensign, 1st Batt., 105th Reg., by Gardner Grant, 21 May 1816.
- Recommended Lieut., 105th Reg., in the room of Patrick Oneal, resigned, 21 May 1816.
- Recommended Captain, in the room of William Buchanan, resigned, 15 Jul 1817.
- Recommendation to Captaincy repeated, 19 May 1818.
- Deceased; replaced as Captain by James Edmondson, Jr., 18 Nov 1823.

BUCHANAN, WILLIAM R.
- Elected 2nd Lieut., 70th Reg., 14 Feb 1835.

BUCHANAN, WILSON
- Recommended Ensign, 2nd Batt., 70th Reg., in the room of Robert Hayton, promoted Captain, 16 May 1820.

BUCHER, JOSHUA
- Recommended Lieut., Washington County Militia, 20 Jun 1780.

BUNCH, JAMES
- Recommended Ensign, 70th Reg., 16 Jun 1829.
- Removed; replaced as Ensign, 2nd Batt., 70th Reg., by Isaac Hutton, 24 Aug 1833.

BURKE, JOSHUA
- Recommended 2nd Lieut., Company of Artillery, 105th Reg., in the room of Joseph Norman, resigned, 19 Jul 1808.
- Commission "not issued", per Officer Roll, 105th Reg., 1808.
- Recommended 1st Lieut., Company of Artillery, in the room of Samuel Keller, removed, 16 May 1809.
- Removed; replaced as 1st Lieut. of Artillery by William Smith, 18 Feb 1812.

BYARS, FLEMING
- Recommended Lieut., 2nd Batt., 70th Reg., in the room of John Beatie, promoted, 20 Feb 1810.

BYARS, GEORGE
- Recommended Ensign, 1st Batt., 70th Reg., in the room of Robert Day, promoted, 17 May 1803.
- Recommended Lieut., in the room of Robert Day, resigned, 20 Nov 1804
- Recommended Captain, 70th Reg., in the room of Arthur Campbell, removed, 20 May

****

1806.
- Resigned; replaced as Captain by Robert Beatie, 16 May 1815.

BYARS, JOHN
- Recommended Ensign, 1st Batt., 70th Reg., in the room of Arthur Campbell, Jr., promoted, 18 Oct 1798.
- Recommended Cornet, Troop of Cavalry, 70th Reg., by Lieut. Colonel Francis Preston, 21 Mar 1800.
- He declined to accept this appointment and was replaced by his brother, William Byars, 21 May 1800.

BYARS, JOHN
- Elected 4th Lieut., Troop of Cavalry, 70th Reg., 13 Feb 1835.

BYARS, WILLIAM
- Recommended Cornet, Troop of Cavalry, 70th Reg., in the room of John Byars, his brother, who had declined to accept, 21 May 1800.
- Recommended 2nd Lieut., in the room of Thomas Edmiston, promoted, 19 Jun 1804.
- Recommended Captain, Troop of Cavalry, 70th Reg., in the room of William Lyon, resigned, 19 May 1807.
- Recommended Major, 2nd Batt., 70th Reg., in the room of Thomas Edmiston, resigned, 20 Dec 1814.
- Recommended Colonel, 70th Reg., in the room of Lieut. Col. Charles Tate, "heretofore resigned", 21 Apr 1818.
- Resigned; replaced as Colonel by James Edmondson, Jr., 22 Mar 1834.

CALDWELL, JAMES
- Earlier recommendation not seen, but because he resigned, replaced as Lieut., 105th Reg., by William Faires, 19 Jun 1804.

CALDWELL (CAULDWELL), JOHN S.
- Recommended Ensign, 1st Batt., 105th Reg., in the room of John Gilliland, promoted, 20 May 1828.
- Recommended Lieut., in the room of John Gilliland, resigned, 18 May 1830.
- Elected Captain, 2nd Batt., 105th Reg. 27, Apr 1832.
- Commission as Captain dated 5 Oct 1832, per Officer Roll, 105th Reg., 1833.
- His company became part of the 70th Reg., 18 May 1833.
- Commission as Captain dated 10 Jul 1833 per Officer Roll, 70th Reg., May 1834.
- Commission as Captain dated 5 Oct 1832, per Officer Roll, 70th Reg., Oct 1834.

CALDWELL, THOMAS
- Recommended Captain, Washington Co. Militia 20 May 1778.

CAMPBELL, ARTHUR
- Took oath of office as County Lieut., Washington Co. Militia, 28 Jan 1777.
- Recommended Lieut. Colonel, Commandant of the Washington County Militia, newly numbered the 70th Reg., 20 Feb 1793.
- Resigned; replaced as Leiut. Col. Commandant of the 70th Reg. by Francis Preston, 21 May 1799.

CAMPBELL, ARTHUR, JR.
- Recommended Ensign, Capt. Patrick Campbell's Company, 1st Batt., 70th Reg., in the room of Thomas Thomas, resigned, 17 Jan 1798.
- Recommended Lieut, in the room of John Anderson, resigned, 18 Oct 1798.
- Recommended Captain, 1st Batt., 70th Reg. in the room of Patrick Campbell, resigned, 17 May 1803.
- Removed; replaced as Captain by George Byars, 20 May 1806.

CAMPBELL, ARTHUR
- Recommended 1st Lieut., Troop of Cavalry, 105th Reg., in the room of William Ireson, who does not accept, 18 Feb 1812.

CAMPBELL, CHARLIE
- Recommended Lieut, Washington Co. Militia, 26 Feb 1777.

CAMPBELL, DAVID, JR
- Recommended Ensign, 2nd Batt., 70th Reg.,

****

in the room of Philip Hawkins, resigned, 19 Nov 1795.
- Resigned; replaced as Ensign by Wallace Willoughby, 17 Jan 1798.
- Clerk of Regimental Court of Enquiry, 70th Reg., 1798.
- Recommended Captain, 2nd Batt., 105th Reg., 21 May 1799.
- Resigned; replaced as Captain by John Preston, Jr., 16 Sep 1800.
- Clerk of Regimental Court of Enquiry, 105th Reg. 1799 through 1804.
- Recommended Captain, Light Infantry Company, 1st Batt., 105th Reg., in the room of Alexander S. Walker, removed, 19 Jul 1808.
- Commission as Captain of Light Infantry "not yet issued", per Officer Roll, 105th Reg., 1808.
- Roll, Light Infantry Company, 1st Batt., 105th Reg., 8 Apr 1809.
- Declined to accept commission; replaced as Captain by Andrew McHenry, 16 May 1809.
- Earlier recommendation not seen, but he was 2nd Lieut., Company of Artillery, 17th Brigade, 3rd Div., attached to the 105th Reg., at the election of Capt. John Crawford, 26 Jun 1815.
- Resigned; replaced as 2nd Lieut., Company of Artillery by Thomas McCulloch, by an invalid court order, 18 May 1819.
- Took oath of office as Colonel, 3rd Reg. of Cavalry, Militia of Virginia, 18 May 1819.
- Properly replaced as 2nd Lieut. of Artillery Company by John Galliher, 21 Dec 1819.

CAMPBELL, EDWARD
- Recommended Ensign, 2nd Batt., 105th Reg., in the room of John Curry, promoted, 21 May 1799.
- Recommended Lieut., in the room of John Corry (sic), promoted, 17 May 1803.
- Resigned; replaced as Lieut by William Gray, 16 July 1805.
- (Appears as Private, Roll of Light Infantry Company, 1st Batt., 105th Reg., 8 Apr 1809.)

CAMPBELL, HUGH
- Recommended Ensign, Washington Co. Militia, 20 Jun 1780.

CAMPBELL, JAMES
- Recommended Ensign, Washington Co. Militia, 13 Oct 1789.
- Recommended Lieut., 1st Batt., 70th Reg., 19 Feb 1793.
- (Recommendation not resubmitted in June, 1793.

CAMPBELL, JAMES
- Recommended Captain, 2nd Batt., 70th Reg., 19 Feb 1793
- (Recommendation not resubmitted in June, 1793)

CAMPBELL, JAMES, JR.
- Recommended Ensign, 105th Reg., in the room of Edmond Henry, "not now a resident of the county", 18 Feb 1812.

CAMPBELL, JAMES
- Earlier recommendation not seen, but because of his promotion, replaced as Ensign, 105th Reg., by Charles Johnston, 19 Mar 1816.
- Recommended Lieut., 1st Batt., 105th Reg., in the room of Henry Parrot, promoted, 19 Mar 1816.
- Recommended Captain, 105th Reg., in the room of Henry Parrott, resigned, 18 May 1819.
- Resigned; replaced as Captain by Daniel Lynch, 15 May 1827.

CAMPBELL, JOHN
- Recommended Captain, Washington Co. Militia, 26 Feb 1777.

CAMPBELL, JOHN, R.O. (Royal Oak)
- Recommended Captain, Washington Co. Militia, 26 Feb 1777.

CAMPBELL, JOHN, SR.
- Recommended by Brigadier General William Tate to be 2nd Lieut., Troop of Horse, 17th Brigade, 12 Dec 1793.

CAMPBELL, JOHN
- Recommended Lieut., 1st Batt., 70th Reg., 19 Feb 1793.
- Recommended Lieut., 5th Company, 1st Batt., 70th Reg., 21 Jun 1793.
- Recommended Captain, 1st Batt., 70th Reg, in the room of Richard Poston, resigned, 19 Jun 1794.
- Resigned; replaced as Captain by Charles Tate, 17 Jan 1798.

CAMPBELL, JOHN
- Recommended Ensign, 70th Reg., in the room of Addison Davis, removed, 19 May 1824.

CAMPBELL, PATRICK
- Recommended Ensign, Washington Co. Militia, 19 Aug 1778.
- Recommended Lieut., 23 Nov 1780.

****

- Recommended Lieut., 1st Batt., 70th Reg., 19 Feb 1793.
- Recommended Lieut., 2nd Company, 1st Batt., 70th Reg., 21 Jun 1793.
- Recommended Captain, 1st Batt., 70th Reg., in the room of Arthur Bowen, resigned, 19 Jun 1794.
- At the Division of the 70th Reg. to create the 105th Reg., his company was assigned to 1st Batt., 70th Reg. 20 Mar 1799.
- Resigned; repalced as Captain by Arthur Campbell, Jr., 17 May 1803.

CAMPBELL, ROBERT
- Recommended Ensign, Washington Co. Militia, 19 Apr 1780.
- Recommended Lieut., 16 May 1781.
- Recommended as officer in the Troop of Horse, 21 Mar 1783.
- Recommended Lieut. of Militia Company, 8 May 1787.
- Recommended Captain of Militia Company, 14 Oct 1788.
- Recommended Captain, 2nd Batt., 70th Reg., 19 Feb 1793.
- Recommended Captain, 2nd Company, 2nd Batt., 70th Reg., 20 Jun 1793.
- Recommended Major, 2nd Batt., 70th Reg., in the room of Alexander Montgomery, removed, 19 Oct 1794. (Replaced as Captain by James Vance.)
- Recommended Major, 1st Batt. of the newly formed 105th Reg., 21 May 1799.
- Commissioned Lieutenant Colonel, Commandant, 105th Reg., on the recommendation of Arthur Campbell (This was a hotly contested action by the Executive, date of commission was probably about Jul 1799.)
- His resignation, "by reason of infirmity under which he has struggled for a considerable time", reported by Brigadier General William Tate, 17th Brigade, 21 Jul 1802.
- Resigned; repalced as Lieut. Colonel by Matthew Willoughby, 17 Aug 1802.

CAMPBELL, WILLIAM
- Took oath of office as Lieut. Colonel, Washington County Militia, 28 Jan 1777.
- Appointed Colonel, Washington Co. Militia, in the room of Evan Shelby, "now a citizen of North Carolina", 19 Apr 1780.
- Recommended Colonel, 1st Batt., 22 Mar 1781

CAMPBELL, WILLIAM
- Recommended Lieut., Company of Grenadiers, 1st Batt., 70th Reg., 19 Feb 1793.
- Recommended Captain of Light Infantry Company, 1st Batt., 70th Reg., in the room of John Greenway, resigned, 22 Jun 1796.
- Resigned; replaced as Captain by David Craig, 15 Aug 1797.

CAMPBELL, WILLIAM
- Recommended Lieut., 70th Reg., 20 May 1823.
- Removed; replaced as Lieut. by Thomas Tate, 19 May 1824.

CAMPBELL, WILLIAM T.
- Recommended Lieut., 2nd Batt, 105th Reg., in the room of William C. Tate, promoted, 19 May 1818.

CARMACK, CORNELIUS
- Recommended Ensign, Washington Co. Militia, 8 May 1787.
- Recommended Lieut., 14 Oct 1788.

CARMACK, JOSEPH
- Recommended Ensign, 2nd Batt., 70th Reg., in the room of Michael Hickman, promoted, 16 May 1815.

CARMACK, WILLIAM
- Recommended Ensign, Captain Joseph Gray's Company, 70th Reg., 16 Apr 1794.
- Recommended Captain, in the room of Joseph Gray, resigned, 19 Oct 1794.
- Removed; replaced as Captain by Walter Preston, 22 Jun 1796.

CARMACK, WILLIAM, JR.
- Recommended Ensign, Capt. Joseph Hensley's Company, 70th Reg., 16 Apr 1794.
- Mention that commission as Ensign not received, 21 Aug 1794.
- Recommended Lieut., in the room of Samuel Hensley, promoted, 19 Nov 1795.
- Resigned; replaced as Lieut., 2nd Batt. 70th Reg., by Fielding Hensley, 21 May 1800.

CARMACK, WILLIAM, JR.
- Recommended Ensign, 2nd Batt., 105th Reg., in the room of Jacob Merchant, who does not accept, 20 May 1823.
- Recommended Lieut., in the room of William Shoemaker, promoted, 21 Jun 1825.
- Removed; replaced as Lieut. by Francis W. Irby, 18 May 1830.

CARR, JOHN
- Elected 2nd Lieut., 2nd Batt., 105th Reg., 14 Apr 1833.
- Did not accept, per Colonel Samuel E.

****

Goodson, 25 Jun 1835.

CARSON, DAVID
- Recommended Ensign, 1st Batt., 70th Reg., 21 May 1799.
- Recommended Lieut., Capt. David Craig's Company of Infantry, 70th Reg., in the room of James Todd, resigned, 19 Aug 1800.
- Resigned; replaced as Lieut. by Joseph Cole, 19 May 1807.
- Elected Captain, new Rifle Company, 1st Batt., 70th Reg., Aug 1807.

CARSON, SAMUEL
- Recommended Ensign, 1st Batt., 70th Reg., in the room of John Moore, removed, 16 Jul 1805.
- Refused to accept; replaced as Ensign by Samuel Carson (sic), 18 Dec 1806.
- Recommended Ensign in the room of Samuel Carson, promoted, 16 May 1809.

CARSON, SAMUEL
- Recommended Ensign, 1st Batt., 70th Reg., in the room of Samuel Carson (sic), who refuses to accept, 18 Dec 1806.
- Recommended Lieut., in the room of Samuel Fulton, promoted, 16 May 1809.
- Resigned; replaced as Lieut. by William Edmiston, 16 May 1815.

CARSON, WILLIAM
- Recommended Ensign, Washington Co. Militia, 14 Feb 1787.
- Recommended Ensign, 1st Batt., 70th Reg., 19 Feb 1793.
- Recommended Ensign, 1st Company, 1st Batt., 70th Reg., 21 Jun 1793.
- Recommended Lieut., Company of Riflemen, 1st Batt., 70th Reg., 15 Aug 1797.
- Muster Fine, "Lieut.", 70th Reg., 1801, $5.00.

CASEY, WILLIAM
- Recommended Ensign, Washington Co. Militia, 26 Feb 1777.

CAWOOD (KEEWOOD), BERRY
- Recommended Ensign, Washington Co. Militia, 14 Feb 1787.
- Recommended Lieut., 13 Oct 1789.
- Recommended Ensign, 1st Batt., 70th Reg., 19 Feb 1793.
- (His recommendation was not resubmitted, 20 Jun 1793)
- Recommended Captain, 70th Reg., in the room of James Logan, resigned, 16 Aug 1796.
- At the division of the 70th Reg. to create the new 105th Reg., his company was assigned to the 2nd Batt., 70th Reg., 20 Mar 1799.

CETCHUM, WILLIAM
- Elected 4th Lieut., 70th Reg., 7 Mar 1835.

CHASTAIN (CHASTEEN), SAMUEL
- Elected Captain, Rifle Company, 2nd Batt., 70th Reg., in the room of Clark G. Gardner. Election certified by Joseph Thomas, Major, 70th Reg., 16 Oct 1830.
- Commission as Captain dated "1832", per Officer Rolls, 70th Reg., May and Oct 1834
- Resigned; replaced as Captain by Solon Buchanan, 22 May 1835.
- Muster Fine, 70th Reg., 1835, $5.00.

CHRISTIAN, GILBERT
- Recommended Captain, Washington Co. Militia, 26 Feb 1777.
- Commission dated 8 May 1777.
- Took oath of Office 20 Nov 1778.

CHURCH, JONATHAN M.
- Recommended Ensign, 1st Batt., 105th Reg., in the room of Bartholomew Neil, who does not accept, 19 Jul 1808.
- Removed "out of the bounds of the company"; replaced as Ensign by Patrick Oneal, 18 Feb 1812.

CLARK, DAVID
- Makes his first appearance as Private on the Muster Roll of the Artillery Company attached to the 105th Reg., 26 Jun 1815
- Muster fine, 105th Reg., 1816, .75.
- Elected 1st Lieut., Artillery Company, 105th Reg., in the room of Thomas McCulloch, promoted. Election certified by John Preston, Colonel, 105th Reg., 13 Oct 1821.
- Elected Captain, Artillery Company, in the room of Thomas McCulloch, promoted. Election certified by Abraham Fulkerson, Colonel, 105th Reg., 29 Oct 1828.
- Resigned; replaced as Captain by Madison Love. Election certified by Samuel E. Goodson, Lieut. Col., 105th Reg., 13 May 1831.

CLARK, JOB
- Earlier recommendation or election not seen, but he was 1st Liuet., Artillery Company, 17th Brigade, 3rd Division, attached to the 105th Reg., at the election of John Crawford to be Capt., 26 Jun 1815.
- Appears as Lieut. on the Musster Roll of the Artillery Company, 26 Jun 1815.
- Resigned; replaced as 1st Lieut. of Artillery by Thomas McCulloch, 21 Dec 1819.
- (Earlier, on 18 May 1819, the county court had improperly recommended Walter

****

Warren to replace Clark.)

CLARK, JOHN
- Recommended Cornet, Troop of Cavalry, 70th Reg., in the room of James Beatie, promoted, 21 May 1811.
- Recommended 2nd Lieut, Troop of Cavalry, in the room of James Beatie, promoted, 20 Dec 1814.
- Recommended 1st Lieut., Troop of Cavalry, in the room of James Beatie, promoted, 19 May 1818.
- Recommended Captain, Troop of Cavalry, 70th Reg., in the room of James Beatie, resigned, 16 May 1820.
- Elected Captain by the men of the Troop of Cavalry, 23 Jun 1820.
- Resigned; replaced as Captain (Election held in Oct 1823) by Matthew Ryburn. Election certified by William Byars, Colonel, 70th Reg., 22 Mar 1824.

CLARK, WILLIAM
- Recommended 2nd Lieut., Troop of Cavalry, 70th Reg., in the room of Matthew Ryburn, promoted, 16 May 1820.
- Elected 2nd Leiut., Troop of Cavalry, by the men of the company, 23 Jun 1820.
- Elected 1st Lieut. (Election held in Oct 1823) Election certified by William Byars, Colonel, 70th Reg., 22 Mar 1824.

CLARK, WILLIAM G.
- Elected Captain of a new company of the militia line, 70th Reg. (Benjamin Lyon, Lieut.; James W. Hill, Ens.) 7 Sep 1833.
- Commission as Captain dated 27 Jan 1834, per Officer Rolls, 70th REg., May and Oct, 1834.
- (Resigned; replaced as Captain by Tobias D. Smith, 3 Apr 1841) (Archives, Virginia State Library).

CLENDENEN, JOHN
- Recommended Ensign, Washington County Militia, 8 May 1787.

COCHRAN, ROBERT B.
- Elected 2nd Lieut, 105th Reg., 30 May 1835.

COCKE, CHARLES
- Recommended Captain, Washington County Militia, 20 Jun 1780.
- Mentioned as Captain, Company No. 6, 1st Batt., 1785.
- (Appears as Major, Russell County Militia 1786).

COLE, ------
- Recommended Ensign, Rifle Company, 70th Reg., in the room of Samuel Edmondson, promoted, 15 Jul 1817.

COLE, JOHN
- Recommended Ensign, Washington County Militia, 9 Mar 1790.
- Recommended Ensign, 1st Batt., 70th Reg., 19 Feb 1793.
- Recommended Ensign, 5th Company, 1st Batt., 70th Reg., 21 Jun 1793.
- Recommended Lieut., of a new company, to be commanded by Capt. Joseph Cole, 1st Batt., 70th Reg., 19 Jun 1794.
- Resigned; replaced as Lieut. by Thomas Tilson, 21 May 1799.

COLE, JOHN JR.
- Recommended Ensign, Capt. Craig's Company of Riflemen, 70th Reg., in the room of John Edmistion, removed, 17 May 1803
- Advice from Colonel Francis Preston, there is no John Cole residing within the bounds of the 70th REg. This commission was intended for Joseph Cole, Jr. 14 May 1804.
- The county court corrected this error, 19 Jun 1804. (See Joseph Cole, Jr.)

COLE, JOSEPH
- Recommended Captain, Washington County Militia, 20 Mar 1782.
- Mentioned as Captain, Company No. 4, 2nd Batt., 1785.
- Recommended Captain "by ballot", 1785.
- A supernumerary officer, recommended Captain of a new militia company, 1st Batt., 70th Reg., 19 Jun 1794.
- Resigned; replaced as Captain by Seberias Main, 15 Aug 1797.

COLE, JOSEPH, JR.
- Recommended Ensign, Capt. Craig's company of Riflemen, 70th Reg., in the room of John Edmiston, removed, 19 Jun 1804. (Recommendation has been erroneously made in the name of "John Cole, Jr." on 17 May 1803. The error was noted by Colonel Francis Preston, 14 May 1804.
- Recommended Lieut., Company of Light Inf. 1st Batt., 70th Reg., in the room of David Carson, resigned, 19 May 1807.
- Did not accept: replaced as Lieut. by David Snodgrass, 18 Jul 1809.

COLE, JOSEPH, "SALUDA"
- First appears as Private, Muster Roll, Volunteer Rifle Company, 1st Batt., 70th Reg., Aug 1807.
- Recommended Ensign, 1st Batt., 70th Reg., in the room of Levi Bishop, promoted, 18 Aug 1807.

****

- Recommended Lieut. in the room of Levi Bishop, promoted 19 Jan 1808.
- Removed; replaced as Lieut. by William Houston, 16 May 1809.

COLE, THOMAS
- Recommended Lieut, Washington County Militia, 20 Mar 1782.

COLVILL, ANDREW
- Recommended Captain, Washington County Militia, 26 Feb 1777.
- Commission dated 17 May 1777.
- Took Oath of Office 19 Aug 1778.

COLVILLE, ANDREW
- Recommended Ensign, Washington County Militia, 13 Oct 1789.
- Recommended Ensign, 2nd Batt., 70th Reg., 19 Feb 1793.
- Recommended Ensign, 1st Company, 2nd Batt., 70th Reg., 21 Jun 1793.

COLVILL, JOSEPH
- Recommended Lieut., Light Infantry Company, Washington County Militia 14 Feb 1787.

CONN, WILLIAM YOUNG
- Recommended Captain, Light Infantry Company, Washington County Militia 14 Feb 1787.
- Recommended Captain, Company of Grenadiers, 2nd Batt., 70th Reg., 19 Feb 1793.
- Mentioned as commander of one of two Rifle Companies in the 70th Reg., 3 Dec 1798.
- Certified as Captain, Company of Infantry, 2nd Batt., 70th Reg., "now 1st Batt., 105th Reg.", 16 Jul 1799. (Date of commission: 17 May 1793).
- Resigned; as an apparent result of the court's recommendation of James Bradley to be Major, 1st Batt., 105th Reg., Jan 1800.

CONNALLY, STEPHEN
- Elected Ensign, Capt. James B. Worley's Company, 2nd Batt., 105th Reg., 18 May 1833.
- Commission as Ensign dated 3 Dec 1833, per Officer roll, 105th Reg, Oct 1834.
- Muster Fine, "Ensign", 105th Reg., 1834, $5.00.
- Refused to accept commission, per Colonel Samuel E. Goodson, 105th Reg., 25 Jun 1835.

COOK, MARCUS
- Elected Lieut., Capt. Andrew Edmondson's Company, 1st Batt., 70th Reg., in the room of Robert Todd, removed, Apr 1832.

COULTER, JOHN
- Recommended Lieut., Washington County Militia, 26 Feb 1777.
- Commission dated 8 May 1777.
- Took oath of office, 18 Aug 1778.

COWAN, ANDREW
- Recommended Lieut., Washington County Militia, 20 Mar 1782.
- Mentioned a Company Commander 23 Aug 1782.
- Mentioned as Captain, Company No. 2, 1st Batt., 1785.
- Appears as Major on board that designated Clinch Mountain the dividing line between 1st and 2nd Batt., 30 Jul 1785.
- (Appears as Lieut. Colonel, Russell County Militia, 1786).

COWAN, WILLIAM
- Recommended Lieut. in Capt. John Snody's Company, Washington Co. Militia, 27 Aug 1777.
- Recommended Capt. 20 Mar 1782.
- Mentioned as Capt., Company No. 9, 1st Batt., 1785.

CRABTREE, JAMES
- Recommended Ensign, Washington County Militia, 26 Feb 1777.
- Recommended Captain 19 Apr 1780.
- Commission dated 9 May 1780.
- Took oath of office 18 Apr 1781.
- Mentioned as Captain, Company No. 6, 2nd Batt., 1785.

CRABTREE, JAMES
- Recommended Ensign, 2nd Batt., 70th Reg., in the room of Reason Roberts, resigned, 21 May 1811.
- Earlier recommendation not seen, but because of his decease, replaced as Lieut. by William C. Tate, 20 Dec 1814.
- (There was a later recommendation that Robert Hayden fill this vacancy, 19 May 1818).

CRABTREE, JOB
- Recommended Ensign, 1st Batt., 70th Reg., in the room of Joseph Scott, promoted, 16 Aug 1796.
- Removed; replaced as Ensign, 2nd Batt., 70th Reg., by David McReynolds, 15 Oct 1799.

CRABTREE, JOHN
- Recommended Lieut., Capt. Berry Cawood's Company, 2nd Batt., 70th Reg., in the room of Joseph Scott, resigned, 18 Mar 1800.

****

- Resigned; replaced as Lieut. by Enoch Smith, 17 May 1803.

CRAIG, DAVID
- Recommended Lieut., 2nd Batt., 70th Reg., 19 Feb 1793.
- Recommended Ensign, 3rd Company, 2nd Batt., 70th Reg., 21 Jun 1793.
- Recommended Lieut. in the room of Benjamin Sharp, "removed out of the county, 19 Jun 1794.
- Removed; replaced as Lieut. by Wallace Willoughby, 23 Jun 1798.

CRAIG, DAVID
- Recommended Ensign, 70th Reg., in the room of John Estill who is "under age and at college", 19 Jun 1794.
- Recommended Lieut, 1st Batt., 70th Reg, in the room of William Campbell, promoted, 22 Jun 1796.
- Recommended Captain, Company of Riflemen in the room of William Campbell, resigned, 15 Aug 1797.
- Mentioned as commander of one of two Rifle Companies, 70th Reg., 3 Dec 1798.
- Resigned; replaced as Captain by Samuel Preston, 18 Jul 1809.

CRAIG, GEORGE
- Recommended Ensign, 105th Reg., in the room of John Preston, promoted, 16 Sep 1800.
- Removed; replaced as Ensign by Allen Mc Donald, 15 Sep 1801.

CRAIG, JAMES, JR.
- Recommended Ensign, Capt. Robert Campbell's Company, 70th Reg., 16 Apr 1794.
- Recommended Lieut. in the room of James Vance, promoted, 19 Oct 1794.

CRAIG, JAMES WHITEHILL
- Recommended Caaptain, 105th Reg., in the room of James Vance, resigned, 19 Sep 1800.
- Resigned; replaced as Captain by Reuben Bradley, 17 Nov 1801.

CRAIG, JOHN
- Recommended 2nd Lieut., Troop of Cavalry, 105th Reg., in the room of William Duff, promoted 18 Aug 1807.
- Removed; replaced as 2nd Lieut. by John Montgomery, 19 Jan 1808.

CRAIG, ROBERT
- Recommended Captain, Washington County Militia, 26 Feb 1777.
- Commission dated 15 May 1777.
- Took oath of office 17 Mar 1779.
- Recommended Lieut. Colonel, 21 Apr 1785.

CRAIG, ROBERT, JR.
- Recommended Captain of Cavalry, Washington County Militia, 11 Apr 1788.

CRAIG, ROBERT, JR.
- Recommended Ensign, Company of Grenadiers, 2nd Batt., 70th Reg., in the room of Wallace Willoughby, promoted, 19 Nov 1795.
- Recommended Lieut. in the room of Wallace Willoughby, resigned, 22 Jun 1796.
- Certified to have been Lieut., Company of Infantry, 2nd Batt., 70th Reg., now 1st Batt., 105th Reg., 16 Jul 1799. (Date of commmission, 16 Jul 1796).
- Recommended Captain, Company of Light Infantry, 1st Batt., 105th Reg., 15 Oct 1799 (This appointment would appear to have been to replace William Y. Conn, resigned.)
- Resigned; replaced as Captain by John Gold, 16 Jul 1805.

CRAIG, ROBERT P.
- Recommended Ensign, 1st Batt., 105th Reg., in the room of Nathan M. Laughlin, promoted, 16 May 1815.
- Removed; replaced as Ensign by Thomas Dryden, Jr., 19 Mar 1816.

CRAIG, WILLIAM
- Recommended Ensign, Washington County Militia, 14 Feb 1787.

CRAIG, WILLIAM DENNY
- Recommended 2nd Lieut., Troop of Cavalry, 3rd Reg., 3rd Division, attached to 105th Reg., 15 Sep 1801.
- Removed; replaced as 2nd Lieut. by Robert Houston, 17 Jun 1802.

CRAWFORD, HUGH
- Recommended Lieut, Washington County Militia, 20 Nov 1778.

CRAWFORD, JAMES
- Recommended Ensign, 2nd Batt., 70th Reg., in the room of John Beatie, promoted 19 Jan 1808.

CRAWFORD, JOHN
- Recommended Ensign, 1st Batt., 105th Reg., in the room of Benjamin Longley, resigned, 21 May 1811.
- Recommended Lieut in the room of John Moffett, promoted, 16 Jun 1812.
- Appears as Private, Muster Roll, Artillery Commpany, 105th Reg., 26 Jun 1815.
- Elected Captain, Artillery Company, in

****

the room of William Smith, reisgned, 26 Jun 1815.
- Had entered service in Tennessee under General Andrew Jackson (in campaign against Creek Indians), per David Campbell letter, 1 Jul 1815.
- Recommended Captain, Artillery Company, 21 May 1816.
- "Reported to be deceased"; replaced as Captain by Thomas McCulloch, 13 Oct 1821.

CRAWFORD, JOHN
- Recommended Lieut., 70th Reg., in the room of Robert Stewart, resigned, 19 May 1824.

CROCKETT, WILLIAM
- Recommended Ensign, Washington County Militia, 20 May 1778.

CUMMINGS, CHARLES J.
- Elected Captain, Artillery Company, 105th Reg., in the room of Madison Love, removed 27 Apr 1832.
- Commission as Captain dated 18 May 1832, per Officer Roll, 105th Reg., 1833.
- Commission as Captain dated 20 Jun 1832, per Officer Roll, 105th Reg., Oct, 1834.

CUMMINGS, JAMES
- Recommended Lieut., Company of infantry, 2nd Batt., 105th Reg., 21 May 1799.
- Resigned; replaced as Lieut. by Thomas McChesney, 19 Sep 1800.

CUMMINGS, ROBERT
- Recommended Ensign, Capt. Reuben Bradley's Company, 1st Batt., 105th Reg., in the room of William Richardson, promoted, 17 Nov 1801.
- Resigned; replaced as Ensign by John Moffett, 16 Jul 1805.

CUNNINGHAM, JONATHAN
- Recommended Ensign, Washington County Militia, "by ballot", 1785.

CUNNINGHAM, SAMUEL
- Recommended Ensign, 70th Reg., in the room of Caleb Logan who refuses to accept, 20 Feb 1810.

CURRIN, WADDY T.
- Earlier recommendation not seen, but because he did not accept, replaced as Ensign, Company of Light Infantry, 70th Reg., by Joseph Trigg, 20 Dec 1814.

CURRY (CORRY), JOHN
- Recommended Ensign, 70th Reg., in the room of Wallace Willoughby, promoted, 23 Jun 1798.
- Recommended Lieut., 2nd Batt., 105th Reg., in the room of Wallace Willoughby, promoted, 21 May 1799.
- Recommended Captain, 2nd Batt., 105th Reg., in the room of Wallace Willoughby, removed, 17 May 1803 (Replaced as Lieut. by Edward Campbell).
- Resigned; replaced as Captain by Robert Davis, 16 Jul 1805.

****

DAVENPORT (DEVENPORT), CLAIBORNE
- Recommended Ensign, 2nd Batt., 70th Reg., in the room of James Doran, resigned, 21 May 1800.

DAVENPORT, DANIEL
- Recommended Ensign, 2nd Batt., 70th Reg., in the room of Charles Morell, resigned, 18 Jul 1826.

DAVIS, ADDISON
- Recommended Ensign, 70th Reg., 20 May 1823.
- Removed; replaced as Ensign by John Campbell, 19 May 1824.

DAVIS, CHARLES
- Recommended Ensign, Company of Light Infantry, 1st Batt., 105th Reg., in the room of William Ireson, removed, 19 Jul 1808.
- Commission as Ensign of Infantry not yet received because "lately nominated", per Officer Roll, 105th Reg., 1808.
- (Jacob Shoen recommended to fill William Ireson's vacancy, 16 May 1809).

DAVIS, JAMES
- Recommended Ensign, Washington County Militia, 18 Sep 1782.

DAVIS, JAMES
- Recommended Lieut., 2nd Batt., 105th Reg., in the room of John Gray, resigned, 19 Mar 1816.
- Earlier recommendation not seen but because of his promotion, replaced as Lieut. by William Ireson, 16 Apr 1817.
- Recommended Captain in the room of William Gray, resigned, 16 Apr 1817.
- Muster fine, "Capt.", 105th Reg., 1820, $1.00.
- Resigned; replaced as Captain by John Hortenstine, 21 Jun 1825.

DAVIS, JAMES L.
- Recommended Ensign, 2nd Batt., 105th Reg., in the room of William Anders, promoted, 20 May 1828.
- Recommended Captain, 2nd Batt., 105th Reg., in the room of John Hortenstine, resigned, 18 May 1830.
- Commission as Captain dated 10 Jun 1830, per Officer Rolls, 105th Reg., 1833 and Oct, 1834.

DAVIS, JOHN
- Recommended Ensign, Washington County Militia, 26 Feb 1777.
- Recommended 2nd Lieut., 20 Nov 1778.
- Recommended Captain, 18 Sep 1782.
- Mentioned as Captain, Company No. 1, 2nd Batt., 1785.
- Recommended Captain, 8 May 1787.

DAVIS, JOHN, JR.
- Recommended Ensign, 2nd Batt., 105th Reg., in the room of Edward Campbell, promoted, 17 May 1803.
- Resigned; replaced as Ensign by Francis McMillan, 16 Jul 1805.

DAVIS, NATHANIEL
- Recommended Ensign, 2nd Batt., 70th Reg., 19 Feb 1793.
- (Recommendation not resubmitted 21 Jun 1793).

DAVIS, ROBERT
- Recommended Ensign, Washington County Militia, 26 Feb 1777.

DAVIS, ROBERT
- Recommended Captain, 2nd Batt., 105th Reg., in the room of John Corry (Curry), resigned, 16 Jul 1805.
- Commission as Captain dated 12 Aug 1805, per Officer Roll, 105th Reg., 1808.
- Resigned; replaced as Captain by William Gray, 16 Apr 1811.

DAVIS, WESLEY
- Elected Ensign, 105th Reg., in the room of William Gray, promoted, 30 Nov 1833.
- Commission as Ensign dated 1 Feb 1834, per Officer Roll, 105th Reg., Oct, 1834.
- Elected 2nd Lieut., 23 May 1835.

DAVISON, DANIEL
- Recommended Ensign, Washington County Militia, 19 Apr 1780.

DAVISON, WILLIAM
- Recommended Ensign, Capt. James Montgomery's Company, Washington County Militia, 22 Apr 1778.
- Recommended Lieut., 19 Apr 1780.
- Commission dated 9 May 1780.
- Took oath of office 16 Aug 1780.

DAY, ROBERT
- Recommended Ensign, 1st Batt., 70th Reg., in the room of Ziba Howard, resigned, 15 Sep 1801.
- Recommended Lieut. in the room of Arthur Campbell, Jr., promoted, 17 May 1803.
- Resigned: replaced as Lieut. by George Byars, 20 Nov 1804.

DEBUSK, ISAAC
- Elected 2nd Lieut., Artillery Company,

****

17th Brigade, 5th Div. of the Virginia Militia, attached to the 105th Reg. Election certified by Capt. Thomas McCulloch, 12 Apr 1823 (He replaced Joseph Blackwell, resigned.)

DENNISON, ROBERT
- Elected Ensign, Capt. Samuel C. Duff's Company, 1st Batt., 70th Reg., 23 Nov 1833.
- Resigned; replaced as Ensign by Archibald Grant, 19 Apr 1834.

DICKINSON (DICKENSON), HENRY
- Recommended Ensign, Washington County Militia, 26 Feb 1777.
- Recommended Lieut., 20 Mar 1782.

DICKINSON (DICKENSON), JOHN
- Elected Lieut., 2nd Batt., 105th Reg., in the room of Thomas (W.) Fleenor, resigned, 28 Dec 1833.
- Commission as Lieut., dated 17 Feb 1834, per Officer Roll, 105th Reg., Oct, 1834.

DIXON, HENRY ST. JOHN
- Earlier recommendation not seen, but his commission as Captain of Riflemen was dated 5 Oct 1807, per Officer Roll, 105th Reg., 1808.

DIXON, RICHARD H.
- Elected 3rd Lieut., 105th Reg., 23 May 1835.

DORAN, ALEXANDER
- Recommended Ensign, Washington County Militia, 22 Mar 1781.
- Commissioned Lieut., 20 Jul 1785, which commission he declined to accept by letter to the Governor, dated 22 Oct 1785.
- Recommended Ensign, 8 May 1787.
- Recommended Lieut., 2nd Batt., 70th Reg., 19 Feb 1793.
- Recommended Lieut., 1st Company, 2nd Batt., 70th Reg., 21 Jun 1793.
- Recommended Captain, in the room of Alexander Montgomery, promoted, 19 Jun 1794.
- At the division of the 70th Reg. to create the 105th Reg., his Company was assigned to the 1st Batt., 105th Reg., 20 Mar 1799.
- "Removed out of the state"; replaced as Captain by Hugh Berry, 15 Sep 1801.

DORAN, JAMES
- Earlier recommendation not seen but because he resigned, replaced as Ensign, 2nd Batt., 70th Reg., by Claiborne Davenport, 21 May 1800.

DORTON, WILLIAM, JR.
- Recommended Ensign, Washington County Militia, 20 Mar 1782.
- (Appears a Captain, Russell County Militia, 1786).

DRYDEN, JONATHAN
- Recommended Ensign, 1st Batt., 105th Reg., in the room of John McCauley, resigned, 20 Sep 1799.
- Recommended Lieut., 1st Batt., 105th Reg., in the room of Hugh Berry, promoted, 15 Sep 1801.
- Resigned; replaced as Lieut. by Nathaniel Dryden, 19 Jun 1804.

DRYDEN, NATHANIEL
- Recommended Ensign, Washington County Militia, 19 Apr 1780.

DRYDEN, NATHANIEL
- Recommended Lieut., 1st Batt., 105th Reg., in the room of Jonathan Dryden, resigned, 19 Jun 1804.
- Commission as Lieut. dated 11 Jul 1804, per Officer Roll, 105th Reg., 1808.
- Earlier recommendation not see but because he resigned, replaced as Captain by William Palmer, 21 Sep 1819.

DRYDEN, THOMAS, JR.
- Recommended Ensign, 1st Batt., 105th Reg., in the room of David P. Craig, removed, 19 Mary 1816.
- He did not accept; replaced as Ensign by Thomas R. McCauley, 21 May 1816.

DRYDEN, WILLIAM
- Recommended an officer of the Troop of Horse, Washington County Militia, 21 Mar 1783.

DUFF, JOHN
- Recommended Ensign, 1st Batt., 105th Reg., in the room of Jonathan Dryden, promoted, 15 Sep 1801
- Resigned; replaced as Ensign by Thomas McSpedden (McSpadden), 19 Jun 1804.

DUFF, SAMUEL C.
- Earlier recommendation not seen but because he was promoted, replaced as Lieut., 105th Reg., by James Mahaffey, 18 May 1830.
- Recommended Captain, 1st Batt., 105th Reg., in the room of John McSpadden, removed, 18 May 1830.
- Commission as Captain dated 10 Jun 1830;

his Comapny transferred to the 70th Reg., in July, 1833; per Officer Roll, 105th Reg., 1833.
- Elected Major, 70th Reg., (over Joseph Stewart, the opposing candidate), 22 Mar 1834.
- Commission as Major dated 29 Mar 1834, per Officer Roll, 70th Reg., May 1834.
- Commission as Major dated 22 Mar 1834, per Officer Roll, 70th Reg., Oct 1834.

DUFF, THOMAS J.
- Elected Ensign, Rifle Company, 1st Batt., 70th Reg., in the room of Robert H. Rhea, promoted Capt., 12 Apr 1834.
- Commission as Ensign dated 12 Apr 1834, per Officer Roll, 70th Reg., May and Oct 1834.
- Resigned; replaced as Ensign by the election of John L. G. Edmondson, 3 Oct 1835.

DUFF, WILLIAM
- Recommended Cornet, Troop of Cavalry, 105th Reg., in the room of Joseph Gray, promoted, 19 Jun 1804.
- Recommended 2nd Lieut., Troop of Cavalry, in the room of Robert Houston, promoted, 20 Nov 1804.
- Recommended 1st Lieut., Troop of Cavalry in the room of Robert Houston, promoted, 18 Aug 1807.
- Commission as 1st Lieut., of Cavalry dated 31 Aug 1807, per Officer Roll, 105th Reg., 1808.
- Recommended Captain of Cavalry, 105th Reg., in the room of Robert Houston, resigned, 15 Nov 1808.
- Appears as Lieut., Muster Roll of the Troop of Cavalry, 1st Batt., 105th Reg., 8 Apr 1809.
- Resigned; replaced as Captain of Cavalry by William Ireson, 16 May 1815.

DUFF, WILLIAM T.
- Earlier recommendation not seen but because of his promotion, replaced as Ensign by Gabriel Apperson, 18 July 1826.
- Recommended Lieut., 1st Batt., 105th Reg., 18 Jul 1826.

DUFFEY, JAMES
- Recommended Ensign, Washington County Militia, 14 Oct 1788.

DUFFEY, JOHN
- Recommended Lieut., 2nd Batt., 70th Reg., in the room of Isaac Hughes, resigned, 19 May 1807.
- Removed; replaced as Lieut., by John Beatie, 19 Jan 1808.

DUNGAN, CHARLES
- Recommended Ensign, 1st Batt., 70th Reg., in the room of Robert Porterfield, promoted, 15 May 1821.
- Did not accept; replaced as Ensign by William Griever, 21 May 1822.

DUNGAN, GEORGE
- Recommended Ensign, Capt. David Craig's Company, 70th Reg., in the room of David Carson, promoted, 19 Aug 1800.
- Resigned: replaced as Ensign by James Edmiston, 15 Sep 1801.

DUNGAN, JESSE
- Recommended Ensign, 1st Batt., 70th Reg., in the room of (William) Griever, promoted, 20 May 1823.

DUNGANS, JOHN
- Recommended Ensign, Capt. William Rowan's Company, 1st Batt., 70th Reg., in the room of William Anderson, resigned, 16 Aug 1796.
- Muster fine, 70th Reg., 1798, $5.00.
- Resigned; replaced as Ensign, 2nd Batt., 70th Reg., by Jesse Meek, 15 Oct 1799.

DUNKIN, JOHN
- Recommended Captain, Washington County Militia, 26 Feb 1777.
- (Mentioned as "prisoner in Canada," 20 Mar 1781).

DUNN, JOHN
- Recommended Ensign, 70th Reg., in the room of William Hayter, promoted, 16 May 1820.

DUNN, SAMUEL
- Appointed Surgeon, 70th Reg., per Officer Rolls, 70th Reg., May and Oct 1834.

DUNN, WILLIAM, JR.
- Recommended Ensign, 70th Reg., in the room of Thomas McCulloch, resigned, 21 May 1816.
- Refused to accept: replaced as Ensign by John McCulloch, 19 May 1818.

DYSART, JAMES
- Recommended Captain, Washington County Militia, 26 Feb 1777.
- Commission dated 3 May 1777.
- Took oath of office 18 Aug 1778.
- Recommended Major 17 Apr 1782.

****

- Commission dated 20 Jun 1782.
- Took Oath of Office 21 Mar 1783.
- Recommended Colonel 21 Apr 1785.

DYSART, SAMUEL, JR.
- Recommended Ensign, 1st Batt., 70th Reg., in the room of David Craig, promoted, 22 Jun 1796.
- Recommended Lieut., Company of Riflemen, 1st Batt., 70th Reg, in the room of David Craig, promoted, 15 Aug 1797.
- Recommended Captain, 2nd Batt., 70th Reg., 21 May 1799.
- Resigned; replaced as Captain by Abraham Funk, 15 Sep 1801.

EAKIN, JOHN
- Recommended Ensign, 70th Reg., 16 May 1820.
- Recommended Capt., 2nd Batt., 70th Reg., in the room of James Talbert, promoted, 19 May 1824.
- Resigned; replaced as Captain by Joseph Stewart, 24 Aug 1833.

EDMISTON, ANDREW
- Recommended Captain, 2nd Batt., 70th Reg., in the room of William Beatie, resigned, 19 Jan 1808.
- Removed; replaced as Captain by John Beatie, 20 Feb 1810.

EDMISTON (EDMONDSON), ANDREW
- Recommended Lieut., 1st Batt., 70th Reg., in the room of (Samuel) Grimes, resigned, 15 May 1821.
- Recommended Captain in the room of Rufus Touse, resigned, 20 Aug 1822.
- Resigned; replaced as Captain by Leandis Love, 23 May 1834.

EMISTON, GENERAL WILLIAM CAMPBELL
- Recommended Lieut., 2nd Batt., 70th Reg., in the room of John Scott, removed, 18 Dec 1806.
- Recommended Captain, Company of Light Infantry, 70th Reg., in the room of Charles Talbutt, resigned, 18 Feb 1812.
- Resigned; replaced as Captain by Joseph C. Trigg, 16 May 1815.

EDMISTON, JAMES
- Recommended Ensign, 70th Reg., in the room of George Dungan, resigned, 15 Sep 1801.

EDMISTON (EDMONDSON), JOHN
- Recommended Ensign, Washington County Militia, 14 Feb 1787.
- Removed; replaced as Ensign, Captain Craig's Company of Riflemen, 70th Regiment, by Joseph Cole, 17 May 1803.

EDMISTON (EDMONDSON, EDMONSON), JOHN
- Recommended Lieut., Washington County Militia, 13 Oct 1789.
- Recommended Captain, 1st Batt., 70th Reg., in the room of James Snodgrass, promoted, 15 Aug 1797.
- At the division of the 70th Reg. to create the 105th Reg., his company was assigned to the 1st Batt., 70th Reg., 20 Mar 1799.
- Recommmeded Major, 1st Batt., 70th Reg., in the room of James Snodgrass, resigned, 16 May 1809.

- Deceased; replaced as Major, 1st Batt. 70th Reg., by Samuel Fulton, 16 May 1815.

EDMISTON, R.
- Mentioned as Captain, Company No. 10, 2nd Batt., Washington County Militia, 1785.

EDMISTON, THOMAS
- Recommended by Lt. Col. Francis Preston to be 2nd Lieut., Troop of Cavalry, 70th Reg., 21 Mar 1800.
- The same recommendation made by the County Court, 21 May 1800.
- He appears as the Clerk of the Court of Enquiry, 70th Reg., from 1803 through 1806.

- Recommended 1st Lieut. in the room of William Lyon, promoted, 19 Jun 1804.
- Recommended Major, 2nd Batt., 70th Reg., in the room of Samuel Meek, resigned, 19 May 1807.

EDMISTON, WILLIAM
- Appears as Lieut. Colonel on the board that designated Clinch Mountain the dividing line between the 1st and 2nd Batt. of the Washington County Militia, 30 Jul 1785.

EDMISTON, WILLIAM
- Recommended Lieut., 1st Batt., 70th Reg., in the room of Samuel Carson, resigned 16 May 1815.
- Recommended Captain in the room of James Harley, removed, 16 Apr 1817.
- Resigned; replaced as Captain by Rufus Rouse, 19 May 1818.
- Muster fine, (Edmondson), 70th Reg., 1818, $5.00.

EDMONDSON, JAMES
- Earlier recommendation not seen but because of his promotion, replaced as Ensign by Benjamin Sharp, 21 May 1816.
- Recommended Lieut., 1st Batt., 105th Reg., in the room of Saumel McGinnis, promoted, 21 May 1816.
- Removed; replaced as Lieut. by Benjamin Sharp, 15 Jul 1817.

EDMONDSON, JAMES, JR.
- Recommended Lieut., 1st Batt., 105th Reg., in the room of William E. Buchanan, promoted, 15 Jul 1817.
- Recommendation to be Lieut. resubmitted 19 May 1818.
- Recommended Captain in the room of William E. Buchanan, deceased, 18 Nov 1823.
- Resigned; replaced as Captain by David Rambo, 20 May 1828.
- Elected Captain of a new Rifle Company, 1st Batt., 105th Reg. Election certified by Abraham Fulkerson, Colonel, 105th Reg. 6 Jun 1829.
- Commission as Captain dated 26 Jun 1829, per Officer Roll, 105th Reg., 1833.
- His company assigned to the 70th Reg., 18 Mar 1833. (At that time, his Lt. was John Ketron, his Ens. was Robert H. Rhea.)
- Elected Colonel, 70th Reg., 22 Mar 1834.
- Commission as Colonel dated 29 Mar 1834, per Officer Roll, 70th Reg., May, 1834.
- Commission as Colonel dated 22 Mar 1834, per Officer Roll, 70th Reg., Oct, 1834.

EDMONDSON, JAMES C.
- Earlier election not seen, but because he resigned, replaced as Lieut. by John Kelly, 23 May 1834.

EDMONDSON, JAMES K.
- Elected Lieut., 1st Batt., 70th Reg., in the room of Robert Todd, resigned, 17 Aug 1833.

EDMONDSON, JOHN L.G.
- Elected 2nd Lieut., Rifle Company, 1st Batt., 70th Reg., 28 Feb 1835.
- Elected 2nd Lieut., Rifle Company, 1st Batt., 70th Reg., 3 Oct 1835.

EDMONDSON (EDMISTON), ROBERT
- Recommended Ensign, 1st Batt., 70th Reg., in the room of John Russell, resigned, 19 Nov 1795.
- Recommended Lieut., Capt. James Keys' Company, 1st Batt., 105th Reg., in the room of Samuel Buchanan, removed (?), 21 Jan 1801.
- Recommended Captain, 105th Reg., in the room of James Keys, resigned, 15 Sep 1801.
- Resigned; replaced as Captain by Welcome Martin, 19 Jun 1804.
- Recommended Captain of a new company, 1st Batt., 105th Reg., 15 Nov 1808.
- "Over age"; replaced as Captain by Samuel McGinnis, 21 May 1816.

EDMONDSON, ROBERT, JR.
- Recommended Ensign, Captain William Edmondson's Company, Washington County Militia, 22 Apr 1778.
- Recommended Lieut. 19 Apr 1780.
- Commission dated 9 May 1780.
- Took oath of office 16 Aug 1780.
- Recommended Captain 23 Nov 1780.

EDMONDSON (EDMISTON), ROBERT B.

****

- Elected 2nd Lieut., Troop of Cavalry, 70th Reg., Oct, 1823. Election certified by William Byars, Colonel, 70th Reg., 22 Mar 1824.
- Elected Captain, Troop of Cavalry, Sep 1832.
- Elected Lieut. Colonel, 70th Reg., over Robert Stewart, the opposing candidate, 22 Mar 1834.
- Commission as Lieut. Colonel dated 29 Mar 1834, per Officer Roll, 70th Reg., May 1834.
- Commission as Lieut. Colonel dated 22 Mar 1834, per Officer Roll, 70th Reg., Oct 1834.

EDMONDSON, SAMUEL
- Recommmended Ensign, Washington County Militia, 17 Apr 1782.

EDMONDSON, SAMUEL
- Recommended Ensign, Company of Riflemen, 70th Reg., in the room of James Meek, Jr., promoted, 16 May 1815.
- Recommended Lieut., Company of Riflemen, in the room of James Meek, Jr., promoted, 15 Jul 1817.
- Recommended Lieut., Company of Riflemen, in the room of James Meek, Jr., promoted 19 May 1818.
- Muster fine, 70th Reg., 1819, $5.00.

EDMONDSON, WILLIAM
- Recommended Captain, Washington County Militia, 26 Feb 1777.
- Recommended Major 19 Apr 1780.
- Recommended Lieut. Colonel, 1st Batt., 22 Mar 1781.
- Recommended Colonel 17 Apr 1782.
- "Declines further service ... about removing into North Carolina", per Arthur Campbell, Apr, 1784.

EDMONDSON, WILLIAM, JR.
- Recommended Captain, Washington County Militia, 19 Apr 1780.
- Commission dated 9 May 1780.
- Took oath of office 16 Aug 1780.

EDMONDSON, WILLIAM M.
- Recommended Ensign, 70th Reg., in the room of Robert Houston, promoted, 18 May 1830.
- Resigned; replaced as Ensign by Levi Lester, 23 May 1834.

ELLINGTON, FRANCIS
- Elected Captain of a new company, 105th Reg., 14 Dec 1833. (His Lt. was Elisha Price, his Ens. was David Kestner.)
- Commission as Captain dated 15 Feb 1834, per Officer Roll, 105th Reg., Oct, 1834.

ELLIOTT, JAMES
- Recommended Ensign, Washington County Militia, 26 Feb 1777.
- Recommended 2nd Lieut., Capt. James Shelby's Company, 22 Apr 1778.

ELLIOTT, THOMAS
- Recommended Captain, Washington County Militia, 8 May 1787.

ESTILL, JOHN
- Recommended Ensign, Company of Grenadiers, 1st Batt., 70th Reg., 19 Feb 1783.
- "Under age and gone to college"; replaced as Ensign by David Craig, 19 Jun 1784.

FAIRES (PHARIS), THOMAS
- Recommended Lieut., Washington County Militia, 20 Nov 1782.
- Recommended Lieut. "by ballot", 1785.

FAIRES, WILLIAM
- Recommended Lieut., 105th Reg., in the room of James Caldwell, resigned, 19 Jun 1804.
- Resigned; replaced as Lieut. by Samuel McGinnis, 18 Dec 1806.

FINDLAY, ALEXANDER
- Mentioned by Lt. Col. David Campbell of the 3rd Regt., as an officer of Volunteer Troop of Cavalry, attached to the 105th Reg., 29 Apr 1817.
- Recommended by John Preston to be Major, 105th Reg., 14 May 1834.

FINLEY, GEORGE
- Recommended Lieut., Washington County Militia, 20 May 1779.
- Recommended Captain, 14 Feb 1787.

FITCHPATRICK, JOHN
- Elected 4th Lieut., 70th Reg., 4 Apr 1835.

FITCHPATRICK, WILLIAM
- Elected Ensign, Capt. John Goode's Company, 70th Reg., 23 May 1834.

FLEENOR, ABRAHAM (ABRAM)
- First appears as Private, Muster Roll of Rifle Company, 2nd Batt., 105th Reg., 10 Apr 1809.
- Recommended Ensign, 2nd Batt., 105th

Reg., in the room of George Gobble, promoted, 16 Apr 1817.
- Recommended Captain, in the room of Thomas Fulkerson, resigned, 19 May 1818.
- Resigned; replaced as Captain by Abraham Mungle, 21 May 1822.

FLEENOR, ADAM, JR.
- Recommended Ensign, Capt. John Gibson's Rifle Company, 2nd Batt., 105th Reg., in the room of Abraham Fulkerson, promoted, 15 Nov 1808.
- Appears on Muster Roll, Rifle Company, 2nd Batt., 105th Reg., 10 Apr 1809.
- Recommended Lieut. in the room of Abraham Fulkerson, promoted, 21 May 1811.
- Recommended Captain, Rifle Company, 2nd Batt., 105th Reg., in the room of Abraham Fulkerson, promoted, 16 Apr 1817.
- Resigned; replaced as Captain by Nathan Smith, 25 Jun 1822.

FLEENOR, HENRY
- Recommended Ensign, 2nd Batt., 105th Reg., in the room of Simon Hensley, promoted, 19 Nov 1805.
- Appears as Private, Muster Roll, Rifle Company, 2nd Batt., 105th Reg., 10 Apr 1809.

FLEENOR, JOHN, JR.
- Recommended Ensign, 2nd Batt., 105th Reg., in the room of John Hawkins, removed, 21 May 1799.
- Recommended Lieut. in the room of Ezekiel Hobbs, resigned 15 Oct 1799.
- Resigned; replaced as Lieut. by Stephen Jett, 17 Nov 1801.

FLEENOR, PETER
- Elected 3rd Lieut., Rifle Company, 105th Reg., 28 May 1835.

FLEENOR, THOMAS W.
- Elected Lieut. in Capt. Ota H. Ward's Company, 2nd Batt., 105th Reg., 2 Aug 1832.
- Commission as Lieut. dated 5 Oct 1832, per Officer Roll, 105th Reg., 1833.
- Resigned; replaced as Lieut. by John Dickinson, 28 Dec 1833.

FORRESTER, JOHN
- Recommended Ensign, 70th Reg., in the room of William Hayter, resigned, 20 May 1823.

FRAZIER, JOHN
- Recommended Lieut., Washington County Militia, 26 Feb 1777.
- Recommended Captain 20 Nov 1782.
- Mentioned as Captain, Company No. 1, 1st Batt., 1785.

FRAZOR, DANIEL
- Recommended Lieut., Washington County Militia, 20 Mar 1782.

FREELAND, GEORGE
- Recommended Lieut., Washington County Militia, 26 Feb 1777.

FROST, JOEL
- Earlier recommendation not seen but because he resigned, replaced as Ensign, 105th Reg., by William Gobble, 19 May 1824.

FROST, JOSEPH
- Recommended Lieut., 2nd Batt., 70th Reg., in the room of Peter Livingston, promoted, 19 Oct 1794.
- Recommended Captain in the room of Peter Livingston, resigned, 22 Jun 1796.
- Resigned; replaced as Captain by Elijah Gillenwaters, 23 Jun 1798.

FUDGE, JOHN
- Recommended Lieut., 70th Reg., in the room of William Hayter, who does not accept, 15 May 1821.
- Recommended Captain, 2nd Batt., 70th Reg., in the room of (Francis) Apperson, resigned, 21 Jun 1825.
- Removed; replaced as Captain by John Goode, 16 Jun 1829.

FULCHER, WILLIAM T.
- Elected 4th Lieut., 2nd Batt., 70th Reg., 14 Feb 1835.

FULKERSON, ABRAHAM
- Recommended Ensign, Rifle Company, 2nd Batt., 105th Reg., in the room of John Smith who does not accept, 19 Jan 1808.
- Commission as Ensign of Riflemen dated 8 Jul 1808, per Officer Roll, 105th Reg., 1808.
- Recommended Lieut. in the Rifle Company in the room of Jacob Teator, resigned, 15 Nov 1808.
- Appears as Ensign, Muster Roll of the Rifle Company, 2nd Batt., 105th Reg., 10 Apr 1809.
- Recommended Captain, Rifle Company, 2nd Batt., 105th Reg., in the room of John Gibson, removed, 21 May 1811.
- Recommended Major, 2nd Batt., 105th Reg., in the room of Abraham Bradley, "over 45 years of age and declines to

act", 16 Apr 1817. (Replaced as Captain by Adam Fleenor.)
- Recommended Lieut. Colonel, 105th Reg., in the room of James White, resigned, 21 May 1822.
- Recommended Colonel, 105th Reg., in the room of John Preston, Jr., resigned, 20 May 1828.
- Resigned; replaced as Colonel by Samuel E. Goodson, 25 Aug 1831.

FULKERSON, FREDERICK
- Recommended Ensign, Company of Infantry, 2nd Batt., 105th Reg., 21 May 1799.
- Resigned; replaced as Ensign by John Preston (Jr.), 21 May 1800.
- Recommended Lieut., 2nd Batt., 105th Reg., in the room of Robert Rhea, promoted, 22 Oct 1800.
- Recommended Captain, Light Infantry Company, 2nd Batt., 105th Reg., in the room of Robert Preston, Jr., resigned, 16 Jul 1805.
- Refused to accept; replaced as Captain by John Gibson, 17 Jun 1806.

FULKERSON, JAMES, SR.
- Recommended Lieut., Washington County Militia, 26 Feb 1777.
- Recommended Captain, 20 May 1779.
- Mention of his "late company", Company No. 11, 2nd Batt., 1785.
- Recommended Major, 21 Apr 1785.
- Appears as Major on the board that designated Clinch Mountain as the dividing line between the 1st and 2nd Batt., 30 Jul 1785.
- Recommended Major, 2nd Batt., 70th Reg., 20 Feb 1793.
- Resigned; replaced as Major by Alexander Montgomery, 19 Jun 1794.

FULKERSON, JOHN
- Recommended Ensign, Company of Grenadiers, 2nd Batt., 70th Reg., 19 Feb 1783.
- Recommended Lieut., in the room of William Bradley, removed out of the state, 19 Jun 1794.
- Removed; replaced as Lieut. by Wallace Willoughby, 19 Nov 1795.
- Recommended Captain, 105th Reg., in the room of Samuel Hensley, resigned, 16 Sep 1800.
- Removed; replaced as Captain by Joseph Gray, Jr., 17 May 1803.
- Mentioned as having "removed out of the county" by Colonel Matthew Willoughby, 18 Oct 1803.

FULKERSON, JOHN
- Recommended Ensign, Capt. Richard Fulkerson's Company, 2nd Batt., 105th Reg., in the room of Isaac Anderson, promoted, 15 Nov 1808.
- Earlier recommendation not seen by because he had removed, replaced as Lieut. by Harry Livingston, 18 Feb 1812.

FULKERSON, RICHARD
- Recommended Lieut., 105th Reg., 18 Jun 1800.
- Recommended Lieut. of a new Company, 105th Reg., 16 Sep 1800. (Appears to have been commissioned on the earlier recommendation.)
- Recommended Captain, 2nd Batt., 105th Reg., in the room of John Sinclair who declined to serve, 22 Oct 1800.
- Resigned; replaced as Captain by James Larkey, 17 May 1803.
- Recommended Captain in the room of James Larkey, cashiered, 18 Aug 1807.
- Commission as Captain dated 31 Aug 1807, per Officer Roll, 105th Reg., 1808.
- (Appears as Captain in South Battalion, 124th Regiment, Scott County, Virginia, Feb 1815.)

FULKERSON, THOMAS
- Recommended Ensign, Rifle Company, 105th Reg., 17 Jun 1806.
- Refused to accept; replaced as Ensign by Benjamin Gray, 18 Dec 1806.
- Appears as Private, Muster Roll, Rifle Company, 2nd Batt., 105th Reg., 10 Apr 1809.
- Recommended Captain of a new company, 2nd Batt., 105th Reg., 19 Mar 1816.
- Resigned; replaced as Captain by Abram Fleenor, 19 May 1818.

FULLEN, WILLIAM
- Recommended Ensign in a new company commanded by Abraham Hayter, Jr., 1st Batt., 70th Reg., 22 Jun 1796.
- Recommended Ensign, 2nd Batt., 70th Reg., in the room of Mordacai Gregory, resigned, 19 Nov 1805.
- Resigned; replaced as Ensign by Robert Mitchell, 18 Aug 1807.

FULTON, JOHN
- Appears as Clerk of the Court of Enquiry, 70th Reg., in 1807 and in 1811.

FULTON, JOHN H.
- Recommended Captain, Company of Riflemen, 1st Batt., 105th Reg., 18 Jun 1824.

****

FULTON, PETER
- Recommended Ensign, 2nd Batt., 70th Reg., in the room of (John) Eakin, promoted, 21 Jun 1825.
- Resigned; replaced as Ensign by William B. Logan, 15 May 1827.

FULTON, SAMUEL
- Recommended Ensign, Company of Riflemen, 1st Batt., 70th Reg., in the room of William Carson, promoted 15 Aug 1797.
- Recommended Lieut. in the room of William Carson, resigned, 15 Sep 1801.
- Recommended Captain in the room of John Edmiston, promoted, 16 May 1809.
- Recommended Major, 1st Batt., 70th Reg., in the room of John Edmondson, deceased, 16 May 1815.

FUNK, ABRAHAM
- Recommended Lieut., 2nd Batt., 70th Reg., 21 May 1799.
- Recommended Captain in the room of Samuel Dysart, resigned, 15 Sep 1801.
- Removed; replaced as Captain by Charles Talbutt, 17 May 1803.

GALLIHER, JOHN
- Recommended 2nd Lieut., Artillery Company, 105th Reg., in the room of David Campbell, resigned, 21 Dec 1819.

GANNAWAY, EDMOND
- Recommended Lieut., 70th Reg., in the room of Jesse Meek, resigned, 16 May 1815
- Removed; replaced as Lieut. by George Winniford, 18 May 1819.

GANNAWAY, ROBERTSON
- Recommended Ensign, 70th Reg., in the room of Joshua Adams, resigned, 20 May 1806.
- Recommended Captain, 1st Batt., 70th Reg., in the room of James Meek, resigned, 16 May 1815.
- Resigned; replaced as Captain by George Winniford, 15 May 1821.

GARDNER, CLARK G.
- His election not seen but he was replaced as Captain, 2nd Batt., 70th Reg., by the election of Samuel Chastain, 16 Oct 1830.
- Muster fine, 70th Reg., 1831, $5.00.

GIBSON, ANDREW
- Recommended Lieut. of a new company, 2nd Batt., 105th Reg., 19 Mar 1816.
- Removed; replaced as Lieut. by George Gobble, 16 Apr 1817.

GIBSON, ANDREW
- Elected Lieut., 1st Batt., 105th Reg., in the room of Robert Bailey, resigned, 14 Apr 1832.
- Elected Captain in the room of Connally F. Trigg, resigned, 13 Apr 1833.
- Elected Captain, but "commission not yet issued", per Officer Roll, 105th Reg., 1833.
- Commission as Captain dated 15 May 1833, per Officer Roll, 105th Reg., Oct, 1834.

GIBSON, GEORGE
- Recommended Ensign, Washington County Militia, 20 Mar 1782.

GIBSON, JOHN
- Recommended 2nd Lieut. in a new Troop of Cavalry, 2nd Batt., 105th Reg., 19 Jun 1804.
- Recommended Captain, Rifle Company, 105th Reg., in the room of Frederick Fulkerson who refuses to accept, 17 Jun 1806.
- Commission as Captain, Rifle Company, dated 4 Aug 1806, per Officer Roll, 105th

Reg., 1808.
- Removed "out of bounds of the batt."; replaced as Captain by Abraham Fulkerson, 21 May 1811.
- Recommended Captain, Company of Light Infantry, 1st Batt., 105th Reg., in the room of Andrew McHenry who does not accept, 21 May 1811.
- Did not accept; replaced as Captain by Peter Mayo, 18 Feb 1812.
- Served as Clerk of Court of Enquiry, 105th Reg., 1814 through 1835.

GIFFORD, GEORGE
- Recommended Lieut. in a new company, 2nd Batt., 105th Reg., 15 Nov 1808.

GILLENWATERS, ELIJAH
- Recommended Captain, 70th Reg., in the room of Joseph Frost, resigned, (with the notation "105th Regt.", the earliest notice of the subsequent division of the 70th to create a new Reg.) 23 Jun 1798.
- At the division of the 70th Reg. to create the new 105th Reg., his company was assigned to the 2nd Batt., 105th Reg., 20 Mar 1799.
- Resigned; replaced as Captain by John Gillenwaters, 20 Nov 1804.

GILLENWATERS, JOHN
- Recommended Captain, 2nd Batt., 105th Reg., in the room of Elijah Gillenwaters, resigned, 20 Nov 1804.
- Commission as Captain dated 31 Dec 1804, per Officer Roll, 105th Reg., 1808.
- Muster fines (2), "Capt.", 105th Reg., 1808, $5.00.

GILLENWATERS, THOMAS
- Elected Ensign, 2nd Batt., 105th Reg., in the room of Ota H. Ward, promoted, 2 Jul 1831.
- Removed; replaced as Ensign by Fleenor Musick, 21 Apr 1832.

GILLILAND, JAMES
- Recommended Ensign, 1st Batt., 105th Reg., in the room of John Keys, promoted 15 Sep 1801.

GILLILAND, JOHN
- Earlier recommendation not seen but because he was promoted, replaced as Ensign, 1st Batt., 105th Reg., by John Caldwell, 20 May 1828.
- Recommended Lieut. in the room of David Rambo, promoted, 20 May 1828.
- Resigned; replaced as Lieut. by John S. Caldwell, 18 May 1830.

GILLILAND, SAMUEL
- Recommended Ensign, 1st Batt., 70th Reg., 19 Feb 1793.
- Recommended Lieut. in the room of James Keys, promoted, 19 Jun 1794.
- Removed; replaced as Lieut. by Samuel Buchanan, 19 Nov 1795.

GLENN, BENJAMIN
- Recommended Ensign, Light Infantry Company, 1st Batt., 70th Reg., in the room of Joseph Cole, promoted, 19 May 1807.
- Did not accept; replaced as Ensign by David Snodgrass, 19 Jan 1808.

GLENN, JAMES
- Recommended Ensign, Company of Riflemen, 1st Batt., 70th Reg., in the room of William Beatie, promoted, 15 Aug 1797.
- Recommended Lieut., 2nd Batt., 70th Reg., 16 Jul 1799.
- Resigned; replaced as Lieut. by Isaac Hughes, 15 Sep 1801.

GLENN, JAMES S.
- Elected 3rd Lieut., 2nd Batt., 70th Reg., 14 Feb 1835.

GLENN (GLEN), SAMUEL
- Recommended by Brig. Gen. William Tate to be 1st Lieut. in a new volunteer Company of Artillery, made up of "young men in the town of Abingdon", 19 Jun 1799.
- Recommended Captain of Artillery Company, 105th Reg., in the room of James White, promoted, 19 Jun 1804.
- Removed; replaced as Captain by John Bradley, 16 Jul 1815.

GOBBLE, GEORGE
- Recommended Ensign, 2nd Batt., 105th Reg., in the room of Stephen Jett, promoted, 17 Nov 1801.
- Recommended Lieut. in the room of Stephen Jett, resigned, 17 May 1803.
- Resigned; replaced as Lieut. by James Jett, 19 Nov 1805.
- Recommended Ensign of a new company, 2nd Batt., 105th Reg., 19 Mar 1816.
- Recommended Lieut. in the room of Andrew Gibson, removed, 16 Apr 1817.
- Resigned; replaced as Lieut. by John Mungle, 19 May 1818.

GOBBLE, JACOB
- Recommended Ensign, 2nd Batt., 105th Reg., in the room of John Linder who refuses to accept, 17 Feb 1807.
- Did not accept; replaced as Ensign by

James Newhouse, 19 Jan 1808.

GOBBLE, WILLIAM (M.)
- Recommended Ensign, 105th Reg., in the room of Joel Frost, resigned, 19 May 1824.
- Recommended Lieut. in the room of Abraham Nordyke, resigned, 16 Jun 1829.

GOFF, ANDREW
- Recommended Ensign, Washington County Militia, 19 Apr 1780.
- Recommended Captain, 8 May 1787.
- Recommended Captain, 2nd Batt., 70th Reg., 19 Feb 1793.
- Recommended Captain, 3rd Company, 2nd Batt., 70th Reg., 20 Jun 1793.
- Resigned; replaced as Captain by Peter Levingston, 19 Oct 1794.

GOFF, GEORGE EMMERY
- Recommeded Captain, 105th Reg., in the room of William Head, resigned, 17 Jun 1806.
- Commission as Captain dated 4 Aug 1804, per Officer Roll, 105th Reg., 1808. (This would appear to be in error.)
- Muster fines (2), 105th Reg., 1808, $8.00.
- "Did not do duty for eight months"; replaced as Captain by James Jett, 18 Feb 1812.

GOFF, WILSON
- Elected 2nd Lieut, Troop of Cavalry, 105th Reg., in the room of William King, removed, 23 May 1835.

GOLD, JOHN
- Recommended Captain, Light Infantry Company, 1st Batt., 105th Reg., in the room of Robert Craig, Jr., resigned, 16 Jul 1805.
- Refused to accept; replaced as Captain by Alexander Stuart Walker, 20 May 1806.
- Appears as Private, Muster Roll, Light Infantry Company, 1st Batt., 105th Reg., 8 Apr 1809.

GOODE, JOHN
- Recommended Captain, 2nd Batt., 70th Reg., in the room of John Fudge, removed, 16 Jun 1829.
- Commission as Captain dated 17 Jul 1829, per Officer Rolls, 70th Reg., May and Oct, 1834.
- Resigned; replaced as Captain by the election of Jefferson Talbert, 4 Apr 1835.

GOODMAN, ISAAC
- Recommended Ensign, 2nd Batt., 105th Reg., in the room of William Carmack, promoted, 21 Jun 1825.

GOODSON, JOHN
- Recommended Captain, 105th Reg., in the room of Joseph Gray who refuses to accept, 17 Jun 1806.
- Commission as Captain dated 4 Aug 1806, per Officer Roll, 105th Reg., 1808.
- Resigned; "being more than 45 years of age"; replaced as Captain by William Rhea, 16 May 1809.
- Muster fine, "Capt.", 105th Reg., 1809, $3.00.

GOODSON, SAMUEL E.
- Recommended Lieut., 2nd Batt., 105th Reg., in the room of John Warfield, resigned, 16 May 1815.
- Muster fine, "Capt.", 105th Reg., 1820, $1.00.
- Earlier recommendation not seen but because of his promotion, replaced as Captain by Nathan Worley, 21 May 1822.
- Recommended Major, 2nd Batt., 105th Reg., in the room of Abraham Fulkerson, promoted, 21 May 1822.
- Recommended Lieut. Colonel, 105th Reg., in the room of Abraham Fulkerson, promoted 20 May 1828.
- Muster fine, "Col.", 105th Reg., 1830, $20.00, "requitted".
- Elected Colonel, 105th Reg., in the room of Abraham Fulkerson, resigned, 25 Aug 1832.
- Commission as Colonel dated 15 Mar 1832, per Officer Rolls, 105th Reg., 1833 and Oct, 1834.

GRAHAM, WILLIAM
- Recommended Ensign, 70th Reg., in the room of Robert Hathorn, resigned, 21 May 1816.
- Removed; replaced as Ensign by Richard Montgomery, 16 Apr 1817.

GRANT, ARCHIBALD S.
- Elected Ensign, 1st Batt., 70th Reg., in the room of Robert Dennison, resigned, 19 Apr 1834.
- Commission as Ensign dated 29 Apr 1834, per Officer Rolls, 70th Reg., May and Oct, 1834.
- Did not qualify; replaced by the election of Joel Adams to be 2nd Lieut., 18 Apr 1835.
- Elected 1st Lieut., 70th Reg., in the room of George McDaniel who omitted to qualify, 7 Nov 1835.

****

GRANT, GARDNER
- Recommended Ensign, 105th Reg., in the room of William E. Buchanan, promoted, 21 May 1816.
- Resigned; replaced as Ensign by James Ryburn, 19 May 1818.

GRANT, ISAAC C.
- Elected Captain, 70th Reg., in the room of Joseph Keller, resigned, 7 Nov 1835.

GRANT, JAMES
- Appointed Quartermaster Sergeant, May, 1834, per Officer Roll, 70th Reg., May, 1834.
- Appointed Quartermaster, Oct, 1834.

GRAY, BENJAMIN
- Recommended Ensign, Rifle Company, 105th Reg., in the room of Thomas Fulkerson, who refuses to accept, 18 Dec 1806.
- Did not accept; replaced as Ensign by John Smith, 19 May 1807.
- Appears as Private, Muster Roll, Rifle Company, 2nd Batt., 105th Reg., 10 Apr 1809.
- Recommended Ensign, 2nd Batt., 105th Reg., in the room of John Warfield, promoted, 16 May 1809.

GRAY, JAMES
- Recommended Ensign, Rifle Company, 105th Reg., in the room of Elisha Pitts, who does not accept, 19 Jun 1821.
- Deceased; replaced as Ensign by William Gray, Jr., 18 May 1830.

GRAY, JAMES
- Recommended Ensign, 2nd Batt., 105th Reg., in the room of John Hortenstine, promoted, 20 May 1823.
- Recommended Lieut., in the room of John Hortenstine, promoted, 21 Jun 1825.
- Resigned; replaced as Lieut. by William Anders, 20 May 1828.

GRAY, JOHN
- Recommended Ensign, Company of Infantry, 105th Reg., in the room of Robert Henderson, who refuses to accept, 20 May 1806.
- Commission as Ensign dated 6 Jul 1806, per Officer Roll, 105th Reg., 1808.
- Recommended Lieut., 2nd Batt., 105th Reg., in the room of William Gray, promoted, 16 Apr 1811.
- Resigned; replaced as Lieut. by James Davis, 19 Mar 1816.

GRAY, JOHN, JR.
- Recommended Ensign, 2nd Batt., 105th Reg., in the room of William Ireson, promoted, 16 Apr 1817.
- Recommended Lieut. in the room of William Ireson, resigned, 19 May 1818.
- Removed; replaced as Lieut. by John Hortenstine, 20 May 1823.

GRAY, JOHN JR.
- Recommended Ensign, 2nd Batt., 105th Reg, in the room of Hugh McClellan, promoted, 21 May 1822.
- Did not accept; replaced as Ensign by Jacob Merchant, 20 Aug 1822.

GRAY, JOSEPH
- Recommended Captain, Washington County Militia, 8 May 1787.
- Recommended Captain, 2nd Batt., 70th Reg., 19 Feb 1793.
- Recommended Captain, 2nd Batt., 105th Reg., "formerly appointed in the same company but resigned, the company being broken up by the raising of a Light Infantry Company", 19 Nov 1805.
- Refused to accept; replaced as Captain by John Goodson, 17 Jun 1806.

GRAY, JOSEPH, JR.
- Recommended Ensign, 2nd Batt., 70th Reg., in the room of William Carmack, promoted, 19 Oct 1794.
- Recommended Cornet, Troop of Cavalry, 3rd Reg., 3rd Division, attached to the 105th Reg., 15 Sep 1801.
- Recommended Captain, 105th Reg., in the room of John Fulkerson, removed, 17 May 1803.
- Recommended 1st Lieut., new Troop of Cavalry, 105th Reg., 19 Jun 1804.
- Refused to accept captaincy; replaced as Captain by John Goodson, 17 Jun 1806.

GRAY, WILLIAM
- Recommended Captain, new Troop of Cavalry, 105th Reg., 19 Jun 1804.
- Recommended Lieut., 2nd Batt., 105th Reg., in the room of Edward Campbell, resigned, 16 Jul 1805.
- Commission as Lieut. dated 12 Aug 1805, per Officer Roll, 105th Reg., 1808.
- Recommended Captain, 2nd Batt., 105th Reg., in the room of Robert Davis, resigned, 16 Apr 1811.
- Resigned; replaced as Captain by James Davis, 16 Apr 1817.

GRAY, WILLIAM, JR.
- Recommended Ensign, 105th Reg., in the room of James Gray, deceased, 18 May 1830.

****

- Commission as Ensign dated 10 Jun 1830, per Officer Roll, 105th Reg., 1833.
- Elected Cornet, Troop of Cavalry, 105th Reg., 24 May 1834.
- Commission as Cornet dated 30 Jul 1834, per Offficer Roll, 105th Reg., Oct, 1834.

GRAY, WILLIAM M.
- Earlier election not seen but his commission as Lieut. dated 4 Sep 1833, per Officer Roll, 105th Reg., Oct, 1834.

GREENWAY, JOHN
- Recommended Captain, Company of Grenadiers, 1st Batt., 70th Reg., 19 Feb 1793.
- Resigned; replaced as Captain by William Campbell, 22 Jun 1796.

GREER, WILLIAM
- Recommended Ensign, Washington County Militia, 23 Nov 1780.

GREGORY, MORDACAI
- Recommended Ensign, 2nd Batt., 70th Reg., in the room of Joseph Miller who refuses to accept, 19 Jun 1804.
- Resigned; replaced as Ensign by William Fullen, 19 Nov 1805.
- Muster fines "Ensign", 70th Reg., 1806, $18.00.

GRIEVER (GREEVER), HIRAM A.
- Recommended Lieut., 1st Batt., 70th Reg., in the room of Robert Porterfield, resigned, 20 May 1828. (Earlier recommendation not seen but because of his promotion, replaced as Ensign by Daniel Walker.)
- Elected Captain, 70th Reg., in the room of William Greever, 26 Aug 1831.

GRIEVER (GREEVER), WILLIAM
- Recommended Ensign, 1st Batt., 70th Reg., in the room of Charles Dungans who does not accept, 21 May 1822.
- Recommended Captain in the room of George Winniford, removed, 20 May 1823.
- Replaced as Captain by Hiram A. Greever, 26 Aug 1831.

GRIMES, SAMUEL
- Recommended Lieut., 1st Batt., 70th Reg., in the room of Rufus Rouse, promoted, 19 May 1818.
- Resigned; replaced as Lieut. by Andrew Edmiston, 15 May 1821.

HAGY, MARTIN
- Elected 2nd Lieut., 2nd Batt., 70th Reg., 14 Feb 1835.

HANBY, PETER S.
- Elected Ensign, Company of Riflemen, 2nd Batt., 105th Reg. Election certified by Capt. Nathan Smith. 4 Oct 1828.
- Elected Lieut., Rifle Company. Election certified by Abraham Fulkerson, Col., 105th Reg., 3 Oct 1829.
- Elected Captain, Rifle Company, 105th Reg., in the room of Joel Barker, resigned, 7 Apr 1832.
- Commission as Captain dated 9 Apr 1832, per Officer Roll, 105th Reg., 1833, and Roll of Oct, 1834.

HAND, JAMES
- Elected Ensign, 2nd Batt., 105th Reg., 27 Apr 1832.
- Resigned; replaced as Ensign in Capt. John S. Caldwell's Company, 70th Reg., by John Buchanan, 16 Nov 1833.

HAND, JOHN
- Elected 4th Lieut., 70th Reg., 14 Feb 1835.

HARKLEROAD, HENRY
- Recommended Ensign, Washington County Militia, 13 Oct 1789.
- Recommended Ensign, 2nd Batt., 70th Reg., 19 Feb 1793. (Recommendation not resubmitted, Jun, 1793.)

HARLE, BALDWIN WASHINGTON
- Recommended Cornet, Troop of Cavalry, Washington County Militia, 11 Apr 1788.

HARLEY, JAMES
- Recommended Ensign, 70th Reg., in the room of Charles Scott, promoted, 18 Feb 1812.
- Recommended Captain, 1st Batt., 70th Reg., in the room of Samuel Fulton, promoted, 16 May 1815.
- Removed; replaced as Captain by William Edmiston, 16 Apr 1817.
- Muster fine, 70th Reg., 1817, $10.00.

HART, ELIJAH
- Recommended Captain, 2nd Batt., 105th Reg., 21 May 1799.

HATHORN, ROBERT
- Recommended Ensign, 70th Reg., in the room of Alexander Robinson, resigned, 16 May 1815.
- Resigned; replaced as Ensign by William

Graham, 21 May 1816.

HAWKINS, JOHN
- Recommended Ensign, 2nd Batt., 70th Reg., in the room of John Kindrick, removed, 23 Jun 1798.
- Removed; replaced as Ensign by John Fleenor, Sr., 21 May 1799.

HAWKINS, PHILIP
- Recommended Ensign, 2nd Batt., 70th Reg., in the room of David Craig, promoted, 19 Jun 1794.
- Resigned; replaced as Ensign by David Campbell, Jr., 19 Nov 1795.

HAYS, CHARLES
- Recommended Lieut. "by ballot", 1785. (Appears as Lieut., Russell County, Virginia, 1786.)

HAYS, DAVID
- Recommended Lieut., Capt. James White's Company of Artillery, 3rd Reg., 3rd Division, attached to the 105th Reg., in the room of James King, removed, 17 Jun 1800.
- Recommended 1st Lieut., Artillery Company, in the room of Samuel Glen, promoted, 19 Jun 1804.

HAYS, SAMUEL
- Recommended Lieut., Washington County Militia, 26 Feb 1777.

HAYTER, ABRAHAM, JR.
- Recommended Ensign, Washington County Militia, 13 Oct 1789.
- Recommended Lieut., 1st Batt., 70th Reg., 19 Feb 1793.
- Recommended Ensign, 2nd Company, 1st Batt., 70th Reg., 21 Jun 1793.
- Recommended Captain of a new company, made up of part of the companies of Vance and Logan, 1st Batt., 70th Reg., 22 Jun 1796.
- At the division of the 70th Reg. to create the 105th Reg., his company was assigned to the 2nd Batt., 70th Reg., 20 Mar 1799.
- Resigned; replaced as Captain by Robert McCulloch, 18 Aug 1807.

HAYTER, JOHN
- Recommended Ensign, 2nd Batt., 70th Reg., in the room of William Shaw Logan, promoted, 18 Aug 1807.

HAYTER, WILLIAM
- Recommended Ensign, 70th Reg., in the room of Lewis Menefee, promoted, 18 May 1819.
- Recommended Lieut., 16 May 1820.
- Did not accept promotion; replaced as Lieut. by John Fudge, 15 May 1821.
- Resigned; replaced as Ensign by John Forrester, 20 May 1823.

HAYTON (HAYDEN), ROBERT
- Recommended Ensign, 2nd Batt., 70th Reg., in the room of James Crabtree, deceased, 19 May 1818.
- Recommended Captain in the room of William C. Tate, resigned, 16 May 1820.
- Resigned; replaced as Captain by Charles C. Taylor, 20 May 1823.

HEAD, GAVIN
- Recommended Lieut. in a new company, 2nd Batt., 105th Reg., in the room of Richard Fulkerson, 22 Oct 1800.
- Resigned; replaced as Lieut. by John Skillern, 17 May 1803.

HEAD, WILLIAM
- Recommended Ensign, Washington County Militia, 14 Oct 1788.
- Recommended Ensign, 2nd Batt., 70th Reg., 19 Feb 1793. (Recommendation was not resubmitted in Jun, 1793.)
- Recommended Ensign in Capt. Samuel Hensley's Company in that part of the 70th Reg. which, in 1799, became the the 105th Reg., 23 Jun 1798.
- Recommended Lieut., 105th Reg., in the room of Fielding Hensley, removed, 18 Jun 1800.
- Earlier recommendation not seen but because of his resignation, replaced as Captain, 105th Reg., by George Emmery Goff, 17 Jun 1806.

HENDERSON, ANDREW
- Recommended Lieut., Company of Light Infantry, 70th Reg., in the room of Robert Mitchell, resigned, 16 May 1815.
- Muster fine, 70th Reg., 1817, $15.00.
- Recommended Captain, 70th Reg., in the room of James Trigg, deceased, 18 May 1819.

HENDERSON, JOHN
- Recommended Cornet, Troop of Cavalry, 105th Reg., 19 Jun 1804.
- Recommended Ensign, 2nd Batt., 105th Reg., in the room of John Gray, promoted, 16 Apr 1811.
- Muster fine, "Lieut.", 105th Reg., 1812, $1.00.
- Resigned; replaced as Ensign by William

****

Ireson, 19 Mar 1816.

HENDERSON, LILBURN L. (OR S.)
- Recommended Lieut., Light Infantry Company, 1st Batt., 105th Reg., in the room of Lewis Toncray, resigned, 15 Nov 1808.
- Appears to Muster Roll, Light Infantry Company, 1st Batt., 105th Reg., 8 Apr 1809.
- Declined to accept; replaced as Lieut. by Henry Shelby, 16 May 1809.

HENDERSON, ROBERT
- Recommended Ensign, 105th Reg., in the room of Francis McMillin who does not accept, 19 Nov 1805.
- Refused to accept; replaced as Ensign by John Gray, 20 May 1806.

HENRY, EDMOND
- Recommended Ensign, 105th Reg., 21 May 1811.

HENSLEY, FIELDING
- Recommended Ensign, 2nd Batt., 70th Reg., in the room of William Carmack, promoted, 18 Oct 1798.
- Recommended Lieut. in the room of William Carmack, resigned, 21 May 1800.
- Removed; replaced as Lieut. by William Head, 18 Jun 1800.

HENSLEY, ICABOD
- Earlier recommendation not seen, but because he removed, replaced as Ensign, 105th Reg., by Simon Hensley, 20 Nov 1804.

HENSLEY, JOSEPH
- Recommended Lieut., Washington County Milita, 8 May 1787.
- Recommended Captain, 14 Oct 1788.
- Recommended Captain, 2nd Batt., 70th Reg., 19 Feb 1793.
- Recommended Captain, 4th Company, 2nd Batt., 70th Reg., 20 Jun 1793.
- Resigned; replaced as Captain by Samuel Hensley, 19 Nov 1795.

HENSLEY, NICHOLAS
- Recommended Lieut., 2nd Batt., 105th Reg., in the room of Simon Hensley who refuses to accept, 18 Dec 1806.
- Commission as Lieut. dated 6 Jun 1807, per Officer Roll, 105th Reg., 1808.
- "Failed for eight months to perform the duties of his office"; replaced as Lieut. by James Jett, 18 Jul 1809.

HENSLEY, ROBERT
- Recommended Lieut., Capt. Walter Preston's Company, 2nd Batt., 70th Reg., 22 Jun 1796.
- Recommended Captain in the room of Walter Preston, removed, 18 Oct 1798.
- At the division of the 70th Reg. to create the 150th Reg., his company was assigned to 2nd Batt., 105th Reg., 20 Mar 1799.
- Resigned; replaced as Captain by Robert Rhea, 22 Oct 1800.
- Muster fines (2), 105th Reg., 1800, $8.00.

HENSLEY, SAMUEL
- Recommended Lieut., 2nd Batt., 70th Reg., 19 Feb 1793. (This recommendation was not resubmitted in Jun, 1793.)
- Recommended Lieut., Joseph Hensley's Company, 70th Reg., 16 Apr 1794.
- Mention that his commission as Lieut., "not received", 21 Aug 1794.
- Recommended Captain in the room of Joseph Hensley, resigned, 19 Nov 1795.
- At the division of the 70th Reg. to create the 105th Reg., his company assigned, 2nd Batt., 105th Reg., 20 Mar 1799.
- Resigned; replaced as Captain by John Fulkerson, 16 Sep 1800. (Appears as Revolutionary War pensioner, age 86, in the Washington County Census of 1840.)

HENSLEY, SAMPSON
- Recommeded Ensign, 2nd Batt., 105th Reg., in the room of Fielding Hensley, promoted, 21 May 1800.
- Earlier recommendation not seen but because he did not accept, replaced as Lieut. by Samuel Wilson, 20 Nov 1804.

HENSLEY, SIMON
- Recommended Ensign, 2nd Batt., 105th Reg., in the room of Icabod Hensley, removed, 20 Nov 1804.
- Recommended Lieut. in the room of Samuel Wilson, who does not accept, 19 Nov 1805.
- Refused to accept; replaced as Lieut. by Nicholas Hensley, 18 Dec 1806.

HENSLEY, THOMAS
- Recommended Ensign, 105th Reg., 18 Aug 1807.
- Commission as Ensign dated 31 Aug 1807, per Officer Roll, 105th Reg., 1808.

HERRON, EZEKIAL
- Elected 1st Lieut., Rifle Company, 2nd Batt., 70th Reg., 21 Feb 1835.

****

HICKAM, JOSEPH
- Recommended Ensign, 2nd Batt., 105th Reg., in the room of Audley Anderson, removed, 19 Nov 1805.
- Recommended Lieut., 19 Jul 1808.
- Appears as Lieut., "lately nominated", on Officer Roll, 105th Reg., 1808.

HICKMAN, MICHAEL
- Earlier recommendation not seen but because of his promotion, replaced as Ensign, 2nd Batt., 105th Reg., by Joseph Carmack, 16 May 1815.
- Recommended Captain, 2nd Batt., 105th Reg., in the room of William Rhea, resigned, 16 May 1815.

HICKMAN, MICHAEL
- Elected Ensign, Company of Riflemen, 2nd Batt., 105th Reg., in the room of William Barker, promoted, 7 Apr 1832.
- Commission as Ensign dated 9 Apr 1832, per Officer Roll, 105th Reg., 1833.
- Removed; replaced as Ensign in Capt. Peter S. Hanby's Company, by Samuel Saffer, 5 Apr 1834.

HILL, JAMES W.
- Elected Ensign, Capt. William G. Clark's newly formed company, 70th Reg., 7 Sep 1833.
- Commission as Ensign dated 27 Jan 1834, per Officer Rolls, 70th Reg., May and Oct, 1834.

HILL, MOSES
- Recommended Ensign, 70th Reg., 21 May 1811.
- Earlier recommendation not seen but because he declined to accept promotion, replaced as Lieut. by John Talbutt, 18 Feb 1812.

HILLAN, BAILEY
- Earlier recommendation not seen but because he was promoted, replaced as Ensign by Sidney Laughlin, 19 Jun 1827.
- Recommended Lieut., 105th Reg., in the room of James Kennedy, resigned, 19 Jun 1827.
- Resigned; replaced as Lieut. by Henry Milbourd, 16 Jun 1829.

HILYARD, WILLIAM
- Elected Ensign, Capt. Samuel C. Duff's Company, 1st Batt., 105th Reg., 27 Apr 1832.
- Commission as Ensign dated 5 Oct 1832, per Officer Roll, 105th Reg., 1833.
- The company to which he belonged, Capt. Caldwell's, transferred to the 70th Reg., 18 May 1833.
- Muster fine, 105th Reg., 1833, $10.00.

HINDS, WILLIAM
- Advice by Col. Francis Preston that HIND'S commission as Ensign, 2nd Batt., 70th Reg., had not been received; requested issuance, 14 May 1804.
- Recommended Ensign in the room of Enoch Smith, promoted, 19 Jun 1804.
- Recommended Captain, 2nd Batt., 70th Reg., in the room of Francis Irby, removed 19 Nov 1805. (Replaced as Ensign by William McHenry, 19 Nov 1805.)
- Removed; replaced as Captain by Jonathan Smith, 19 Jan 1808.

HINNEGAR, JACOB
- Recommended Ensign, Washington County Militia, 19 Nov 1783.
- Recommended Ensign, 8 May 1787.

HOBBS, EZEKIAL
- Recommended Ensign, 2nd Batt., 70th Reg.,in the room of John Russell, who declines serving, 19 Oct 1794.
- Recommended Lieut. in the room of Joseph Frost, promoted, 22 Jun 1796.
- Resigned; replaced as Lieut. by John Fleenor, 15 Oct 1799.

HOCKETT, JOHN
- Earlier recommendation not seen but because of his resignation, replaced as Ensign, 70th Reg., by Christopher Morrell, 18 Feb 1812.

HOLLEY, BARNABAS
- Elected 2nd Lieut., Rifle Company, 2nd Batt., 70th Reg., 21 Feb 1835.

HOPKINS, GEORGE W.
- Elected 3rd Lieut., Troop of Cavalry, 70th Reg., 13 Feb 1835.
- Elected 2nd Lieut., Troop of Cavalry, 22 May 1835.

HORN, HENRY
- Elected Captain of a new Company of Artillery, 70th Reg. Election cerified by Col. Robert B. Edmondson, 19 Jul 1834. (The formation of this company was not approved by the State Adjutant General; a new election was specified.)
- Elected Captain, Company of Artillery, 70th Reg., 11 Apr 1835.

HORTENSTINE, JOHN
- Recommended Ensign, 2nd Batt., 105th

****

Reg., in the room of Samuel Snoddy, resigned, 19 Jun 1821.
- Recommended Lieut. in the room of John Gray, removed, 20 May 1823.
- Recommended Captain, 2nd Batt., 105th Reg., in the room of James Davis, resigned, 21 Jun 1825.
- Resigned; replaced as Captain by James S. Davis, 18 May 1830.

HOUSTON, JAMES
- Recommended Ensign, Washington County Militia, 19 Apr 1780.
- Recommended Lieut., 23 Nov 1780.

HOUSTON, JOHN
- Recommended Lieut., Washington County Militia, 17 Mar 1784.
- Recommended Lieut., 8 May 1787.
- Recommended Lieut., 1st Batt., 70th Reg., 19 Feb 1793. (Recommendation not resubmitted, Jun 1793.)

HOUSTON, ROBERT
- Recommended 2nd Lieut., Troop of Cavalry, 3rd Reg., 17th Brigade, 3rd Division, attached to the 150th Reg. of Washington County, in the room of William D. Craig, removed, 17 Jun 1802.
- Recommended 1st Lieut. in the room of Jacob Baker, promoted, 20 Nov 1804.
- Recommended Captain, Troop of Cavalry, 105th Reg., in the room of Jacob Baker, resigned, 18 Aug 1807.
- Commission as Captain of Cavalry dated 31 Aug 1807, per Officer Roll, 105th Reg., 1808.
- Resigned; replaced as Captain by William Duff, 15 Nov 1808.

HOUSTON, ROBERT
- Recommended Ensign, 70th Reg., in the room of (Edmond) Roe, resigned, 21 Jun 1825.
- Recommended Ensign, 70th Reg., in the room of R. Todd, resigned, 15 May 1827.
- Earlier recommendation not seen but because of his promotion (not seen), replaced as Ensign by William M. Edmondson, 18 May 1830.

HOUSTON, WILLIAM
- Recommended Ensign, 1st Batt., 70th Reg., in the room of Joseph Cole, promoted, 19 Jan 1808.
- Recommended Lieut. in the room of Joseph Cole, removed, 16 May 1809.
- Recommended Captain, 1st Batt., 70th Reg., in the room of Levi Bishop, resigned, 16 May 1815.

HOWARD, ZIBA
- Recommended Ensign, 1st Batt., 70th Reg., in the room of Arthur Campbell, Jr., promoted, 21 May 1799.
- Resigned; replaced as Ensign by Robert Day, 15 Sep 1801.

HUBBLE, JOHN
- Elected Lieut., Capt. William Greever's Company, 70th Reg., 12 May 1831.

HUGHES, ISAAC
- Recommended Ensign, 2nd Batt., 70th Reg., 16 Jul 1799.
- Recommended Lieut. in the room of James Glenn, resigned, 19 May 1801.
- Muster fine, Capt. Beatie's Company, 70th Reg., 1805, $2.00.
- Muster fine, "Lt.", 70th Reg., 1806, $2.00.
- Resigned; replaced as Lieut. by John Duffey, 19 May 1807.

HULL, THOMAS
- Elected Ensign, 70th Reg. Election certified by Capt. John Thomas, 2 Apr 1831.

HUTTON, ISAAC
- Elected Ensign, 2nd Batt., 70th Reg., in the room of James Bunch, removed, 24 Aug 1833.
- Commission as Ensign dated 17 Aug 1833, per Officer Rolls, 70th Reg., May and Oct, 1834.

HUTTON, WILLIAM, JR.
- Elected 3rd Lieut., 70th Reg., 14 Feb 1835.

HUTTON, WILLIAM D.
- Elected 1st Lieut., 70th Reg., in the room of John Painter, promoted, 22 May 1835.

****

IRBY, FRANCIS

- Earlier recommendation not seen but because he was promoted, replaced as Ensign, 2nd Batt., 70th Reg., by Augustine Jenkins, 21 May 1799.
- Recommended Lieut., in the room of Isaac Leonard, removed, 21 May 1799.
- Recommended Capt., 70th Reg., in the room of Francis Smith, commissioned Capt. of Cavalry, 18 Jun 1800.
- Removed; replaced as Captain by William Hinds, 19 Nov 1805.

IRBY, FRANCIS W.

- Recommended Lieut., 2nd Batt., 105th Reg., in the room of William Carmack, removed, 18 May 1830. (This was a contested nomination; Isaac Goodman had been elected by the men of the company.)
- Resigned; replaced as Lieut. by James M. Martin, 18 May 1833.
- Elected Capt., Troop of Cavalry, 105th Reg., 24 May 1834.
- Commission as Capt. of Cavalry dated 30 Jul 1834, per Officer Roll, 105th Reg., Oct 1834.

IRESON, WILLIAM

- Recommended Ensign, Company of Light Infantry, 1st Batt., 105th Reg., in the room of Lewis Toncray, promoted, 19 May 1807.
- Removed; replaced as Ensign by Charles Davis, 19 Jul 1808.
- Appears as Private on Muster Roll, Troop of Cavalry, 105th Reg., 8 Apr 1809.
- Additional recommendation that Jacob Shoen fill his vacancy, 16 May 1809.
- Recommended 1st Lieut., Troop of Cavalry, 105th Reg., in the room of Peter Mayo, recommended in the Light Infantry, 21 May 1811.
- Did not accept; replaced as 1st Lieut. by Arthur Campbell, 18 Feb 1812.
- Earlier recommendation not seen but because of his promotion, replaced as 1st Lieut. by William McConnell, 16 May 1815.
- Recommended Captain, Troop of Cavalry, 105th Reg., in the room of William Duff, resigned, 16 May 1815.

IRESON, WILLIAM

- Recommended Ensign, 2nd Batt., 105th Reg., in the room of John Henderson, resigned, 19 Mar 1816.
- Recommended Lieut. in the room of James Davis, promoted, 16 Apr 1817.
- Resigned; replaced as Lieut. by John Gray, Jr., 19 May 1818.

JAMISON, JOHN

- Recommended Lieut., Washington County Militia, 16 May 1781.
- Recommended Lieut., Capt. William Russell's Company, 21 Mar 1783.
- Recommended Captain, 19 Nov 1783.
- Recommended Captain "by ballot", 1785.
- Mentioned as Captain, Company No. 3, 2nd Batt., 1785.
- Recommended Captain, 8 May 1787.
- Recommended Captain, 1st Batt., 70th Reg., 19 Feb 1793.
- Recommended Captain, 1st Company, 1st Batt., 70th Reg., 20 Jun 1793.
- Recommended Major, 1st Batt., 70th Reg., in the room of John Lowry, deceased. (In this recommendation, William Edmiston dissented, because Arthur Bowen outranked Jamison.) 16 Apr 1794.
- Resigned; replaced as Major by James Snodgrass, 15 Aug 1797.

JENKINS, AUGUSTINE (AUSTIN)

- Recommended Ensign, 2nd Batt., 70th Reg., in the room of Francis Irby, promoted, 21 May 1799.
- Recommeded Lieut. in the room of Francis Irby, promoted, 18 Jun 1800.

JENNINGS, JESSE

- Recommended Ensign, 2nd Batt., 70th Reg., in the room of David McHenry who refuses to accept, 19 May 1807.
- Recommended Lieut. in the room of Jonathan Smith, promoted, 19 Jan 1808.
- Resigned; replaced as Lieut. by William Scott, 18 Feb 1812.

JETT, JAMES

- Recommended Ensign, 2nd Batt., 105th Reg., in the room of Philip Taylor, removed, 20 Nov 1804.
- Recommended Lieut., in the room of George Gobble, resigned, 19 Nov 1805.
- Commission as Lieut. dated 31 Dec 1804, per Officer Roll, 105th Reg., 1808. (This would appear to be an error.)
- Recommended Lieut., 2nd Batt., 105th Reg., in the room of Nicholas Hensley, "who did not perform his duties", 18 Jul 1809.
- Recommended Captain, in the room of George E. Goff, "who has not done his duty for eight months", 18 Feb 1812.

JETT, STARK

- Recommended Lieut., 105th Reg., in the room of James Jett, promoted, 18 Feb 1812.

JETT, STEPHEN

- Recommended Ensign, 2nd Batt., 105th

****

Reg., in the room of John Fleenor, promoted, 15 Oct 1799.
- Recommended Lieut. in the room of John Fleenor, resigned, 17 Nov 1801.
- Resigned; replaced as Lieut. by George Gobble, 17 May 1803.

JOHNSON, HUGH
- Elected Ensign, Company of Light Infantry, 2nd Batt., 70th Reg., 27 Apr 1821.

JOHNSTON, CHARLES
- Recommended Ensign, 1st Batt., 105th Reg., in the room of James Campbell, promoted, 19 Mar 1816.
- Did not accept; replaced as Ensign by William Tankersley, 21 May 1816.

JOHNSTON, PETER C.
- "...Spring of 1822, when I commanded the performance of the duties of Inspector of (17th) Brigade", 21 May 1823.
- Inspector of (17th) Brigade, 15 Sep 1834.

JONES, WILLIAM
- Recommended 2nd Lieut., Artillery Company, 105th Reg., in the room of George Spangler, promoted, 20 Nov 1804.
- Resigned; replaced as 2nd Lieut. of Artillery by Joseph Norman, 19 Nov 1805.
- Recommended Lieut. of Artillery, in the room of James Withroe, promoted, 20 May 1806.
- Recommended Captain, Artillery Company, 105th Reg., in the room of James Withroe, deceased, 15 Mar 1808.
- Commission as Captain of Artillery dated 30 Apr 1808, per Officer Roll, 105th Reg., 1808.

JONES, WILLIAM
- Elected 4th Lieut., Rifle Company, 1st Batt., 70th Reg., 28 Feb 1835.

KALOR, ABRAM
- Elected 4th Lieut., Rifle Company, 105th Reg., 28 May 1835.

KATRINE, CHRISTOPHER
- Recommended Lieut., 1st Batt., 105th Reg., in the room of William Buchanan, promoted, 18 Feb 1812.

KELLER, GEORGE
- Elected 1st Lieut., 70th Reg., 28 Feb 1835.

KELLER, JOHN
- Mentioned by Lt. Col. David Campbell, 3rd Va. Regt. of Militia, as an officer of the volunteer Troop of Cavalry, attached to the 105th Reg., 29 Apr 1817.

KELLER, JOSEPH
- Elected Lieut., Capt. Samuel C. Duff's Company, 70th Reg., 23 Nov 1833.
- Elected Captain, 1st Batt., 70th Reg., in the room of Samuel C. Duff, promoted, 19 Apr 1834.
- Commission as Captain dated 29 Apr 1834, per Officer Rolls, 70th Reg., May and Oct, 1834.
- Resigned; replaced as Captain by the election of Isaac C. Grant, 7 Nov 1835.

KELLER, SAMUEL
- Recommended Cornet, Troop of Cavalry, 105th Reg., in the room of John Vance, removed, 16 Jul 1805.
- Did not accept; replaced as Cornet by Thomas Rowland, 19 Jan 1808.
- Recommended 1st Lieut., Company of Artillery, 105th Reg., in the room of William Jones, promoted, 15 Mar 1808.
- Commission as 1st Lieut. of Artillery dated 30 Apr 1808, per Officer Roll, 105th Reg., 1808.
- Removed; replaced as 1st Lieut. of Artillery by Joshua Burke, 16 May 1809.

KELLY, JOHN
- Elected Lieut., 70th Reg., in the room of James C. Edmondson, resigned, 23 May 1834.
- Commission as Lieut. dated 23 May 1834, per Officer Roll, 70th Reg., Oct, 1834.

KELLY, MILTON F.
- Elected 4th Lieut., Rifle Company, 2nd Batt., 70th Reg., 21 Feb 1835.

KENDRICK, JOHN
- Recommended Ensign, 2nd Batt., 70th Reg., in the room of Ezekial Hobbs, promoted, 22 Jun 1796.
- Removed; replaced as Ensign by John Hawkins, 23 Jun 1798.

KENNEDY, JAMES
- Earlier recommendation not seen but because he resigned, replaced as Lieut., 105th Reg., by Bailey Hillan, 19 Jun 1827.

KENNEDY, JOHN
- Recommended Ensign, Washington County Militia, 23 Nov 1780.

KENNEDY, ROBERT
- Recommended to be an officer in the Troop

****

of Horse, Washington County Militia, 21 Mar 1783.

KESTNER (KISTNER), DAVID
- Elected Ensign of a new company, 105th Reg., commanded by Francis Ellington, Capt., 14 Dec 1833.
- Commission as Ensign dated 15 Feb 1834, per Officer Roll, 105th Reg., Oct, 1834.

KETRON, CHRISTLEY
- Recommended Ensign, 1st Batt., 105th Reg., in the room of John S. Caldwell, promoted, 18 May 1830.

KETRON (CATRON), JOHN
- Recommended Ensign, 1st Batt., 105th Reg., in the room of David Rambo, promoted, 18 Nov 1823.
- Elected Lieut., new Rifle Company, 1st Batt., 105th Reg. Election certified by Abraham Fulkerson, Col., 105th Reg., 6 Jun 1829.
- Commission as Lieut. dated 26 Jun 1829, per Officer Roll, 105th Reg., 1833.
- His company (Capt. James Edmondson's) transferred to the 70th Reg., 18 May 1833.
- Appointed Adjutant, 70th Reg.; replaced as Lieut. by George Keys, 12 Apr 1834.
- Commission as Adjutant dated May, 1834, per Officer Roll, 70th Reg., May, 1834.

KEYS, GEORGE B.
- Elected Lieut., Rifle Company, 1st Batt., 70th Reg., in the room of John Ketron, appointed Adjutant of the 70th Reg., 12 Apr 1834.
- Commission as Lieut. dated 12 Apr 1834, per Officer Rolls, 70th Reg., May and Oct, 1834.
- Elected 1st Lieut., 28 Feb 1835.
- Elected 1st Lieut., 3 Oct 1835.

KEYS, JAMES
- Recommended Lieut., Washington County Militia, 18 Sep 1782.
- Commission dated 20 Aug 1783.
- Took oath of office 20 Aug 1783.
- Recommended Lieut., 8 May 1783.
- Recommended Captain, 1st Batt., 70th Reg., 19 Feb 1793.
- Recommended Lieut., 1st Company, 1st Batt., 70th Reg., 21 Jun 1793.
- Recommended Captain, 1st Batt., 70th Reg., in the room of John Lowry, promoted, 15 Oct 1793 and 21 Aug 1794.
- At the division of the 70th Reg. to create the 105th Reg., his company was assigned to the 1st Batt., 105th Reg., 20 Mar 1799.
- Resigned; replaced as Captain by Robert Edmiston, 15 Sep 1801.
(Appears as Revolutionary War pensioner in the Washington County Census of 1840.)

KEYS, JAMES
- Elected 3rd Lieut., 70th Reg., 14 Feb 1835.

KEYS, JOHN
- Recommended Ensign, 1st Batt., 105th Reg., in the room of Robert Edmiston, promoted, 21 Jan 1801.
- Recommended Lieut. in the room of Robert Edmiston, promoted, 15 Sep 1801.

KILLINGER, JACOB
- Elected Cornet, Troop of Cavalry, 70th Reg., 23 Jun 1820.

KINKEAD, JOHN
- Recommended Captain, Washington County Militia, 26 Feb 1777.
- Commission dated 13 May 1777.
- Took oath of office 18 Aug 1778.

KINCAID, ROBERT
- Recommended Ensign, Washington County Militia, 14 Feb 1787.
- Recommended Ensign in Capt. James Vance's Company, in the room of Abraham Bradley, promoted cornet in a Troop of Cavalry, 17 Aug 1798.
- Resigned; replaced as Ensign by William Richardson, 19 Sep 1800.

KINCANNON, ANDREW
- Recommended Lieut., Washington County Militia, 26 Feb 1777.
- Commission dated 3 May 1777.
- Took oath of office 16 Feb 1779.
- Recommended Captain, 17 Apr 1782.
- Mentioned as Captain, Company No. 7, 2nd Batt., 1785.

KINCANNON, FRANCIS
- Recommended Lieut., 70th Reg., in the room of Robert Stewart, promoted, 20 May 1823.

KINCANNON, JAMES
- Recommended Captain, Washington County Militia, 14 Feb 1787.
- Mentioned as having "declined serving under the late (militia) law", 8 May 1794.
- Mentioned as having resigned as Captain, 21 Aug 1794.
- Recommended Ensign, 1st Batt., 70th Reg., in the room of Abijah Thomas, promoted, 20 May 1806.

****

- Removed; replaced as Ensign by Robert Beatie, 18 Feb 1812.

KINCANNON, MATTHEW
- Recommended Ensign, Washington County Militia, 17 Apr 1782.
- Recommended Lieut., 1st Batt., 70th Reg., 19 Feb 1793.
- Recommended Lieut., 4th Company, 1st Batt., 70th Reg., 21 Jun 1793.
- Resigned; replaced as Lieut. by William Beatie, 15 Aug 1797.

KING, JAMES
- Recommended by Brig. Gen. William Tate to be 2nd Lieut. in a volunteer Company of Artillery "made up of young men in the town of Abingdon", 19 Jun 1799.
- Removed; replaced as Lieut. by David Hays, 17 Jun 1800.

KING, WILLIAM
- Elected 2nd Lieut., Troop of Cavalry, 105th Reg., 24 May 1834.
- Commission as Lieut. dated 30 Jul 1834, per Officer Roll, 105th Reg., Oct, 1834.
- Removed; replaced as 2nd Lieut. by Wilson Goff, 23 May 1835.

LANDERS, ANDREW K.
- Elected Ensign, 1st Batt., 105th Reg., in the room of William N. or (V.) Ruley, promoted, 13 Apr 1833.

LARKEY, JAMES
- Recommended Captain, 2nd Batt., 105th Reg., in the room of Richard Fulkerson, resigned, 17 May 1803. (Earlier recommendation not seen - probably "LARKIN", following herein, but replaced as Ensign by Adley Anderson.)
- Cashiered; replaced as Captain by Richard Fulkerson, 18 Aug 1807. (Court material proceedings not seen.)

LARKIN (probably LARKEY), JAMES
- Recommended Ensign, 105th Reg., 18 Jun 1800.
- Recommended Ensign of a new company, 105th Reg., 16 Sep 1800. (Commissioned on earlier recommendation.)

LATHEM, EDWARD
- Recommended Ensign, 105th Reg., in the room of Allen McDonald, removed, 17 May 1803.
- "Having resigned in the Light Infantry", recommended Lieut., 2nd Batt., 105th Reg., 19 Nov 1805.
- Commission as Lieut. dated 6 Jan 1806, per Officer Roll, 105th Reg., 1808.
- Muster fines (2), "Lt.", 105th Reg., 1808, $5.00.
- Resigned; replaced as Lieut. by William Rhea, 15 Nov 1808.

LAUGLIN, NATHAN M. (OR W.)
- Earlier recommendation not seen but because he was promoted, replaced as Ensign, 1st Batt., 105th Reg., by Robert P. Craig, 16 May 1815.
- Recommended Lieut., in the room of Thoams McConnell, removed, 16 May 1815.
- Removed; replaced as Lieut. by William Palmer, 19 Mar 1816. (There was a later recommendation that John Berry fill Laughlin's vacancy as Ensign, 19 May 1818.)

LAUGLIN, NELSON
- Earlier recommendation not seen, but because he resigned, replaced as Ensign by Jonathan Palmer, 16 Jun 1829.

LAUGHLIN, SIDNEY
- Recommended Ensign, 105th Reg., in the room of Bailey Hillan, promoted, 19 Jun 1827.

LEEPER, JAMES
- Recommended Ensign, Capt. John Campbell's (of Royal Oak) Company, Washington County Militia, 3 Oct 1777.
- Recommended 2nd Lieut., 19 Aug 1778.

LEONARD, ISAAC
- Recommended Lieut., a new Company, 1st Batt., 70th Reg., 21 Nov 1798. (Commanded by Capt. Francis Preston.)
- Removed; replaced as Lieut. by Francis Irby, 21 May 1799.

LESTER, LEVI
- Advice by Col. Francis Preston that Lester's commission, 1st Batt., 70th Reg., not received; requests issuance, 14 May 1804.
- Recommended Lieut. in the room of John Rouse, who refuses to accept, 19 Jun 1804.
- Recommended Captain, 70th Reg., in the room of Thomas Tilson, resigned, 18 Aug 1807.
- Refused to accept; replaced as Captain by Levi Bishop, 19 Jan 1808.

LESTER, LEVI
- Elected Ensign, 70th Reg., in the room of William Edmondson, resigned, 23 May 1834.
- Commission as Ensign dated 23 May 1834, per Officer Roll, 70th Reg., Oct, 1834.

****

LEWIS, AARON
- Recommended Captain, Washington County Militia, 26 Feb 1777.
- Recommended Major, 1st Batt., 22 Mar 1781.
- Recommended Lieut. Colonel, 1st Batt., 17 Apr 1782.
- Commission dated 20 Jun 1782.
- Took oath of office 21 Mar 1783.
- Recommended Colonel, 21 Apr 1785. (A note at the foot of this court order: "Is removed to Kentucky".)

LEWIS, JOHN
- Recommended Ensign, Washington County Militia, 20 Mar 1782.

LINDER, ABRAM
- Elected Lieut., 2nd Batt., 105th Reg., in the room of Elijah Mongle, resigned, 2 Jul 1831.

LINDER, JOHN
- Recommended Ensign, 2nd Batt., 105th Reg., in the room of James Jett, promoted, 19 Nov 1805.
- Refused to accept; replaced as Ensign by Jacob Gobble, 17 Feb 1807.

LITERAL, LEWIS
- Elected 4th Lieut., 70th Reg., 28 Feb 1835.

LITTEN (LITTON), SOLOMON
- Recommended Ensign, Washington County Militia, 26 Feb 1777.
- Recommended 2nd Lieut., 19 Aug 1778.
- Mentioned as "prisoner in Canada", 20 Mar 1781.
(Appears as Ensign, Russell County, Virginia, 1786.)

LIVINGSTON, HARRY
- Recommended Lieut., 2nd Batt., 105th Reg., in the room of John Fulkerson, removed, 18 Feb 1812.

LEVINGSTON (LIVINGSTON), PETER
- Recommended Lieut., 2nd Batt., 70th Reg., 19 Feb 1793.
- Recommended Lieut., 4th Company, 2nd Batt., 70th Reg., 21 Jun 1793.
- Recommended Captain, in the room of Andrew Goff, resigned, 19 Oct 1794.
- Resigned; replaced as Captain by Joseph Frost, 22 Jun 1796.

LOGAN, CALEB
- Recommended Ensign, 70th Reg., in the room of Samuel McReynolds, promoted, 16 May 1809.
- Refused to accept; replaced as Ensign by Samuel Cunningham, 20 Feb 1810.

LOGAN, JAMES
- Recommended Lieut., Washington County Militia, 14 Feb 1787.
- Recommended Captain, 13 Oct 1789.
- Recommended Captain, 1st Batt., 70th Reg., 19 Feb 1793.
- Recommended Captain, 4th Company, 1st Batt., 70th Reg., 20 Jun 1793.
- Resigned; replaced as Captain by Berry Cawood, 16 Aug 1796.

LOGAN, WILLIAM B.
- Recommended Ensign, 2nd Batt., 70th Reg., in the room of Peter Fulton, resigned, 15 May 1827.
- Removed; replaced as Ensign by James C. Black, 20 May 1828.

LOGAN, WILLIAM SHAW
- Recommended Ensign, 2nd Batt., 70th Reg., in the room of David McReynolds, resigned, 18 Dec 1806.
- Recommended Lieut., in the room of Robert McCulloch, promoted, 18 Aug 1807.
- Recommended Captain, in the room of Robert McCulloch, resigned 16 May 1809.
- Resigned; replaced as Captain by William Apperson, 16 May 1815.

LONG, JOHN
- Recommended Lieut., Washington County Militia, 8 May 1787.

LONGLEY, BENJAMIN
- Recommended Ensign, 1st Batt., 105th Reg., in the room of John Moffitt, promoted, 18 Jul 1809.
- Resigned; replaced as Ensign by John Crawford, 21 May 1811.

LOONY, JOHN
- Recommended Ensign, Washington County Militia, 26 Feb 1777.

LOONY, MOSES
- Recommended Lieut., Washington County Militia, 20 Nov 1778.

LOONY, ROBERT
- Recommended Ensign, Washington County Militia, 20 Nov 1778.

LOVE, LEANDIS (LEONDUS)
- Elected Captain, 70th Reg., in the room of Andrew Edmondson, resigned, 23 May 1834.

****

- Commission as Captain dated 23 May 1834, per Officer Roll, 70th Reg., Oct, 1834.

LOVE, LEONIDAS
- Recommended Ensign, 70th Reg., in the room of Josiah N. Beatie, resigned, 21 May 1822.
- Resigned; replaced as Ensign by Chapman A. Spotts, 15 May 1827.

LOVE, MADISON
- Elected Captain, Company of Artillery, 105th Reg., in the room of David Clark, resigned. Election certified by Samuel E. Goodson, Lt. Col., 105th Reg. 13 May 1831.
- Removed; replaced as Captain by Charles J. Cummings, 27 Apr 1832.

LOVE, WILLIAM
- Recommended Lieut., 70th Reg., in the room of Elisha Thomas, who does not accept, 18 Feb 1812.
- Resigned; replaced as Lieut. by Arthur Bowen, Jr., 16 May 1815.

LOVELACE, JAMES
- Recommended Ensign, 1st Batt., 105th Reg., in the room of James Mahaffey, promoted, 18 May 1830.

LOWRY, JAMES H.
- Elected 3rd Lieut., Rifle Company, 1st Batt., 70th Reg., 28 Feb 1835.
- Elected 3rd Lieut., Rifle Company, 1st Batt., 70th Reg., 3 Oct 1835.

LOWRY, JOHN
- Recommended Ensign, Washington County Militia, 26 Feb 1777.
- Commission as Lieut. (sic) dated 1 Nov 1777.
- Took oath of office as Lieut., 18 May 1779.
- Recommended Captain, 16 May 1781.
- Commission dated 20 Jul 1785. (The original commission is in the Archives Department, Virginia State Library.)
- Mentioned as Captain, Company No. 5, 2nd Batt., 1785.
- Recommended Major, 1st Batt., 70th Reg., 20 Feb 1793. (Replaced as Captain by James Keys, 15 Oct 1793.)
- Deceased; replaced as Major by John Jamison, 16 Apr 1794.
- Arthur Campbell mentions, "first promoted to be a major, and since deceased", 8 May 1794.

LYNCH, DANIEL
- Recommended Lieut., 1st Batt., 105th Reg., in the room of David Spyker, who does not accept, 16 May 1820.
- Recommended Captain, in the room of James Campbell, resigned, 15 May 1827.
- Resigned; replaced as Captain by William K. Trigg, 16 Jun 1829.

LYNCH, JOHN
- Recommended Ensign, Capt. John Skillern's Company, 2nd Batt., 70th Reg., in the room of William Anderson, promoted, 19 Jun 1794.
- Recommended Lieut., 105th Reg., 18 Jun 1800.

LYON, BENJAMIN
- Elected Lieut., a new Company to be commanded by Capt. William G. Clark, 70th Reg., 7 Sep 1833.
- Commission as Lieut. dated 27 Jan 1833, per Officer Roll, 70th Reg., May, 1834.
- Commission as Lieut. dated 27 Jan 1834, per Officer Roll, 70th Reg., Oct, 1834.
- Elected 1st Lieut., 2nd Batt., 70th Reg., 13 May 1835.

LYON, HUMBERSON
- Recommended Lieut., Washington County Militia, 19 Apr 1780.

LYON, JACOB
- Recommended Ensign, a new Company, 70th Reg., 19 Jan 1808.
- Recommended Lieut., in the room of Nicholas Reagan, who refuses to accept, 19 Jul 1808.
- (An additional court order recommends Reason Roberts to fill Reagan's vacancy, 20 Feb 1810.)

LYON, WILLIAM
- Recommended Ensign, 2nd Batt., 70th Reg., 21 May 1799.
- Resigned; replaced as Ensign by John Sayers, 16 Jul 1799.
- Recommended by Lt. Col. Francis Preston to be 1st Lieut. Troop of Cavalry, 70th Reg., 21 Mar 1800. (The same recommendation made by the court, 21 May 1800.)
- Recommended Captain, Troop of Cavalry, 70th Reg., in the room of Francis Smith, removed, 19 Jun 1804.
- Resigned; replaced as Captain by William Byars, 19 May 1807.

****

McCARTY, BENJAMIN
- Recommended Ensign, 2nd Batt., 70th Reg., in the room of Henry Rogers, resigned, 19 Jun 1804.
- Refused to accept; replaced as Ensign by Mitchell Tate, 16 Jul 1805. (A later court order recommends Eli McCravy to fill this vacancy, 20 Feb 1810.)

McCARTY, ENOCH
- Recommended Ensign, 1st Batt., 70th Reg., in the room of Charles Tate, promoted, 19 Jun 1794.
- Resigned; replaced as Ensign by William Posten, 15 Aug 1797.

McCARTY, JAMES
- Recommended Lieut., 2nd Batt., 70th Reg., in the room of Thomas Tate, promoted, 20 Feb 1810.

McCAULEY, JOHN
- Recommended Ensign, 2nd Batt., 70th Reg., in the room of William Berry, resigned, 16 Aug 1796.
- Resigned; replaced as Ensign, 1st Batt., 105th Reg., by Jonathan Dryden, 20 Sep 1799.

McCAULEY, THOMAS R.
- Recommended Ensign, 1st Batt., 105th Reg., in the room of Thomas Dryden, who does not accept, 21 May 1816.

McCHESNEY, LEANDER
- Recommended Lieut., 105th Reg., in the room of William Palmer, promoted, 21 Sep 1819.
- Earlier recommendation not seen, but because he resigned, replaced as Captain by Thomas McConnell, 16 Jun 1829.

McCHESNEY, THOMAS
- Recommended Lieut., Company of Infantry, 2nd Batt., 105th Reg., in the room of James Cummings, resigned, 19 Sep 1800.
- Resigned; replaced as Lieut. of Light Infantry, by Peter Whistenand, 17 May 1803.

McCLELLAND, ABRAHAM
- Recommended Ensign, Washington County Militia, 26 Feb 1777.

McCLELLAN, HUGH
- Earlier recommendation not seen, but because he was promoted, replaced as Ensign by John Gray, Jr., 21 May 1822.
- Recommended Lieut., 2nd Batt., 105th Reg., in the room of Nathan Worley, promoted, 21 May 1822.
- Did not accept; replaced as Lieut. by William Shoemaker, 20 Aug 1822.

McCONNELL, THOMAS
- Recommended Ensign, 1st Batt., 105th Reg., in the room of Moses Maxwell, who does not accept, 16 Jun 1812.
- Earlier recommendation not seen, but because he removed, replaced as Lieut. by Nathan M. Laughlin, 16 May 1815.

McCONNELL, THOMAS
- Recommended Captain, 105th Reg., in the room of Leander McChesney, resigned, 16 Jun 1829.
- Commission as Captain dated 20 Jul 1829, per Officer Rolls, 105th Reg., 1833 and Oct, 1834.

McCONNELL, WILLIAM
- Earlier recommendation not seen, but because he was promoted, replaced as 2nd Lieut., Troop of Cavalry, 105th Reg., by Thomas McQuown, 16 May 1815.
- Recommended 1st Lieut. of Cavalry, in the room of William Ireson, promoted, 16 May 1815.

McCONNELL, WILLIAM K.
- Elected 3rd Lieut., 105th Reg., 30 May 1835.

McCORMICK, JOHN
- His commission as 1st Lieut., Troop of Cavalry, 3rd Reg., 3rd Division of the Militia of Virginia, attached to the 105th Reg. of Washington County and commanded by Capt. Claiborne Watkins, dated 12 May 1797.
- He appeared in court and certified he had resigned his commission as 1st Lieut. of Cavalry before Abraham Bradley was recommended as Captain, 18 Aug 1802.

McCRAVY, ELI
- Recommended Ensign, 2nd Batt., 70th Reg., in the room of Benjamin McCarty, who refuses to accept, 20 Feb 1810.

McCULLOCH (McCULLOUGH), JOHN
- Recommended Lieut., Washington County Militia, 13 Oct 1787.

McCULLOCH, JOHN
- Recommended Ensign, 70th Reg., in the room of William Dunn, who refuses to accept, 19 May 1818.

McCULLOUGH, ROBERT

****

- Recommended Lieut. of a new company commanded by Capt. Abraham Hayter, Jr., 1st Batt., 70th Reg., 22 Jun 1796.
- Recommended Captain, in the room of Abraham Hayter, Jr., resigned, 18 Aug 1807.
- Resigned; replaced as Captain by William S. Logan, 16 May 1809.

McCULLOCH, ROBERT
- Elected 2nd Lieut., Company of Artillery, 105th Reg. Election certified by Abraham Fulkerson, Col., 105th Reg., 29 Oct 1828.

McCULLOUGH, THOMAS
- Recommended Lieut., Washington County Militia, 19 Aug 1778.

McCULLOCH, THOMAS
- Recommended Ensign, 70th Reg., in the room of Christian Morrell, resigned, 16 May 1815.
- Resigned; replaced as Ensign by William Dunn, Jr., 21 May 1816.
- Recommended 2nd Lieut., Artillery Company, 105th Reg., in the room of David Campbell, resigned, 18 May 1819. (This court order was invalid.)
- Elected 1st Lieut., Company of Artillery, in the room of Job Clark, resigned, 21 Dec 1819.
- Elected 1st Lieut., "by a large majority" of the men of the Artillery Company, in the room of Job Clark, resigned, 23 May 1820.
- Elected Captain, Company of Artillery, in the room of (John) Crawford, "reported to be deceased". Election certified by John Preston, Col., 105th Reg., 13 Oct 1821.
- Recommended Major, 2nd Batt., 105th Reg., in the room of Samuel E. Goodson, promoted, 20 May 1828. (Replaced as Captain of Artillery by David Clark.)
- Elected Lieut. Colonel, 105th Reg., in the room of Samuel E. Goodson, promoted, 25 Aug 1831.
- Muster fine, "Major", 105th Reg., 1831, $5.00.
- Commission as Lieut. Colonel dated 15 Mar 1832, per Officer Rolls, 105th Reg., 1833 and Oct, 1834.
- Muster fine, "Col.", 105th Reg., 1834, $5.00.

McCUTCHAN, SAMUEL
- Recommended Ensign, Washington County Militia, 16 May 1781.

McCUTCHAN, WILLIAM
- Recommended Ensign, Washington County Militia, 20 Mar 1782.

McDANIEL, GEORGE
- Elected 2nd Lieut., 70th Reg., 28 Feb 1835.
- Elected 1st Lieut., 70th Reg., 18 Apr 1835.
- "Omitted to qualify"; replaced as 1st Lieut. by the election of Archibald S. Grant, 7 Nov 1835.

McDANIEL, WILLIAM
- Elected Lieut., 1st Batt., 70th Reg., in the room of Joseph Keller, promoted, 19 Apr 1834.
- Commission as Lieut. dated 29 Apr 1834, per Officer Rolls, 70th Reg., May and Oct, 1834.
- Removed; replaced as Lieut. by George McDaniel, 18 Apr 1835.

McDONALD (McDONNALD), ALLEN
- Recommended Ensign, 105th Reg., in the room of George Craig, removed, 15 Sep 1801.
- Removed; replaced as Ensign by Edward Lathim, 17 May 1803.

McFARLAND, ROBERT
- Recommended Ensign, Washington County Militia, 23 Nov 1780.

McFERREN, JOHN
- Recommended Ensign, Washington County Militia, 19 Apr 1780.

McGINNIS, SAMUEL
- Recommended Lieut., 105th Reg., in the room of William Faires, resigned, 18 Dec 1806.
- Did not accept; replaced as Lieut. by William Buchanan, 19 May 1807.
- Recommended Ensign, 1st Batt., 105th Reg., in the room of (William) Steel, who refuses to accept, 15 Aug 1809.
- Earlier recommendation not seen, but because of his promotion, replaced as Lieut. by James Edmondson, 21 May 1816.
- Recommended Captain, 1st Batt., 105th Reg., in the room of Robert Edmondson, "over age", 21 May 1816.
- Muster fine, "Capt.", 105th Reg., 1820, $1.00.
- Resigned; replaced as Captain by John McSpadden, 18 Jul 1826.

McHENRY, ANDREW
- Recommended Captain, Light Infantry

****

****

Lovelace, 18 May 1830.
- Recommended Lieut., in the room of Samuel C. Duff, promoted, 18 May 1830.
- Commission as Lieut. dated 10 Jun 1830, per Officer Roll, 105th Reg., 1833.
- His company assigned to the 70th Reg., when new boundary line was designated, 13 May 1833.

MAIN, SABIAS (SABERS, SEBERIAS)
- Recommended Ensign, Washington County Militia, 17 Mar 1784.
- Recommended Lieut. "by ballot", 1785.
- Recommended Lieut., 9 Mar 1790.
- Recommended Captain, 1st Batt., 70th Reg., in the room of Joseph Cole, resigned, 15 Aug 1797.
- At the division of the 70th Reg. to created the 150th Reg., his company was assigned to 1st Batt., 70th Reg., 20 Mar 1799.

MAIN, TIMOTHY
- Earlier recommendation not seen, but because of his promotion, replaced as Ensign by Rufus Rouse, 16 May 1815.
- Recommended Lieut., 1st Batt., 70th Reg., in the room of William Houston, "resigned" (sic) - (This should read "promoted".) 16 May 1815.

MARTIN, JAMES M.
- Elected Lieut., Capt. Worley's Company, 2nd Batt., 105th Reg., in the room of Francis W. Irby, resigned, 18 May 1833.
- Commission as Lieut. dated 3 Dec 1833, per Officer Roll, 105th Reg., Oct, 1834.
- "Removed", per Col. Samuel E. Goodson, 25 Jun 1835.

MARTIN, JOHN
- Recommended Ensign, 70th Reg., in the room of Samuel Beatie, removed, 18 May 1819.

MARTIN, JOSEPH
- Recommended Captain, Washington County Militia, 26 Feb 1777.
- Recommended Lieut. Colonel, 2nd Batt., 22 Mar 1781.

MARTIN, WELCOME
- Recommended Captain, 1st Batt., 105th Reg., in the room of Robert Edmiston, resigned, 19 Jun 1804.
- Commission as Captain dated 10 Jul 1804, per Officer Roll, 105th Reg., 1808.
- Removed; replaced as Captain by William Buchanan, 18 Feb 1812.

MASTIN, THOMAS
- Recommended Captain, Washington County Militia, 26 Feb 1777.
- Recommended Major, 2nd Batt., 22 Mar 1781.

MAXWELL, GEORGE
- Recommended Lieut., Washington County Militia, 26 Feb 1777.
- Recommended Captain, 20 Nov 1778.

MAXWELL, JAMES
- Recommended Lieut., Washington County Militia, 26 Feb 1777.

MAXWELL, JAMES
- Recommended Ensign, 2nd Batt., 70th Reg., in the room of Robert Craig, Jr., promoted, 22 Jun 1796.
- Certified to be Ensign, Company of Infantry, 2nd Batt., 70th Reg., now the newly formed 1st Batt., 105th Reg., 16 Jul 1799.
- Recommended Lieut., Company of Light Infantry, 1st Batt., 105th Reg., 15 Oct 1799.
- Resigned or removed (illegible); replaced as Lieut. by Michael Shaver, 19 Jun 1804.

MAXWELL, MOSES
- Recommended Ensign, 1st Batt., 105th Reg., in the room of Thomas McSpedden, promoted in a new company, 15 Nov 1808.
- Did not accept; replaced as Ensign by Thomas McConnell, 16 Jul 1812.

MAYO, PETER
- Recommended 1st Lieut., Troop of Cavalry, 105th Reg., in the room of James Shelby, who will not accept, 18 Jul 1809.
- Recommended Lieut., Company of Light Infantry, 105th Reg., in the room of Henry Shelby, removed, 21 May 1811. (Replaced as 1st Lieut. of Cavalry by William Ireson.)
- Recommended Captain, Company of Light Infantry, 105th Reg., in the room of John Gibson, who does not accept, 18 Feb 1812.

MAYO, WILLIAM H.
- Elected 3rd Lieut., 105th Reg., 6 Jun 1835.

MEEK, ARCHIBALD
- Recommended Ensign, 2nd Batt., 70th Reg., 20 Feb 1810.
- Recommended Captain, in the room of James Scott, removed, 19 May 1818. (This recommendation was contested by James Talbutt.)

****

MEEK, JAMES
- Recommended Lieut., Capt. William Rowan's Company, 1st Batt., 70th Reg., 16 Apr 1794.
- Identical recommendation repeated, 21 May 1799.
- Earlier recommendation not seen, but because he resigned, replaced as Captain by Robertson Gannaway, 16 May 1815.

MEEK, JAMES, JR.
- Earlier recommendation not seen, but because of his promotion, replaced as Ensign, 70th Reg., by Samuel Edmondson, 16 May 1815.
- Recommended Lieut., Company of Riflemen, 70th Reg., in the room of James Allen, resigned, 16 May 1815.
- Recommended Captain, in the room of Andrew Patterson, resigned, 15 Jul 1817.
- Again recommended Captain, same unit, in the room of Andrew Patterson, resigned, 19 May 1818.
- "James Meek, Sr." certified the election of John Allen to be ensign in the Rifle Company, 1 Jan 1821.

MEEK, JESSE
- Recommended Ensign, 2nd Batt., 70th Reg., in the room of John Dungans, resigned, 15 Oct 1799.
- Earlier recommendation not seen, but because he resigned, replaced as Lieut. by Edmond Gannaway, 16 May 1815.

MEEK, SAMUEL
- Recommended Lieut., Washington County Militia, 14 Feb 1787.
- Recommended Captain, 1st Batt., 70th Reg., 19 Feb 1793.
- Recommended Lieut., 3rd Company, 1st Batt., 70th Reg., 21 Jun 1793.
- Recommended Captain, 1st Batt., 70th Reg., 15 Oct 1793.
- Mentioned as Captain, in the room of James Kincannon, resigned, 21 Aug 1794.
- At the division of the 70th Reg., to create the 105th Reg., his company was assigned to 2nd Batt., 70th Reg., 20 Mar 1799.
- Recommended Major, 2nd Batt., 70th Reg., 21 May 1799.
- Resigned; replaced as Major by Thomas Edmiston, 19 May 1807.

MELTON, JOHN
- Elected 4th Lieut., 105th Reg., 30 May 1835.

MENEFEE, -----
- Earlier recommendation not seen, but because he resigned, replaced as Ensign, 70th Reg., by Lewis Morell, 15 May 1821.

MENEFEE, LEWIS
- Recommended Lieut., 70th Reg., in the room of Spencer White, who did not accept, 18 May 1819.

MERCHANT, JACOB
- Recommended Ensign, 2nd Batt., 105th Reg., in the room of John Gray, who does not accept, 20 Aug 1822.
- Did not accept; replaced as Ensign by William Carmack, Jr., 20 May 1823.

MILBOURN, HENRY
- Recommended Lieut., 105th Reg., in the room of Bailey Hillan, resigned, 16 Jun 1829.
- Did not accept; replaced as Lieut. by Jonathan Palmer, 18 May 1830.

MILLAR, JOHN
- Recommended Captain, 2nd Batt., 70th Reg., 19 Feb 1793.
- Removed out of the state; replaced as Captain by John Skillern, 19 Jun 1794.

MILLER, JOHN
- Recommended Ensign, Rifle Company, 105th Reg., in the room of Abram Barb, removed, 19 May 1818. (Abraham Nordyke had been recommended earlier to fill Barb's vacancy, 19 Mar 1816.)

MILLER, JOSEPH
- Recommended Ensign, 2nd Batt., 70th Reg., in the room of John Scott, promoted, 17 May 1803.
- Refused to accept; replaced as Ensign by Mordacai Gregory, 19 Jun 1804.
- Recommendation not seen, but he appears as Captain, 2nd Batt., 70th Reg., on the Militia Fines List of 1811.

MITCHELL, ROBERT
- Recommended Ensign, 2nd Batt., 70th Reg., in the room of William Fullen, resigned, 18 Aug 1807.
- Recommended Lieut., in the room of General William Campbell Edmiston, promoted, 18 Feb 1812.
- Resigned; replaced as Lieut. by Andrew Henderson, 16 May 1815.

MOFFETT (MOFFITT), JOHN
- Recommended Ensign, 105th Reg., in the room of Robert Cummings, resigned, 16 Jul

****

1805.
- Commission as Ensign dated 12 Jul 1805, per Officer Roll, 105th Reg., 1808.
- Recommended Lieut., 1st Batt., 105th Reg., in the room of William Richardson, removed, 18 Jul 1809.
- Recommended Captain, in the room of (Reuben) Bradley, resigned, 16 Jun 1812.
- Resigned; replaced as Captain by Henry Parrott, 19 Mar 1816.

MONTGOMERY, ALEXANDER
- Recommended Lieut., Washington County Militia, 23 Nov 1780.
- Recommended Captain, 21 Apr 1785.
- Mentioned as Captain, Company No. 13, 2nd Batt., 1785.
- Recommended Captain, 2nd Batt., 70th Reg., 19 Feb 1793.
- Recommended Captain, 1st Company, 2nd Batt., 70th Reg., 20 Jun 1793.
- Recommended Major, 2nd Batt., 70th Reg., in the room of James Fulkerson, resigned, 19 Jun 1794. (Replaced as Captain by Alexander Doran.)
- Removed; replaced as Major by Robert Campbell, 19 Oct 1794.

MONTGOMERY, JAMES
- Recommended Captain, Washington County Militia, 26 Feb 1777.
- Commission dated 5 May 1777.
- Took oath of office 20 Nov 1778.

MONTGOMERY, JOHN
- Recommended 2nd Lieut., Troop of Cavalry, 105th Reg., in the room of John Craig, removed, 19 Jan 1808.
- Commission as 2nd Lieut. of Cavalry dated 8 Feb 1808, per Officer Roll, 105th Reg., 1808.
- Recommended 1st Lieut., in the room of William Duff, promoted, 15 Nov 1808.
- Appears on Muster Roll, Troop of Cavalry, 1st Batt., 105th Reg., 8 Apr 1809.
- Refused to accept promotion; replaced as 1st Lieut. by James Shelby, 16 May 1809.

MONTGOMERY, MICHAEL
- Recommended Major, Washington County Militia, 21 Apr 1785.

MONTGOMERY, RICHARD
- Recommended Ensign, 70th Reg., in the room of William Graham, removed, 16 Apr 1817.

MONTGOMERY, WASHINGTON
- Recommended Ensign, 105th Reg., in the room of Jonathan Palmer, promoted, 18 May 1830.
- Commission as Ensign dated 10 Jun 1830, per Officer Rolls, 105th Reg., 1833 and Oct, 1834.
- Resigned, per Col. Samuel E. Goodson, 25 Jun 1835.

MOORE, JOHN
- Recommended Ensign, 1st Batt., 70th Reg., in the room of Samuel Fulton, promoted, 15 Sep 1801.
- Removed; replaced as Ensign by Samuel Carson, 16 Jul 1805.

MOORE, WILLIAM
- Elected 3rd Lieut., 70th Reg., 7 Mar 1835.

MORELL, CHARLES
- Recommended Lieut., 2nd Batt., 70th Reg., in the room of John Fudge, promoted, 21 Jun 1825.
- Resigned; replaced as Ensign by Daniel Davenport, 18 Jul 1826.

MORELL, CHRISTOPHER (CHRISTIAN)
- Recommended Ensign, 70th Reg., in the room of John Hickett, resigned, 18 Feb 1812.
- Resigned; replaced as Ensign by Thomas McCulloch, 16 May 1815.

MORELL, LEWIS
- Recommended Ensign, 70th Reg., in the room of ---- Menefee, resigned, 15 May 1821.

MORRISON, GEORGE
- Recommended Ensign, 2nd Batt., 105th Reg., 2 May 1799.
- Recommended Captain, 18 Jun 1800.
- Muster fines (3), "Capt.", 105th Reg., 1802, $3.00.

MUMPOWER, HENRY
- Elected Lieut., Capt. James B. Worley's Company, 105th Reg., 10 Oct 1835.

MUNGLE (MONGLE), ABRAHAM (ABRAM)
- First appears as Private, Muster Roll, of Artillery Company, 105th Reg., 26 Jun 1815.
- Recommended Ensign, 2nd Batt., 105th Reg., in the room of Abram Fleenor, promoted Captain, 19 May 1818.
- Recommended Captain, in the room of Abram Fleenor, resigned, 21 May 1822.
- Resigned; replaced as Captain by Ota H. Ward, 2 Jul 1831.

****

- Recommended Major, 2nd Batt., 105th Reg., in the room of Thomas McCulloch, promoted, 25 Aug 1831.
- Commission as Major dated 15 Mar 1832, per Officer Rolls, 105th Reg., 1833 and Oct, 1834.

MUNGLE (MONGLE), ELIJAH
- Recommended Ensign, 105th Reg., in the room of William M. Gobble, promoted, 16 Jun 1829.
- Earlier recommendation not seen, but because he resigned, replaced as Lieut. by Abram Linder, 2 Jul 1831.
- Elected 2nd Lieut., Company of Artillery, 105th Reg., 27 Apr 1832.
- Commission as Ensign (sic) dated 18 May 1832, per Officer Roll, 105th Reg., 1833.
- Commission as Ensign dated 20 Jun 1832, but marked "Lieut. of Cavalry", Officer Roll, 105th Reg., Oct, 1834.

MUNGLE, JOHN
- Appears on Muster Roll, Troop of Cavalry, 1st Batt., 105th Reg., 8 Apr 1809.
- Recommended Lieut., 2nd Batt., 105th Reg., in the room of George Gobble, resigned, 19 May 1818.

MUSICK, FLEENOR
- Elected Ensign, Capt. Ota H. Ward's Company, 2nd Batt., 105th Reg., in the room of Thomas Gillenwaters, removed, 21 Apr 1832.
- Commission as Ensign dated 18 May 1832, per Officer Roll, 105th Reg., 1833.
- Resigned; replaced as Ensign by John Felps, 28 Dec 1833.
- Earlier election not seen, but a later commission as Ensign dated 17 Feb 1834, per Officer Roll, 105th Reg., Oct, 1834.

NEEL (NEILL), BARTHOLOMEW
- Earlier recommendation not seen, but because he resigned, replaced as Ensign, 105th Reg., by William Berry, 19 Jun 1804.
- Recommended Ensign, 1st Batt., 105th Reg., in the room of James Reed, who does not accept, 18 Aug 1807.
- Did not accept; replaced as Ensign by Jonathan M. Church, 19 Jul 1808.

NEAL (NEIL), WILLIAM
- Recommended Ensign, Washington County Militia, 26 Feb 1777.
- Recommended 2nd Lieut., Capt. Aaron Lewis' Company, 22 Apr 1778.
- Recommended Captain, 19 Aug 1778.
- Mentioned as Captain, Company No. 9, 2nd Batt., 1785.
- Recommended Captain, 8 May 1787.

NEWELL, SAMUEL, JR.
- Recommended 2nd Lieut., Capt. Andrew Colvill's Company, 22 Apr 1778.
- Commission dated 1 Jun 1778.
- Took oath of office 17 Mar 1779.
- Recommended Captain, 22 Mar 1781.

NEWHOUSE, JAMES
- Recommended Ensign, 2nd Batt., 105th Reg., in the room of Jacob Gobble, who does not accept, 19 Jan 1808.
- Commission as Ensign dated 8 Feb 1808, per Officer Roll, 105th Reg., 1808.

NEWLAND, ISAAC
- Recommended Ensign, Washington county Militia, 22 Mar 1781.
- Recommended Lieut., 14 Feb 1787.
- Commission dated 24 Mar 1787.
- Refused to accept, per Arthur Campbell, 23 Oct 1787.

NORDYKE, ABRAHAM
- Recommended Ensign, Company of Riflemen, 105th Reg., "in the room of Abram Barb, removed", 16 May 1815.
- Recommended Ensign, Capt. (Abraham) Fulkerson's Rifle Company, 105th Reg., in the room of Abraham Barb, removed, 19 Mar 1816.
- Recommended Lieut., Company of Riflemen, 2nd Batt., 105th Reg., in the room of Adam Fleenor, promoted, 16 Apr 1817.
- Resigned; replaced as Lieut. by Nathan Smith, 19 May 1818.
- Recommended Ensign, 2nd Batt., 105th Reg., in the room of Abraham Mungle, promoted, 21 May 1822.
- Earlier recommendation not seen, but because he resigned, replaced as Leiut. by

****

William M. Gobble, 16 Jun 1829.
- Recommended Captain, in the room of Ota H. Ward, removed, 28 Dec 1833.
- Commission as Captain dated 17 Feb 1834, per Officer Roll, 105th Reg., Oct , 1834.

NORMAN, JOSEPH
- Recommended 2nd Lieut., Artillery Company, 105th Reg., in the room of William Jones, resigned, 19 Nov 1805.
- Resigned; replaced as 2nd Lieut. of Artillery by Joshua Burke, 19 Jul 1808.

OGDEN, ELIAS
- Recommended Lieut., 1st Batt., 105th Reg., in the room of Daniel Lynch, promoted, 15 May 1827.
- Did not accept; replaced as Lieut. by William K. Trigg, 19 Jun 1827.

ONEAL, PATRICK
- Recommended Ensign, 1st Batt., 105th Reg., in the room of Jonathan M. Church, removed, 18 Feb 1812.
- Earlier recommendation not seen, but because he resigned, replaced as Lieut. by William E. Buchanan, 21 May 1816.

ORR, JAMES
- Recommended Cornet, Troop of Cavalry, 70th Reg., in the room of William Byars, promoted, 19 Jun 1804.
- Recommended 1st Lieut., in the room of Thoams Edmiston, promoted, 19 May 1807.
- Recommended Captain, Troop of Cavalry, 70th Reg., in the room of William Byars, promoted, 20 Dec 1814.
- Resigned; replaced as Captain by James Beaty, 19 May 1818.
- Appears as Clerk of Court of Enquiry, 70th Reg., 1807, 1809-1810, 1812-1835.

ORR, JAMES, JR.
- Elected Lieut., 2nd Batt., 70th Reg., in the room of Joseph Stewart, promoted, 24 Aug 1833.
- Commission as Lieut. dated 17 Aug 1833, per Officer Roll, 70th Reg., May, 1834.
- Elected Captain, in the room of Joseph Stewart, resigned. Election certified by Col. Robert B. Edmondson, 19 Jul 1834.
- Commission as Captain dated 19 Jul 1834, per Officer Roll, 70th Reg., Oct, 1834.
- Resigned; replaced as Captain by John Painter, 22 May 1835.

ORR, JOHN
- Recommended 2nd Lieut., Troop of Cavalry, 70th Reg., in the room of William Byars, promoted, 19 May 1807.
- Resigned; replaced as 2nd Lieut. by James Beatie, 21 May 1811.

ORR, MOSES C.
- Elected 2nd Lieut., Troop of Cavalry, 70th Reg., Sep, 1832.
- Commission as Lieut. dated 5 Jan 1833, per Officer Roll, 70th Reg., May, 1834.
- Resigned; replaced as 2nd Lieut. by William M. Ryburn, 23 May 1834.

OWENS, JOHN
- Recommended Lieut., Capt. Joseph Gray's Company, 2nd Batt., 70th Reg., 16 Apr 1794.
- Removed; replaced as Lieut. by David Worley, 19 Oct 1794.

PAINTER, JOHN
- Elected 1st Lieut., 70th Reg., in the room of James Orr, Jr., promoted, 19 Jul 1834.
- Commission as Lieut. dated 19 Jul 1834, per Officer Roll, 70th Reg., Oct, 1834.

PALMER, JONATHAN
- Recommended Ensign, 105th Reg., in the room of Nelson Laughlin, resigned, 16 Jun 1829.
- Recommended Lieut., in the room of Henry Milbourn, who does not accept, 18 May 1830.
- Commission as Lieut. dated 20 Jul 1829, per Officer Roll, 105th Reg., 1833.
- "Vacated by removal to Missouri", per Officer Roll, 105th Reg., Oct, 1834.
- Removed; replaced as Lieut. by William Woods, 30 May 1835.

PALMER, WILLIAM
- Recommended Lieut., 1st Batt., 105th Reg., in the room of Nathan M. Laughlin, removed, 19 Mar 1816.
- Recommended Captain, 105th Reg., in the room of Nathaniel Dryden, resigned, 21 Sep 1819.

PARROTT, HENRY
- Recommended Ensign, 1st Batt., 105th Reg., in the room of John Crawford, promoted, 16 Jun 1812.
- Earlier recommendation not seen, but because he was promoted, replaced as Lieut. by James Campbell, 19 Mar 1816.
- Recommended Captain, 1st Batt., 105th Reg., in the room of John Moffett, resigned, 19 Mar 1816.
- Resigned; replaced as Captain by James Campbell, 18 May 1819.

****

PATTERSON, ANDREW
- Recommended Ensign, Company of Light Infantry, 1st Batt., 70th Reg., in the room of William P. Thompson, promoted, 20 Feb 1810.
- Recommended Lieut., in the room of William P. Thompson, who does not accept, 21 May 1811.
- Earlier recommendation not seen, but because he resigned, replaced as Captain by James Meek, Jr., 15 Jul 1817.

PATTERSON, THOMAS E.
- Elected 2nd Lieut., 70th Reg., 7 Mar 1835.

PATTERSON, WILLIAM
- Recommended Lieut., Washington County Militia, 20 Mar 1782.

PERREN, JOSEPH
- Recommended Lieut., in Capt. John Kinkead's "bounds", Washington County Militia, 19 Nov 1782.

PHELPS (FELPS), JOHN
- Elected Ensign, 2nd Batt., 105th Reg., in the room of Fleenor Musick, resigned, 28 Dec 1833.
- Refused to accept, per Col. Samuel E. Goodson, 25 Jun 1835.

PIERCE, JOHN
- Recommended Ensign, Washington County Militia, 8 May 1787.

PIRTLE, GEORGE
- Recommended Ensign, Washington County Militia, 19 Aug 1778.

PITMAN, WILLIAM
- Recommended Lieut., Capt. Dunkin's Company, Washington County Militia, 21 Apr 1779.

PITTS, ELISHA
- Earlier recommendation not seen, but because he did not accept, replaced as Ensign, Rifle Company, 105th Reg., by James Gray, 19 Jun 1821.

PORTERFIELD, ROBERT
- Recommended Ensign, 1st Batt., 70th Reg., in the room of Thomas St. John, removed, 18 May 1819.
- Recommended Lieut., in the room of George Winniford, promoted, 15 May 1821. (Replaced as Ensign by Charles Dungan.)
- Muster fine, 70th Reg., 1824, $15.00.
- Resigned; replaced as Lieut. by William Sanders, 18 Jul 1826.
- Additional recommendation to fill his vacancy as Lieut., by Hiram A. Griever, 20 May 1828.

POSTON, ALEXANDER B.
- Recommended Lieut., 70th Reg., 16 May 1820.

POSTON, HATCH D.
- Recommended Lieut., 2nd Batt., 70th Reg., in the room of (Robert) Hayton, promoted, 15 May 1821.

POSTON, RICHARD
- Recommended Captain, Washington County Militia, 21 Apr 1785.
- Recommended Captain, 1st Batt., 70th Reg., 19 Feb 1793.
- Recommended Captain, 3rd Company, 1st Batt., 70th Reg., 20 Jun 1793.
- Resigned; replaced as Captain by John Campbell, 19 Jun 1794.

POSTON, WILLIAM
- Recommended Ensign, 1st Batt., 70th Reg., in the room of Enoch McCarty, resigned, 15 Aug 1797.
- Recommended Lieut., in the room of Charles Tate, promoted, 17 Jan 1798.
- Resigned; replaced as Lieut., 2nd Batt., 70th Reg., by Mitchell Tate, 19 Nov 1805.

PRESTON, FRANCIS
- (He had been made a Captain of a Company of Light Infantry in Montgomery County in 1788.)
- Recommended Captain, a new Company, 1st Batt., 70th Reg., 21 Nov 1798.
- At the division of the 70th Reg., to create the 105th Reg., his company was assigned to the 2nd Batt., 70th Reg., 20 Mar 1799.
- Mention that he had been "a Captain in Montgomery County before Samuel Meek was a subaltern in Washington County", 26 Mar 1799.
- Recommended Lieut. Colonel, Commandant of the 70th Reg., in the room of Arthur Campbell, resigned, 21 May 1799.
- Promoted in the 17th Brigade Virginia Militia; replaced as Lieut. Colonel, 70th Reg., by Charles Tate, 20 Dec 1814.
- (A record of Francis Preston's subsequent service in the Virginia Militia is not preserved among the Washington County Militia papers.)

PRESTON, JOHN, JR.
- Recommended Ensign, 2nd Batt., 105th

****

****

- Elected Ensign, Capt. William Greever's Company, 70th Reg., 12 May 1831.

REDPATH, JAMES
- Recommended Ensign, Company of Light Infantry, 1st Batt., 105th Reg., 15 Oct 1799.
- Removed; replaced as Ensign by John R. Acklin, 17 Jun 1800.

REED, JAMES
- Recommended Ensign, 105th Reg., in the room of John Trimble, resigned, 19 May 1807.
- Did not accept; replaced as Ensign by Bartholomew Neel, 18 Aug 1807.

RHEA, JOSEPH
- Recommended Ensign, Washington County Militia, 20 Mar 1782.

RHEA, ROBERT
- Recommended Ensign, Capt. Walter Preston's Company, 2nd Batt., 70th Reg., 22 Jun 1796.
- Recommended Lieut., in the room of Robert Hensley, promoted, 18 Oct 1798.
- Recommended Captain, 2nd Batt., 105th Reg., in the room of Robert Hensley, resigned, 22 Oct 1800.

RHEA, ROBERT H.
- Elected Ensign, a new Rifle Company, 1st Batt., 105th Reg., 6 Jun 1829.
- Commission as Ensign dated 26 Jun 1829, per Officer Roll, 105th Reg., 1833.
- His company (Capt. James Edmondson's) transferred to 70th Reg., 18 May 1833.
- Elected Captain, Rifle Company, 1st Batt., 70th Reg., in the room of James Edmondson, Jr., promoted Colonel of the 70th Reg., 12 Apr 1834.
- Commission as Captain dated 12 Apr 1834, per Officer Rolls, 70th Reg., May and Oct, 1834.

RHEA, WILLIAM
- Recommended Lieut., 2nd Batt., 105th Reg., in the room of Edward Lathem, resigned, 15 Nov 1808.
- Recommended Captain in the room of John Goodson, resigned, 16 May 1809.
- Resigned; replaced as Captain by Michael Hickman, 16 May 1815.

RICHASON, DAVID
- Recommended Ensign, 70th Reg., in the room of Armstrong Beatie, who does not accept, 18 Feb 1812.
- Did not accept; replaced as Ensign by John Smith, 16 Jun 1812.

RICHARDSON, WILLIAM
- Recommended Ensign, 105th Reg., in the room of Robert Kincaid, resigned, 16 Sep 1800.
- Recommended Lieut., 1st Batt., 105th Reg., in the room of Reuben Bradley, promoted, 17 Nov 1801.
- Commission as Lieut. dated 8 Dec 1801, per Officer Roll, 105th Reg., 1808.
- Removed; replaced as Lieut. by John Moffitt, 18 Jul 1809.

RILEY, CHARLES
- Recommended Ensign, 1st Batt., 70th Reg., in the room of Robertson Gannaway, promoted, 16 May 1815.
- Removed; replaced as Ensign by Thomas St. John, 19 May 1818.

RITCHIE, ALEXANDER
- Recommended Ensign, Capt. John Snody's Company, Washington County Militia, 27 Aug 1777.
- Recommended Captain, 20 Mar 1782.
- Mentioned as Captain, Company No. 7, 1st Batt., 1785.

ROBERTS, HENRY
- Recommended Ensign, 2nd Batt., 70th Reg., in the room of John Epperson, resigned, 15 Oct 1799.
- Resigned; replaced as Ensign by Benjamin McCarty, 19 Jun 1804.

ROBERTS, JAMES
- Recommended Ensign, Washington County Militia, 20 Mar 1782.
- Recommended Lieut., 17 Apr 1782.

ROBERTS, REASON
- Recommended Ensign, a new Company, 70th Reg., in the room of Jacob Lyon, promoted, 19 Jul 1808.
- Recommended Lieut., in the room of Nicholas Reagan, who does not accept, 20 Feb 1810.
- Resigned; replaced as Ensign by James Crabtree, 21 May 1811.
- Muster fine, "Lieut.", 70th Reg., 1811, $15.00.

ROBERTS, WILLIAM
- Recommended Lieut., 2nd Batt., 70th Reg., 19 Feb 1793.
- (Recommendation not resubmitted, Jun, 1793.)

ROBERTSON, JAMES

****

- Recommended Captain, Washington County Militia, 26 Feb 1777.

ROBINSON, ALEXANDER
- Earlier recommendation not seen, but because he resigned, replaced as Ensign, 70th Reg., by Robert Hathorn, 16 May 1815.

ROBINSON, JAMES
- Elected Lieut., new Rifle Company, 1st Batt., 70th Reg., Aug, 1807.

ROBINSON, JOHN
- Recommended 2nd Lieut., Capt. James Dysart's Company, Washington County Militia, 3 Oct 1777.

ROE, EDMOND
- Recommended Ensign, 70th Reg., 19 May 1818.
- Resigned; replaced as Ensign by Robert Houston, 21 Jun 1825.

ROSEBROUGH, WILLIAM
- Recommended Ensign, Washington County Milita, 26 Feb 1777.
- Recommended Lieut., 20 May 1778.

ROUSE, JOHN
- Recommended Ensign, 1st Batt., 70th Reg., in the room of Thomas Tilson, promoted, 21 May 1799.
- Advice by Col. Francis Preston that Rouse's commission as Lieut. not received; requests issuance, 14 May 1804.
- Refused to accept; replaced as Lieut. by Levi Lester, 19 Jun 1804.

ROUSE, PHILLIP
- Elected Ensign, new Rifle Company, 1st Batt., 70th Reg., Aug, 1807.

ROUSE, RUFUS
- Recommended Ensign, 1st Batt., 70th Reg., in the room of Timothy Main, promoted, 16 May 1815.
- Recommended Lieut., in the room of William Edmiston, promoted, 16 Apr 1817.
- Recommended Captain, in the room of William Edmiston, promoted, 19 May 1818.
- Resigned; replaced as Captain by Andrew Edmiston, 20 Aug 1822.

ROWAN, WILLIAM
- Recommended Ensign, Washington County Militia, 13 Oct 1789.
- Recommended Ensign, 1st Batt., 70th Reg., 19 Feb 1793.
- (Recommendation not resubmitted, Jun 1793.)
- Recommended Captain, 1st Batt., 70th Reg., in the room of John Jamison, promoted, 16 Apr 1794.
- At the division of the 70th Reg. to create the 150th Reg., his Company was assigned to 1st Batt., 70th Reg., 20 Mar 1799.
- Cashiered by Court Martial, 16 Oct 1801.

ROWLAND, THOMAS
- Recommended Cornet, Troop of Cavalry, 105th Reg., in the room of Samuel Keller, who does not accept, 19 Jan 1808.
- Commission as Cornet of Cavalry dated 8 Feb 1808, per Officer Roll, 105th Reg., 1808.
- Appears on Muster Roll, Troop of Cavalry, 1st Batt., 105th Reg., 8 Apr 1809.
- Muster fine, "Cornet", 105th Reg., 1811, $6.00.
- Muster fine, "Cornet", 105th Reg., 1812, $7.00.

RUGGLES, SOLOMON
- Elected 3rd Lieut., Company of Artillery, 70th Reg., 11 Apr 1835.
- "Omitted to qualify"; replaced as 3rd Lieut. by William Allin, 10 Oct 1835.

RULY (RULEY), NICHOLAS H.
- Recommended Ensign, 105th Reg., in the room of Joseph Vance, resigned, 15 May 1827
- Recommended Lieut., in the room of William K. Trigg, promoted, 16 Jun 1829.
- Resigned; replaced as Lieut. by Robert Bailey, 13 May 1831.

RULEY, WILLIAM V. (OR N.)
- Elected Ensign, 1st Batt., 105th Reg., in the room of Addison A. Spotts, resigned, 14 Apr 1832.
- Elected Lieut., in the room of Andrew Gibson, promoted, 13 Apr 1833.
- Commission as Lieut. dated 15 May 1833, per Officer Roll, 105th Reg., Oct, 1834.

RUSSELL, JOHN
- Recommended Ensign, Capt. Andrew Goff's Company, 70th Reg., 16 Apr 1794.
- Declined to serve; replaced as Ensign by Ezekial Hobbs, 19 Oct 1794.

RUSSELL, JOHN
- Recommended Ensign, 1st Batt., 70th Reg., in the room of Samuel Gilliland, promoted, 19 Jun 1794.
- Resigned; replaced as Ensign by Robert Edmiston, 19 Nov 1795.

RUSSELL, ROBERT

****

- Recommended Ensign, Washington County Militia, 20 Mar 1782.

RUSSELL, WILLIAM, JR.
- Recommended Captain, 1st Batt., Washington County Militia, 22 Mar 1781.
- Appears as President of board that designated Clinch Mountain the dividing line between the 1st and 2nd Batt., 30 Jul 1785.

RUST, DANIEL
- Elected 4th Lieut., 105th Reg., 23 May 1835.

RYBURN, JAMES
- Recommended Ensign, 105th Reg., in the room of Gardner Grant, resigned, 19 May 1818.

RYBURN, MATTHEW
- Recommended Cornet, Troop of Cavalry, 70th Reg., in the room of David Beatie, resigned, 19 May 1818.
- Earlier recommendation not seen, but because he was promoted, replaced as 2nd Lieut. by William Clark, 16 May 1820.
- Recommended 1st Lieut., in the room of John Clark, promoted, 16 May 1820.
- Elected 1st Lieut. by men of the Troop of Cavalry, 23 Jun 1820.
- Elected Captain, Troop of Cavalry, 70th Reg., in the room of John Clark, resigned, 22 Mar 1824.

RYBURN, WILLIAM M.
- Elected 2nd Lieut., Troop of Cavalry, 70th Reg., in the room of Moses C. Orr, resigned, 23 May 1834.
- Commission as Lieut. dated 7 Jul 1834, per Officer Roll, 70th Reg., Oct, 1834.

SANDERS, ANDREW K.
- Earlier election not seen, but his commission as Ensign, was dated 15 May 1833, per Officer Roll, 105th Reg., Oct, 1834.
- Muster fine, "Ensign", 105th Reg., 1834, $20.00.

SANDERS, WILLIAM
- Recommended Lieut., 1st Batt., 70th Reg., in the room of Robert Porterfied, resigned, 18 Jul 1826.

SAWYERS, JOHN
- Recommended Ensign, Washington County Militia, 20 Nov 1778.

SAYERS, JOHN
- Recommended Ensign, Company of Infantry, 2nd Batt., 70th Reg., in the room of William Lyon, resigned, 16 Jul 1799.
- Because of apparent loss in the mail, recommendation resubmitted by Lt. Col. Francis Preston, 15 May 1800.
- Resigned; replaced as Ensign by John Scott, 15 Sep 1801.

SCOTT, BAZEL
- Recommended Ensign, 2nd Batt., 70th Reg., in the room of Mitchell Tate, promoted, 19 Nov 1805.
- Recommended Captain of a new Company, 70th Reg., 19 Jan 1808.
- Deceased; replaced as Captain by Mitchell Scott, 18 Feb 1812.

SCOTT, CHARLES
- Recommended Ensign, 70th Reg., in the room of Reason Roberts, promoted, 20 Feb 1810.
- Recommendation not seen, but because he was promoted, replaced as Ensign by James Harley, 18 Feb 1812.

SCOTT, JAMES
- Recommended Captain, 2nd Batt., 70th Reg., in the room of John Beatie, removed, 21 May 1811.
- Removed; replaced as Captain by Archibald Meek, in a contested recommendation, 19 May 1818.

SCOTT, JOHN
- Recommended Ensign, 2nd Batt., 70th Reg., in the room of John Sayers, resigned, 15 Sep 1801.
- Recommended Lieut., in the room of Charles Talbutt, promoted, 17 May 1803.
- Removed; replaced as Lieut. by General Willaim Campbell Edmiston, 18 Dec 1806.

****

SCOTT, JOSEPH
- Recommended Lieut., Washington County Militia, 19 Apr 1780.

SCOTT, JOSEPH
- Recommended Ensign, 1st Batt., 70th Reg., in the room of Abraham Hayter, Jr., promoted, 22 Jun 1796.
- Recommended Lieut. in the room of Berry Cawood, promoted, 16 Aug 1796.
- Resigned; replaced as Lieut. in Berry Cawood's Company by John Crabtree, 18 Mar 1800.

SCOTT, MITCHELL
- Recommended Captain, 2nd Batt., 70th Reg., in the room of Bazel Scott, deceased, 18 Feb 1812.

SCOTT, WILLIAM
- Recommended Lieut., Washington County Militia, 22 Mar 1781.

SCOTT, WILLIAM
- Recommended Lieut., 2nd Batt., 70th Reg., in the room of Jesse Jennings, resigned, 18 Feb 1812.

SHAFFER (SAFFER), SAMUEL
- Elected Ensign, Rifle Company, 105th Reg., in the room of Michael Hickman, removed, 5 Apr 1834.
- Elected 2nd Lieut., 28 May 1835.

SHARP, BENJAMIN
- Recommended Lieut., Washington County Militia, 8 May 1787.
- Recommended Lieut., 2nd Batt., 70th Reg., 19 Feb 1793.
- Recommended Lieut., 2nd Company, 2nd Batt., 70th Reg., 21 Jun 1793.
- Removed from county; replaced as Lieut. by David Craig, 19 Jun 1794.

SHARP, BENJAMIN
- Recommended Ensign, 1st Batt., 105th Reg., in the room of James Edmondson, promoted, 21 May 1816.
- Recommended Lieut., in the room of James Edmondson, removed, 15 Jul 1817.
- This recommendation was repeated, 19 May 1818.
- Appointed Sergeant Major, 70th Reg., May, 1834, per Officer Rolls, 70th Reg., May and Oct, 1834.

SHARP, THOMAS
- Recommended Ensign, Washington County Militia, 20 Nov 1778.

SHAVER, MICHAEL
- Recommended Lieut., Company of Light Infantry, 1st Batt., 105th Reg., in the room of James Maxwell, 19 Jul 1805.
- Resigned; replaced as Lieut. by James Bailey, 16 Jul 1805.
- Appears as Private, Muster Roll, Artillery Company, 105th Reg., 26 Jun 1815.

SHAW, JAMES
- Recommended Ensign, Washington County Militia, 26 Feb 1777.

SHEFFY, JAMES W.
- Elected 4th Lieut., Troop of Cavalry, 105th Reg., 23 May 1835.

SHELBY, EVAN
- Took oath of office as Colonel, Washington County Militia, 29 Jan 1777.

SHELBY, HENRY
- Recommended Lieut., Light Infantry Company, 105th Reg., in the room of Lilburn S. Henderson, who declines to accept, 16 May 1809.
- Removed; replaced as Lieut. by Peter Mayo, 21 May 1811.

SHELBY, JAMES
- Recommended Captain, Washington County Militia, 26 Feb 1777.

SHELBY, JAMES
- Appears as Private, Roll of Light Infantry Company, 1st Batt., 105th Reg., 8 Apr 1809.
- Recommended 1st Lieut., Troop of Cavalry, 105th Reg., in the room of John Montgomery, who refuses to accept, 16 May 1809.
- Would not accept; replaced as 1st Lieut. by Peter Mayor, 18 Jul 1809.

SHELBY, JOHN, SR.
- Recommended Captain, Washington County Militia, 26 Feb 1777.
- Commission dated 4 May 1777.
- Took oath of office, 19 Aug 1778.

SHOEMAKER, WILLIAM S.
- Recommended Lieut., 2nd Batt., 105th Reg., in the room of Hugh McClellan, who does not accept, 20 Aug 1822.
- Recommended Captain, in the room of Nathan Worley, resigned, 21 Jun 1825.
- Muster fine, "Capt.", 105th Reg., 1826, $25.00.

- Muster fine, "Capt.", 105th Reg., 1830, $5.00.
- Muster fine, "Capt.", 105th Reg., 1832, $1.00.
- Replaced as Captain by James B. Worley, 14 Apr 1833.

SHOEN (OR SHOER), JACOB
- Recommended Ensign, Company of Light Infantry, 105th Reg., in the room of William Ireson, removed, 16 May 1809. (It has been recommended earlier that Charles Davis fill this vacancy, 19 Jul 1808.)

SINCLAIR, JOHN
- Recommended Captain, 105th Reg., 18 Jun 1800.
- Recommended Captain of a new Company, 105th Reg., 16 Sep 1800.
- Declined to serve; replaced as Captain by Richard Fulkerson, 22 Oct 1800.

SKILLERN, ANDREW
- Recommended Ensign, 105th Reg., 18 Jun 1800.

SKILLERN, JAMES
- Recommended Lieut., 105th Reg., in the room of John Skillern, recommended through error, 19 Jun 1804.

SKILLERN, JOHN
- Recommended Lieut., 2nd Batt., 70th Reg., 19 Feb 1793.
- Recommended Lieut., 5th Company, 2nd Batt., 70th Reg., 21 Jun 1793.
- Recommended Captain, 2nd Batt., 70th Reg., in the room of John Millar, "removed out of the state", 19 Jun 1794.

SMITH (SMYTH), ALEXANDER
- Of Wythe County
- Recommended by Brig. Gen. William Tate to be Captain of a Troop of Horse (Cavalry), 17th Brigade, 12 Dec 1793.
- Mentioned as Brigade Major, 25 Nov 1794.

SMITH, DANIEL
- Took oath of office as Major, Washington County Militia, 29 Apr 1777.
- Recommended Lieut. Colonel, 19 Apr 1780.
- Recommended Colonel, 2nd Batt., 22 Mar 1781.
- "Declines further service ... about removing into North Carolina", per Arthur Campbell, Apr, 1784.

SMITH (SMYTH), DAVID R.
- Elected 1st Lieut., Troop of Cavalry, 70th Reg., Sep, 1832.
- Elected Captain, Troop of Cavalry, 70th Reg., in the room of Robert B. Edmondson, promoted, 23 May 1834.
- Commission as Captain dated 7 Jul 1834, per Officer Roll, 70th Reg., Oct, 1834.

SMITH, ENOCH
- Recommended Ensign, Capt. Francis Irby's Company, 70th Reg., in the room of Austin Jenkins, promoted, 18 Jun 1800.
- Resigned; replaced as Ensign by Matthew Buchanan, 15 Sep 1801.
- Recommended Lieut., 2nd Batt., 70th Reg., in the room of James Crabtree, resigned, 17 May 1803.
- Removed; replaced as Lieut. by Jonathan Smith, 19 Nov 1805.

SMITH, FRANCIS
- Recommended Ensign in a new Company, commanded by Francis Preston, 1st Batt., 70th Reg., 21 Nov 1798.
- Recommended Captain, 2nd Batt., 70th Reg., in the room of Francis Preston, promoted, 21 May 1799.
- Recommended by Lt. Col. Francis Preston to be Captain, Troop of Cavalry, 70th Reg., 21 Mar 1800.
- Recommendation to be Captain of Cavalry made by the County Court, 21 May 1800.
- Removed; replaced as Captain of Cavalry by William Lyon, 19 Jun 1804.

SMITH, HENRY
- Recommended Ensign, Washington County Militia, 23 Nov 1780.
- Recommended Captain, 20 Mar 1782.
- Mentioned as Captain, Company No. 5, 1st Batt., 1785.
- (Appears as Colonel, Russell County, VA, 1786.)

SMITH, JACOB
- Elected 3rd Lieut., Rifle Company, 2nd Batt., 70th Reg., 21 Feb 1835.

SMITH, JOHN
- Recommended Ensign, Rifle Company, 2nd Batt., 105th Reg., in the room of Benjamin Gray, who does not accept, 19 May 1807.
- Did not accept; replaced as Ensign by Abraham Fulkerson, 19 Jan 1808.

SMITH, JOHN
- Recommended Ensign, 70th Reg., in the room of David Ricason, who does not accept, 16 Jun 1812.
- Resigned; replaced as Ensign by Samuel Beaty, 16 May 1815.

****

SMITH, JONAS, JR.
- Recommended Ensign, 70th Reg., in the room of John Eakin, promoted, 19 May 1834.
- Recommended Lieut., in the room of Robert Stewart, resigned, 21 Jun 1825.
- Resigned; replaced as Lieut. by Joseph Stewart, 15 May 1827.

SMITH, JONATHAN
- Recommended Lieut., 2nd Batt., 70th Reg., in the room of Enoch Smith, removed, 16 Nov 1805.
- Recommended Captain, 2nd Batt., 70th Reg., in the room of William Hinds, removed, 19 Jan 1808.

SMITH, NATHAN
- Recommended Lieut., Company of Riflemen, 105th Reg., in the room of Abram Nordyke, resigned, 19 May 1818.
- Recommended Lieut., in the room of Adam Fleenor, promoted, 18 May 1819.
- Elected Captain, Rifle Company, 2nd Batt., 105th Reg., in the room of Adam Fleenor, resigned, 25 Jun 1822.
- Muster fine, 105th Reg., 1827, $10.00.
- Muster fine, "Capt.", 105th Reg., 1828, $5.00.
- Muster fine, "Capt.", 105th Reg., 1829, $3.00.

SMITH, PLEASANT
- Recommended Ensign, 70th Reg., in the room of Robert Mitchell, promoted, 18 Feb 1812.

SMITH, SAMUEL
- Elected Lieut., Rifle Company, 2nd Batt., 105th Reg. ("by 23 votes, over 20 votes cast for Israel Nordyke"). Election certified by Capt. Nathan Smith. 15 Jun 1824.

SMITH, TOBIAS
- Recommended Cornet, Troop of Cavalry, 70th Reg., in the room of John Clark, promoted, 20 Dec 1814.
- Removed; replaced as Cornet by David Beaty ("son of William"), 16 May 1815.

SMITH, TOBIAS D.
- (Elected Captain, 70th Reg., in the room of William G. Clark, resigned, 3 Apr 1841.)

SMITH, WILLIAM
- Earlier recommendation not seen, but because he did not accept, replaced as Ensign, 70th Reg., by Armstrong Beatie, 21 May 1811.
- Recommended 1st Lieut., Company of Artillery, 105th Reg., in the room of Joshua Burke, removed, 18 Feb 1812.
- Earlier recommendation not seen, but because he removed, replaced as Captain of Artillery by John Crawford, 21 May 1816. (Smith had appeared "resigned" on 26 Jun 1815.)

SNODDY (SNODY), JOHN
- Recommended Lieut., Washington County Militia, 26 Feb 1777.
- Appears to have been acting as Captain, 27 Aug 1777.
- Recommended Captain, in the room of Joseph Martin, named Indian Agent, 1 Oct 1777.

SNODDY, SAMUEL
- Recommended Ensign, 2nd Batt., 105th Reg., in the room of Andrew Balfour, who does not accept, 21 Dec 1819.
- Muster fine, "Ensign", 105th Reg., 1820, $5.00.
- Resigned; replaced as Ensign by John Hortenstine, 19 Jun 1821.

SNODGRASS, DAVID ("Son of James")
- Recommended Ensign, Company of Light Infantry, 1st Batt., 70th Reg., in the room of Benjamin Glen, who does not accept, 19 Jan 1808.
- Recommended Lieut., in the room of Joseph Cole, who does not accept, 18 Jul 1809.
- Resigned; replaced as Lieut. by William P. Thompson, 20 Feb 1810.

SNODGRASS, JAMES
- Recommended Captain, Washington County Militia, 14 Feb 1787.
- Recommended Captain, 1st Batt., 70th Reg., 19 Feb 1793.
- Recommended Captain, 5th Company, 1st Batt., 70th Reg., 20 Jun 1793.
- Recommended Major, 1st Batt., 70th Reg., in the room of John Jamison, resigned, 15 Aug 1797.
- Resigned; replaced as Major by John Edmiston, 16 May 1809.

SNODGRASS, JAMES M.
- Elected Cornet, Troop of Cavalry, 70th Reg., in the room of Madison Beaty, promoted, 23 May 1834.
- Commission as Cornet dated 7 Jul 1834, per Officer Roll, 70th Reg., Oct, 1834.
- Commission as Cornet dated 19 Jul 1834, per Col. James Edmondson, Jr., 21 Jun

****

1835.

SNODGRASS, JOHN
- Recommended Ensign, Rifle Company, 70th Reg., in the room of William Tomlinson, 18 May 1819.
- Elected Cornet, Troop of Cavalry, Oct, 1823. Election certified by William Byars, Col., 70th Reg., 22 Mar 1824.

SNODGRASS, JOSEPH
- Elected Ensign, a new Company of Artillery, 70th Reg., 19 Jul 1834.
(This company was not then approved; Snodgrass was not mentioned in additional elections, 11 Apr 1835.)

SNODGRASS, ROBERT
- Recommended 2nd Lieut., Company of Artillery, 105th Reg., in the room of Joshua Burke, promoted, 16 May 1809.

SNODGRASS, WILLIAM
- Elected 2nd Lieut., a new Company of Artillery, 70th Reg., 11 Apr 1835.

SPANGLER, GEORGE
- Recommended 2nd Lieut., Company of Artillery, 105th Reg., in the room of David Hays, promoted, 19 Jun 1804.
- Recommended 1st Lieut., Company of Artillery, in the room of Samuel Glen, promoted, 20 Nov 1804.
- Resigned; replaced as 1st Lieut. by James Withroe, 19 Nov 1805.

SPENCER, JAMES
- Recommended Ensign "in Robert Hensley's old Company", 2nd Batt., 105th Reg., 19 Nov 1805.
- Commission as Ensign dated 6 Jan 1806, per Officer Roll, 105th Reg., 1808.
- Muster fine, "Ensign", 105th Reg., 1808, $2.00.
- Resigned; replaced as Ensign by John Warfield, 15 Nov 1808.

SPAHR, ISAAC
- Recommended Ensign, Company of Riflemen, 2nd Batt., 105th Reg., in the room of Abraham Nordyke, promoted, 16 Apr 1817.

SPOTTS, ADDISON A.
- Elected Ensign, 1st Batt., 105th Reg., in the room of Connally F. Trigg, promoted, 13 May 1831.
- Resigned; replaced as Ensign by William Ruley, 14 Apr 1832.

SPOTTS, CHAPMAN A.
- Recommended Ensign, 70th Reg., in the room of Leonidas Love, resigned, 15 May 1827.

SPYKER, DAVID
- Recommended Lieut., 1st Batt., 105th Reg., in the room of James Campbell, promoted, 18 May 1819.
- Did not accept; replaced as Lieut. by Daniel Lynch, 16 May 1820.

STATZER, GEORGE
- Elected Ensign, 2nd Batt., 105th Reg., 14 Apr 1833.
- Did not receive commission, per Col. Samuel E. Goodson, 25 Jun 1835. (This compiler believes the oversight was due to manuscript illegibility. G.H.C.)

STEEL, JOHN
- Recommended Ensign, Capt. James Shelby's Company, Washington County Militia, 22 Apr 1778.
- Commission dated 1 Jun 1778.
- Took oath of office, 17 Mar 1779.

STEEL, WILLIAM
- Recommended Ensign, a new Company, 1st Batt., 105th Reg., 15 Nov 1808.
- Refused to accept; replaced as Ensign by Samuel McGinnis, 15 Aug 1809.

STEVENS, CONRAD
- First appears as Private, Troop of Cavalry, 1st Batt., 105th Reg., Muster Roll, 8 Apr 1809.
- Recommended Lieut., Light Infantry Company, 105th Reg., in the room of Peter Mayo, promoted, 18 Feb 1812.

STEVENS, JOHN W.
- Recommended Lieut., Company of Riflemen, 1st Batt., 105th Reg., 18 Jun 1824.
- Elected 2nd Lieut., Company of Artillery, 105th Reg., 2 Nov 1827.
- Elected 1st Lieut., Company of Artillery, 29 Oct 1828.
- Resigned; replaced as 1st Lieut. by John Woodsides, 13 May 1831.

STEWART, JOSEPH
- Recommended Lieut., 70th Reg., in the room of Jonas Smith, resigned, 15 May 1827.
- Recommended Lieut., 16 Jun 1829.
- Elected Captain, 2nd Batt., 70th Reg., in the room of John Eakin, resigned, 24 Aug 1833.
- Commission as Captain dated 17 Aug 1833, per Officer Roll, 70th Reg., May, 1834.

****

- Resigned; replaced as Captain by James Orr, 19 Jul 1834.

STEWART, ROBERT
- Recommended Lieut., 2nd Batt., 70th Reg., in the room of James Talbert, promoted, 18 May 1819.
- Recommended Major, 70th Reg., in the room of Robert Beatie, resigned, 20 May 1823. (This recommendation was contested. The court refused to reconsider its recommendation. 16 Sep 1823.)
- Resigned; replaced as Lieut. by John Crawford, 19 May 1824.
- Resigned; replaced as Lieut. by Jonas Smith, Jr., 21 Jun 1825.
- Appointed Pay Master, 70th Reg., May, 1834, per Officer Rolls, 70th Reg., May and Oct, 1834.

ST. JOHN, THOMAS
- Recommended Ensign, 1st Batt., 70th Reg., in the room of Charles Riley, removed, 19 May 1818.
- Removed; replaced as Ensign by Robert Porterfield, 18 May 1819.

SURBER, ADAM T.
- Elected Lieut., 70th Reg., 22 May 1835.

SYLER, WYMUS
- Recommended Ensign, "by ballot", Washington County Militia, 1785.

TALBERT, CHARLES
- Recommended Lieut., 2nd Batt., 70th Reg., in the room of Abraham Funk, promoted, 15 Sep 1801.
- Recommended Captain, in the room of Abraham Funk, removed, 17 May 1803.
- Resigned; replaced as Captain, Company of Light Infantry, by General William Campbell Edmiston, 18 Feb 1812.
- Recommended Ensign, Company of Light Infantry, 70th Reg., in the room of Joseph C. Trigg, promoted, 16 May 1815.

TALBERT (TALBUTT), JAMES
- Recommended Lieut., 2nd Batt., 70th Reg., in the room of James Scott, promoted, 21 May 1811.
- He contested the promotion of Archibald Meek to Captain, 19 May 1818; and in consequence, was promoted Captain "on advice", Feb, 1819.
- Was involved in the Beatie-Trigg controversy in 1823, and in consequence was promoted Major. He was replaced as Captain by John Eakin, 19 May 1824.
- Removed; replaced as Major by Joseph Thomas, 16 Jun 1829.

TALBERRT, JEFFERSON
- Elected Captain, 70th Reg., in the room of John Goode, resigned, 4 Apr 1835.

TALBUTT, JOHN
- Recommended Lieut., 70th Reg., in the room of Moses Hill, who does not accept, 18 Feb 1812.

TALBERT, THOMAS
- Recommended Lieut., Company of Light Infantry, 70th Reg., in the room of Andrew Henderson, promoted, 18 May 1819.

TANKERSLEY, WILLIAM
- Recommended Ensign, 1st Batt., 105th Reg., in the room of Charles Johnston, who does not accept, 21 May 1816.
- Resigned; replaced as Ensign by Joseph Vance, 18 May 1819.

TATE, CHARLES
- Recommended Ensign, 1st Batt., 70th Reg., 19 Feb 1793.
- Recommended Ensign, 3rd Company, 1st Batt., 70th Reg., 21 Jun 1793.
- Recommended Lieut., John Campbell's Company (replacing him as Lieut.), 1st Batt., 70th Reg., 19 Jun 1794.
- Recommended Captain, in the room of Joh Campbell, resigned, 17 Jan 1798.
- At the division of the 70th Reg. to

****

create the 105th Reg., his Company was assigned to the 2nd Batt., 70th Reg., 20 Mar 1799.
- Resigned; replaced as Captain by Thomas Tate, 20 Feb 1810.
- Recommended Lieut. Colonel, Commandant, 70th Reg., in the room of Francis Preston, promoted, 20 Dec 1814.
- Resigned; replaced as Commandant, 70th Reg., by William Byars, recommended Colonel, (William P. Thompson was recommended Lieut. Colonel, second in command), 21 Apr 1818.

TATE, JOHN M.
- Recommended Ensign, 70th Reg., in the room of William Buchanan, who does not accept, 15 May 1821.

TATE, MITCHELL
- Recommended Lieut., 2nd Batt., 70th Reg., in the room of William Poston, resigned, 19 Nov 1805. (Earlier recommendation not seen, but he was replaced as Ensign by Bazel Scott.)
- Removed; replaced as Lieut. by Thomas Tate, 19 Jan 1808.

TATE, THOMAS
- Recommended Lieut., 2nd Batt., 70th Reg., in the room of Mitchell Tate, removed, 19 Jan 1808.
- Recommended Captain, in the room of Charles Tate, resigned, 20 Feb 1810.
- Recommended Major, 2nd Batt., 70th Reg., in the room of William P. Thompson, promoted, 21 Apr 1818. (Replaced as Captain by William C. Tate, 19 May 1818.)
- Resigned; replaced as Major by Robert Beaty, 16 May 1820.
- Muster fine, "Major", 70th Reg., 1820, $20.00.

TATE, THOMAS
- Recommended Lieut., 70th Reg., in the room of William Campbell, removed, 19 May 1824.

TATE, WILLIAM
- Recommended Lieut. Colonel, Washington County Militia, 21 Apr 1785.
- Promoted to Brigadier General, commanding the 17th Brigade of the Virginia Militia, 1793.
- Replaced as Brigadier General by Frances Preston, 1814.

TATE, WILLIAM C.
- Recommended Lieut., 2nd Batt., 70th Reg., in the room of James Crabtree, deceased, 20 Dec 1814.
- Recommended Captain, in the room of Thomas Tate, promoted, 19 May 1818.
- Resigned; replaced as Captain by Robert Hayton, 16 May 1820.
- Muster fine, "Lieut.", 70th Reg., 1820, $40.00.

TAYLOR, CHARLES
- From Montgomery County, Virginia.
- Recommended Cornet, Troop of Horse (Cavalry), 17th Brigade, by William Tate, 12 Dec 1799.

TAYLOR, CHARLES C.
- Recommended Captain, 2nd Batt., 70th Reg., in the room of Robert Hayton, resigned, 20 May 1823.

TAYLOR, JAMES "of Washington Co."
- Advice he had resigned his commission as Major, 1st Batt., 3rd Reg. of Artillery, Virginia Militia, 17 Jan 1811.

TAYLOR, PHILIP
- Recommended Ensign, 2nd Batt., 105th Reg., in the room of George Gobble, promoted, 17 May 1803.
- Removed; replaced as Ensign by James Jett, 20 Nov 1804.

TEATOR, JACOB
- Recommended Lieut., Rifle Company, 105th Reg., 17 Jun 1806.
- Commission as Lieut. of Riflemen dated 4 Aug 1806, per Officer Roll, 105th Reg., 1808.
- Muster fines (2), 105th Reg., 1808, $5.00.
- Resigned; replaced as Lieut. by Abraham Fulkerson, 15 Nov 1808.

TESTER, GEORGE
- Recommended Ensign, Washington County Militia, 19 Aug 1778.

THOMAS, ABIJAH
- Recommended Lieut., 1st Batt., 70th Reg., in the room of George Byars, promoted, 20 May 1806.

THOMAS, ELISHA
- Earlier recommendation not seen, but because he did not accept, replaced as Lieut., 70th Reg., by William Love, 18 Feb 1812.

THOMAS, JOHN, SR.
- Recommended Lieut., 70th Reg., in the room of Arthur M. Bowen, resigned, 16 May

****

1820.
- Recommended Captain, in the room of Joseph Thomas, promoted, 16 Jun 1829.

THOMAS, JOHN, JR.
- Recommended Ensign, 70th Reg., 16 Jun 1829.

THOMAS, JOSEPH
- Recommended Ensign, 1st Batt., 70th Reg., in the room of Robert Beaty, promoted, 16 May 1815.
- Recommended Captain, 1st Batt., 70th Reg., in the room of Robert Beaty, promoted, 16 May 1820.
- Recommended Major, 2nd Batt., 70th Reg., in the room of James Talbutt, removed, 16 Jun 1829. (Replaced as Captain by John Thomas, Sr.)

THOMAS, JOSEPH
- Elected 4th Lieut., Company of Artillery, 70th Reg., 11 Apr 1835.

THOMAS, THOMAS
- Recommended Lieut., Capt. Patrick Campbell's Company, 70th Reg., 18 Nov 1794.
- Resigned; replaced as Ensign (sic) by Arthur Campbell, Jr., 17 Jan 1798.

THOMPSON, WILLIAM
- Recommended Lieut., Washington County Militia, 20 Mar 1782.
- (Appears a Captain, Russell County, Virginia, 1786.)

THOMPSON, WILLIAM P.
- Recommended Ensign, Company of Light Infantry, 1st Batt., 70th Reg., in the room of David Snodgrass, promoted, 18 Jul 1809.
- Recommended Lieut., in the room of David Snodgrass, resigned, 20 Feb 1810.
- Did not accept; replaced as Lieut. by Andrew Patterson, 21 May 1811.
- Recommended Major, 1st Batt., 70th Reg., 21 May 1816.
- Recommended Lieut. Colonel, 70th Reg., in the room of Charles Tate, resigned, 21 Apr 1818.
- Took oath of office as Lieut. Colonel, 18 May 1819.
- Removed; replaced as Lieut. Colonel by Joseph C. Trigg, 20 May 1823. (This recommendation was protested.)

TILSON, THOMAS
- Recommended Ensign, a new Company commanded by Joseph Cole, 1st Batt., 70th Reg., 19 Jun 1794.
- Recommended Lieut., in the room of John Cole, resigned, 21 May 1799.
- Appears as Captain at Court of Enquiry, 70th Reg., 1803.
- Earlier recommendation not seen, but because of his resignation, replaced as Captain by Levi Lester, 18 Aug 1807.

TODD, JAMES
- Recommended Ensign, Company of Riflemen, 1st Batt., 70th Reg., in the room of Samuel Dysart, promoted, 15 Aug 1797.
- Recommended Lieut. of Infantry, 21 May 1799.
- Resigned; replaced as Lieut. by David Carson, 19 Aug 1800.

TODD, R---
- Earlier recommendation not seen, but because he resigned, replaced as Ensign, 70th Reg., by Robert Houston, 15 May 1827.

TODD, ROBERT
- Recommended Lieut., 1st Batt., 70th Reg., in the room of James Beaty, resigned, 21 Jun 1825.
- Removed; replaced as Lieut. by Marcus Cook, Apr, 1832. (James K. Edmondson later recommended to fill this vacancy. 17 Aug 1833.)

TOMLINSON, WILLIAM
- Recommended Ensign, Company of Riflemen, 70th Reg., in the room of Samuel Edmondson, promoted, 19 May 1818.
- Did not accept; replaced as Ensign by John Snodgrass, 18 May 1819.

TONCRAY, LEWIS
- Recommended Ensign, Company of Light Infantry, 1st Batt., 105th Reg., in the room of James Bailey, promoted, 16 Jul 1805.
- Recommended Lieut., in the room of William Berryhill, who does not accept, 19 May 1807.
- Commission as Lieut. of Infantry dated 6 Jun 1807, per Officer Roll, 105th Reg., 1808.
- Resigned; replaced as Lieut. by Lilburn L. Henderson, 15 Nov 1808.
- Appears as Private on Roll of Light Infantry Company, 1st Batt., 105th Reg., 8 Apr 1809.
- Appears as Private on Roll of Artillery Company, 105th Reg., 26 Jun 1815.

TOPP, ROGER
- Recommended Lieut., Washington County

****

Militia, 26 Feb 1777.
- Commission dated 4 May 1777.
- Took oath of office, 19 Aug 1778.

TRIGG, ABRAM B.
- Recommended Cornet, Troop of Cavalry, 105th Reg., in the room of John M. Preston, promoted, 19 May 1818.

TRIGG, ABRAHAM (?) B.
- Elected Cornet, Troop of Cavalry, 70th Reg., 14 Apr 1827.

TRIGG, CONNALLY F.
- Recommended Ensign, 1st Batt., 105th Reg., in the room of Nicholas H. Ruly, promoted, 16 Jun 1829.
- Elected Captain, 1st Batt., 105th Reg., in the room of William K. Trigg, 13 May 1831.
- Resigned; replaced as Captain by Andrew Gibson, 13 Apr 1833.

TRIGG, JAMES
- Recommended Captain, Company of Light Infantry, 70th Reg., in the room of Joseph C. Trigg, resigned, 21 May 1816.
- Muster fine, 70th Reg., 1818, $20.00.
- Deceased; replaced as Captain by Andrew Henderson, 18 May 1819.
- Muster fine, 70th Reg., 1819, $5.00.

TRIGG, JOSEPH C.
- Recommended Ensign, Company of Light Infantry, 70th Reg., in the room of Waddy T. Currin, who does not accept, 20 Dec 1814.
- Recommended Captain, Company of Light Infantry, in the room of General William Campbell Edmiston, resigned, 16 May 1815. (Replaced as Ensign by Charles Talbutt.)
- Resigned; replaced as Captain by James Trigg, 21 May 1816.
- Elected Captain, Company of Light Infantry, 2nd Batt., 70th Reg., 27 Apr 1821.
- Recommended Lieut. Colonel, 70th Reg., in the room of William P. Thompson, removed, 20 May 1823. (This recommendation was vigorously contested by Robert Beatie)
- The County Court refused to reconsider his recommendation to be Lieut. Colonel, 16 Sep 1823.
- Recommended by Andrew Russell and David Campbell to high position in the Virginia Militia outside the county, Dec, 1823.

TRIGG, WILLIAM K.
- Recommended Lieut., 1st Batt., 105th Reg., in the room of Elias Ogden, who does not accept, 19 Jun 1827.
- Recommended Captain, 1st Batt., 105th Reg., in the room of Daniel Lynch, resigned, 16 Jun 1829.
- Resigned; replaced as Captain by Connally F. Trigg, 13 May 1831.
- Appointed Surgeon's Mate, 70th Reg., May, 1834, per Officer Rolls, 70th Reg., May and Oct, 1834.

TRIMBLE, JOHN
- Recommended Ensign, 105th Reg., in the room of William Berry, resigned, 17 Feb 1807.
- Resigned; replaced as Ensign by James Reed, 19 May 1807.

TRIMBELL, ROBERT
- Recommended Captain, Washington County Militia, 22 Mar 1781.
- Mention of his "late company", Company No. 12, 2nd Batt., 1785.

TURNER, REUBEN
- Earlier recommendation not seen, but because of his removal, replaced as 2nd Lieut., Troop of Cavalry, 105th Reg., by John M. Preston, 19 May 1818.

VANCE, G. W.
- Elected 2nd Lieut., 70th Reg., 4 Apr 1835.

VANCE, JAMES
- Recommended Ensign, Washington County Militia, 16 May 1781.
- Recommended Ensign, 8 May 1787.
- Recommended Lieut., 14 Oct 1788.
- Recommended Lieut., 2nd Batt., 70th Reg., 19 Feb 1793.
- Recommended Lieut., 3rd Company, 2nd Batt., 70th Reg., 21 Jun 1793.
- Recommended Captain, in the room of Robert Campbell, promoted, 19 Oct 1794.
- At the division of the 70th Reg. to create the 105th Reg., his company was assigned to the 1st Batt., 105th Reg., 20 Mar 1799.
- Resigned; replaced as Captain by James Whitehall Craig, 19 Sep 1800.

VANCE, JOHN
- Recommended Cornet, Troop of Cavalry, 105th Reg., in the room of William Duff, promoted, 20 Nov 1804.
- Removed; replaced as Cornet by Samuel Keller, 16 Jul 1805.

VANCE, JOSEPH

****

- Recommended Ensign, 1st Batt., 105th Reg., in the room of William Tankersly, resigned, 18 May 1819.
- Resigned; replaced as Ensign by Nicholas H. Ruly, 15 May 1827.

VANHOOK, SAMUEL
- Recommended Ensign, Washington County Militia, 19 Aug 1778.

WALKER, ALEXANDER STUART
- Recommended Captain, Company of Lighy Infantry, 1st Batt., 105th Reg., in the room of John Gold, who refuses to accept, 20 May 1806.
- "Removed out of the county and bounds of the Reg., and ceased to perform the duties of his office for eight months"; replaced as Captain by David Campbell, 19 Jul 1808.

WALKER, DANIEL
- Recommended Ensign, 1st Batt., 70th Reg., in the room of Hiram A. Griever, promoted, 20 May 1828.

WARD, DAVID
- Recommended Lieut., Washington County Militia, 26 Feb 1777.
- Mentioned as Captain, Company No. 4, 1785.
- (Appears as Captain, Russell County, Virginia, 1786.)

WARD, OTA H.
- Elected Captain, 2nd Batt., 105th Reg., in the room of Abram Mongle, resigned, 2 Jul 1831.
- Commission as Captain dated 2 Jul 1831, per Officer Roll, 105th Reg., 1833.
- Removed; replaced as Captain by Abram Nordyke, 28 Dec 1833.

WARFIELD, JOHN
- Recommended Ensign, 2nd Batt., 105th Reg., in the room of James Spencer, resigned, 15 Nov 1808.
- Recommended Lieut., in the room of William Rhea, promoted, 16 May 1809.
- Resigned; replaced as Lieut. by Samuel E. Goodson, 16 May 1815.

WARREN, WALTER
- Recommended 1st Lieut., Company of Artillery, 105th Reg., in the room of Job Clark, resigned, 18 May 1819. (This court recommendation was invalid; Thomas McCulloch was elected to fill this vacancy, 21 Dec 1819.)

WATKINS, CLAIBORNE
- Recommended by Brig. Gen. William Tate to be 1st Lieut., Troop of Horse (Cavalry), 17th Brigade, 12 Dec 1793.
- Received commission, dated 12 May 1797, appointing him Captain, Troop of Cavalry, 3rd Reg., 3rd Division, Militia of Virginia, per his letter, 1 Jul 1797.
- Mention of order by Brig. Gen. Tate that his Troop assigned for duty to the 105th Reg., 1 Feb 1800.
- Resigned; replaced as Captain by Abraham Bradley, 15 Sep 1801.

WATSON, WILLIAM
- Recommended Lieut., Washington County Militia, 14 Feb 1787.
- Commission dated 24 Mar 1787.
- Refused to qualify, per Arthur Campbell, 23 Oct 1787.
- Recommended Captain, 1st Batt., 70th Reg., 19 Feb 1793. (Recommendation not resubmitted, Jun, 1793.)

WHISTENAND, PETER
- Recommended Lieut., Company of Light Infantry, 105th Reg., in the room of Thomas McChesney, resigned, 17 May 1803.

WHITAKER, BENJAMIN
- Recommended Ensign, 70th Reg., 16 Jun 1829.

WHITE, JAMES
- Recommended by Brig. Gen. William Tate to be Captain of a volunteer Company of Artillery, made up of "young men in the town of Abingdon", 19 Jun 1799.
- Muster fine, "Capt.", 105th Reg., 1802, $5.00.
- Recommended Major, 1st Batt., 105th Reg., in the room of James Bradley, resigned, 19 Jun 1804.
- Commission as Major dated 10 Jul 1804, per Officer Roll, 105th Reg., 1808.
- Muster fine, "Major", 105th Reg., 1811, $5.00.
- Muster fine, "Major", 105th Reg., 1812, $5.00.
- Recommended Lieut. Colonel, 105th Reg., in the room of John Preston, Jr., promoted Colonel, 21 Apr 1818.
- Took oath of office as Lieut. Colonel, 18 May 1819.
- Resigned; replaced as Lieut. Colonel by Abraham Fulkerson, 21 May 1822.

WHITE, SPENCER
- Earlier recommendation not seen, but because he refused to accept, replaced as

****

Lieut., 70th Reg., by Lewis Menefee, 18 May 1819.

WHITTEN, THOMAS
- Recommended Ensign, Washington County Militia, 26 Feb 1777.

WILLIAMS, JOHN R.
- Elected 2nd Lieut., 70th Reg., 14 Feb 1835.

WILLOUGHBY, ANDREW
- Appears as Clerk of the Court of Enquiry, 105th Reg., 1805-1813.
- Recommended Cornet, Troop of Cavalry, 105th Reg., in the room of Thomas McQuown, promoted, 16 May 1815.

WILLOUGHBY, MATTHEW
- Recommended Lieut., Washington County Militia, 8 May 1787.
- Recommended Captain, 2nd Batt., 70th Reg., 19 Feb 1793.
- Recommended Captain, 5th Company, 2nd Batt., 70th Reg., 20 Jun 1793.
- At the division of the 70th Reg. to create the 105th Reg., his Company was assigned to the 2nd Batt., 105th Reg., 20 Mar 1799.
- Recommended Major, 2nd Batt. of the newly formed 105th Reg., 21 May 1799. (Replaced as Captain by Wallace Willoughby.)
- Recommended Lieut. Colonel, Commandant, 105th Reg., in the room of Robert Campbell, resigned, 17 Aug 1802.
- Resigned; replaced as Lieut. Colonel, Commandant, 105th Reg., by John Preston, Jr., 20 Nov 1804.

WILLOUGHBY, WALLACE
- Recommended Ensign, Company of Grenadiers, 2nd Batt., 70th Reg., 19 Jun 1794.
- Recommended Lieut., in the room of John Fulkerson, removed, 19 Nov 1795.
- Resigned; replaced as Lieut. by Robert Craig, Jr., 22 Jun 1796.
- Recommended Ensign, Capt. Matthew Willoughby's Company, 2nd Batt., 70th Reg., in the room of David Campbell, resigned, 17 Jan 1798.
- Recommended Lieut., in the room of David Craig, removed, 23 Jun 1798.
- Recommended Captain, 2nd Batt., 105th Reg., in the room of Matthew Willoughby, promoted, 21 May 1799.
- Removed; replaced as Captain by John Corry, 17 May 1803.

WILLOUGHBY, WILLIAM
- Recommended Lieut., Washington County Militia, 18 Sep 1782.

WILSON, JOHN
- Recommended Ensign, Washington County Militia, 26 Feb 1777.

WILSON, JOSEPH
- Recommended Ensign, 2nd Batt., 70th Reg., 19 Feb 1793. (Recommendation not resubmitted, Jun, 1793.)

WILSON, SAMUEL
- Recommended Lieut., 2nd Batt., 105th Reg., in the room of Sampson Hensley, who does not accept, 20 Nov 1804.
- Did not accept; replaced as Lieut. Simon Hensley, 19 Nov 1805.

WINNIFORD, GEORGE
- Recommended Lieut., 1st Batt., 70th Reg., in the room of Edmond Gannaway, removed, 18 May 1819.
- Recommended Captain, in the room of Robertson Gannaway, resigned, 15 May 1821. (Replaced as Lieut. by Robert Porterfield)
- Removed; replaced as Captain by William Griever, 20 May 1823.

WISE, WILLIAM
- Recommended Ensign, Company of Riflemen, 1st Batt., 105th Reg., 18 Jun 1824.

WITHROE, JAMES
- Recommended 1st Lieut., Company of Artillery, 105th Reg., in the room of George Spangler, resigned, 19 Nov 1805.
- Recommended Captain of Artillery, in the room of John Bradley, who refuses to accept, 20 May 1806.
- Deceased; replaced as Captain of Artillery by William Jones, 15 Mar 1808.

WOODS, JOHN W.
- Recommended Ensign, 105th Reg., in the room of John Berry, who does not accept, 21 Sep 1819.

WOODS, WILLIAM
- Elected 1st Lieut., 105th Reg., 30 May 1835.

WOODSIDES, HUGH
- Elected 2nd Lieut., Company of Artillery, 105th Reg., in the room of David Campbell, resigned, 23 May 1820.

WOODSIDES, JOHN
- Elected 1st Lieut., Company of

****

Artillery, 105th Reg., in the room of John W. Stevens, resigned, 13 May 1831.

WOODWARD, BARTLEY
- Elected 3rd Lieut., 70th Reg., 4 Apr 1835.

WORLEY, DAVID
- Recommended Lieut., 2nd Batt., 70th Reg., in the room of John Owens, removed, 19 Oct 1794.

WORLEY, GEORGE S.
- Elected Lieut., Capt. James B. Worley's Company, 105th Reg., 10 Oct 1835.

WORLEY, JAMES B.
- Elected Captain, 2nd Batt., 105th Reg., in the room of William Shoemaker, 14 Apr 1833.
- Commission as Captain dated 29 Apr 1832 (sic), per Officer Roll, 105th Reg., Oct, 1834.

WORLEY, NATHAN
- Earlier recommendation not seen, but because he was promoted, replaced as Lieut., 2nd Batt., 105th Reg., by Hugh McClellan, 21 May 1822.
- Recommended Captain, 2nd Batt., 105th Reg., in the room of Samuel E. Goodson, promoted, 21 May 1822.
- Resigned; replaced as Captain by William Shoemaker, 21 Jun 1825.

WRIGHT (RIGHT), ISAAC
- Elected 4th Lieut., 70th Reg., 14 Feb 1835.
- Elected Lieut., 70th Reg., 22 May 1835.

WRIGHT, JAMES W.
- Elected Lieut., 2nd Batt., 105th Reg., 27 Apr 1832.
- Commission as Lieut. dated 5 Oct 1832, per Officer Roll, 105th Reg., 1833.
- His Company (Capt. Caldwell's) assigned to the 70th Reg., 18 May 1833.

WRIGHT, ROBERT
- Elected 4th Lieut., Rifle Company, 1st Batt., 70th Reg., 3 Oct 1835.

WYLIE, ALEXANDER
- Recommended Lieut., Washington County Militia, 26 Feb 1777.
- Recommended Lieut., 8 May 1787.

WYLIE, JAMES
- Recommended Ensign, 2nd Batt., 70th Reg., 19 Jan 1808.

YOUNG, DANIEL
- Recommended Ensign, Washington County Militia, 8 May 1787.

YOUNG, WILLIAM
- Recommended Ensign, Washington County Militia, 26 Feb 1777.

****

ABLE, WILLIAM
- 105th Reg., 1815 - 1820.

ACALTREE, THOMAS
- 70th Reg., 1830.

ACKLAND, ALEXANDER S.
- Light Infantry Company, 105th Reg., 1808.

ACKLIN, CHRISTOPHER
- 1st Batt., 105th Reg., 1802; Capt. Bradley's Company, 1808; Sergeant, 1813, 1814.

ACKLIN, CHRISTOPHER, JR.
- 1st Batt., 105th Reg., 1803.

ACKLIN, JOHN
- 2nd Batt., 70th Reg., 1798.

ACKLIN, JOSEPH
- 1st Batt., 105th Reg., 1800.

ADAMS, JONATHAN
- Capt. Tate's Company, 2nd Batt., 70th Reg., 1811, 1812, 1821, 1825.

ADCOCK, GEORGE
- Capt. Jones' Light Infantry Company, 1st Batt., 105th Reg., 1807; Capt. Jones' Artillery Company, 105th Reg., 1808, 1809, 1810.

ADCOCK, JOSEPH
- Capt. Bradley's Company, 1st Batt., 105th Reg., 1805, 1806; Capt. Jones' Artillery Company, 1808; Capt. Bradley's Company, 1810.

ADKINS, HIRAM
- Artillery Company, 105th Reg, 1815, 1816

ADKINS, JOHN
- 1st Batt., 105th Reg., 1805, 1806.

ADKINS, NOAH
- 105th Reg., 1822; 70th Reg., 1825; 105th Reg., 1829, 1831, 1834.

ADKINS, THOMAS
- Capt. Fulkerson's Company, 2nd Batt., 105th Reg., 1809.

ADKINS, WADE
- 105th Reg., 1823; 70th Reg., 1825.

ADKISON, WILLIAM
- Capt. Fulkerson's Company, 2nd Batt., 105th Reg., 1808, 1812.

AGEE (AGY), WILLIAM
- 2nd Batt., 105th Reg., 1802, 1804; Capt. Fulkerson's Company, 1809, 1810, 1811.

AICOCK, BURR
- 70th Reg., 1800.

AIRS, DANIEL
- 70th Reg., 1812, 1826.

AIRS, JEREMIAH
- 70th Reg., 1817, 1819, 1820, 1823, 1825, 1827.

AIRS, JIRE (?)
- 70th Reg., 1830.

AJAY, MICHAEL
- Capt. Fulkerson's Company, 2nd Batt., 105th Reg., 1808.

AKEN, JOHN
- 105th Reg., 1817.

AKERS, BENJAMIN
- 70th Reg., 1800.

ALES, WILLIAM
- Capt. Berry's Company, 1st Batt., 105th Reg., 1806.

ALEXANDER, DAVID
- 70th Reg., 1809.

ALEXANDER, JAMES
- 105th Reg., 1831, 1832.

ALEXANDER, JOHN
- 70th Reg., 1801; Capt. Irby's Company, 2nd Batt., 1803.

ALLEN, CHARLES
- 70th Reg., 1814-1816, 1819-1822.

ALLEN, DANIEL
- 2nd Batt., 105th Reg., 1803; Capt. Goff's Company, 1807, 1819.

ALLEN, ELI
- Rifle Company, 1st Batt., 70th Reg., 1807.

ALLEN, GEORGE
- 70th Reg., 1826.

ALLEN, ISAAC
- Rifle Company, 1st Batt., 70th Reg., 1807.

****

****

- Capt. Meek's Company, 1st Batt., 70th Reg., 1811.

ANDERSON, THOMAS
- Capt. Campbell's Company, 70th Reg., 1805.

ANDERSON, WILLIAM
- Capt. Meek's Company, 1st Batt., 70th Reg., 1806, 1809; Capt. George Byar's Company, 1811, 1813.

ANDERSON, WILLIAM
- 1st Batt., 70th Reg., 1798, 1800; 1st Batt., 105th Reg., 1812.

ANDREWS, EZRA
- 105th Reg., 1834, 1834.

ANDREWS, JOHN
- 2nd Batt., 70th Reg., 1798.

ANDREWS, PETER
- 105th Reg., 1835.

ANDIS (ANDRIS), JOHN
- 1st Batt., 105th Reg., 1802; Capt. Jones' Light Infantry Company, 1807; Capt. Jones' Artillery Company, 1808.

APPERSON, FRANCIS
- 70th Reg., 1818.

APPERSON, REUBEN
- 105th Reg., 1819.

APPERSON, RICHARD
- 70th Reg., 1815, 1818, 1824-1827.

APPERSON, WILLIAM
- 70th Reg., 1824; 105th Reg., 1825, 1828, 1829, 1831.

ARBOUGH, FRANCIS
- 70th Reg., 1800.

ARBUCKLE, WILLIAM B.
- 105th Reg., 1818.

ARCHER, MEREDITH
- 1st Batt., 70th Reg., 1798, 1802.

ARMS, EVAN BROOK
- 1st Batt., 105th Reg., 1800; 2nd Batt., 1800; Capt. Gillenwaters' Company, 1806.

ARMSTRONG, JOHN
- 70th Reg., 1800, 1802; Capt. Smyth's Company, 2nd Batt., 1803.

ARMSTRONG, SAMUEL
- 105th Reg., 1817.

ARNETT, ANDREW
- Capt. Talbert's Company, 2nd Batt., 70th Reg., 1803.

ARNETT, DANIEL
- 70th Reg., 1799-1802, 1809; Capt. Talbert's Company, 70th Reg., 1811, 1815-1817.

ARNOLD, JAMES
- 105th Reg., 1829.

ARNOLD, JOHN
- 105th Reg., 1828.

ARNOTT, ANDREW
- 2nd Batt., 105th Reg., 1803.

ARTHURS, JOSEPH
- Rifle Company, 1st Batt., 70th Reg., 1807.

ASHLY, CARY
- 1st Batt., 105th Reg., 1801.

ATHY, JOHN
- 70th Reg., 1799, 1820.

ATKINS, WILLIAM
- Capt. Larkey's Company, 2nd Batt., 105th Reg., 1806.

ATLY, HENRY D.
- Capt. Gillenwaters' Company, 105th Reg., 1808; Capt. Fulkerson's Company, 2nd Batt., 1809, 1810, 1818.

ATHY, HENRY D.
- 70th Reg., 1819.

ATWOOD, MOSES
- 1st Batt., 105th Reg., 1799.

AUSTIN, EDWARD
- 105th Reg., 1824, 1825.

AUSTIN, JAMES
- 105th Reg., 1827; Rifle Company, 1st Batt., 1829.

AUSTEN, JOHN
- Capt. Preston's Company, 1st Batt., 70th Reg., 1811.

AVERY, SAMUEL
- 105th Reg., 1811.

****

AWFIELD, PRESTON
- 105th Reg., 1828, 1829.

AYLES, WILLIAM
- Capt. Fulkerson's Company, 2nd Batt., 105th Reg., 1809.

BACON, JAMES
- 105th Reg., 1820.

BAILEY, JAMES
- 1st Batt., 105th Reg., 1806; Capt. Dixon's Rifle Company, 1808.

BAILEY, ROBERT
- 105th Reg., 1811, 1813, 1832, 1835.

BAILEY, SAMUEL
- 70th Reg., 1799; Capt. Bradley's Company, 1st Batt., 105th Reg., 1810.

BAILEY, THOMAS
- Troop of Cavalry, 1st Batt., 105th Reg., 1809.

BAIRD, JOHN
- 2nd Batt., 70th Reg., 1798; 1st Batt., 105th Reg., 1803.

BAKER, GEORGE
- Troop of Cavalry, 1st Batt., 105th Reg., 1809.

BAKER, HENRY
- 2nd Batt., 70th Reg., 1798; 2nd Batt., 105th Reg., 1812.

BAKER, ISAAC
- 2nd Batt., 70th Reg., 1798; 2nd Batt., 105th Reg., 1799.

BAKER, JACOB
- Capt. Duff's Troop of Cavalry, 1st Batt., 105th Reg., 1809, 1810.

BAKER, JAMES
- Rifle Company, 1st Batt., 70th Reg., 1807.

BAKER, JOHN
- 105th Reg., 1826.

BAKER, JOSEPH
- Capt. Hayter's Company, 2nd Batt., 70th Reg., 1803.

BAKER, JOSIAH
- Capt. Campbell's Company, 70th Reg., 1804.

BAKER, MARTIN
- 70th Reg., 1801, 1802; Capt. Hayter's Company, 2nd Batt., 1803; Capt. Campbell's Company, 1st Batt., 1804.

BAKER, WILLIAM
- 2nd Batt., 70th Reg., 1798, 1819.

BAKER, WILLIAM
- 105th Reg., 1824.

BALFOUR, ANDREW
- 105th Reg., 1825.

BALFOUR, CHARLES C.
- 105th Reg., 1818-1821, 1824.

BALFOUR, JOHN
- 1st Batt., 105th Reg., 1800.

BALLARD, MOSES
- 70th Reg., 1825, 1827.

BALTZELL, PHILIP
- 1st Batt., 105th Reg., 1812, 1813.

BANKS, WILLIAM
- 70th Reg., 1801.

BANNISTER, HENDERSON
- Capt. Jones' Artillery Company, 105th Reg., 1808.

BANNISTER, WILLIAM
- Rifle Company, 1st Batt., 105th Reg., 1829.

BARB, JACOB
- Rifle Company, 2nd Batt., 105th Reg., 1809, 1811.

BARKER, CHARLES (JR.)
- 2nd Batt., 70th Reg., 1798; 2nd Batt., 105th Reg., 1803, 1813, 1814, 1818, 1819.

BARKER, CHARLES, SR.
- 2nd Batt., 105th Reg., 1799.

BARKER, CHARLES, JR. "son of Charles"
- 105th Reg., 1832, 1833.

BARKER, EDWARD
- 70th Reg., 1812.

BARKER, GEORGE
- 105th Reg., 1835.

BARKER, HENRY
- 105th Reg., 1813.

****

BARKER, JOEL
- 105th Reg., 1827.

BARKER, JOHN
- Capt. Goff's Company, 2nd Batt., 105th Reg., 1807, 1813, 1818, 1819.

BARKER, OBIDIAH
- 70th Reg., 1823, 1824.

BARKER, SHERRARD (SHERWOOD)
- 2nd Batt., 105th Reg., 1812, 1814, 1817, 1819, 1820.

BARKER, WILLIAM
70th Reg., 1822.

BARKER, WILLIAM W.
- 105th Reg., 1828, 1829, 1834, 1835.

BARLOW, JAMES
- 105th Reg., 1811; 70th Reg., 1812.

BARLOW, JESSE
- Rifle Company, 1st Batt., 70th Reg., 1807.

BARLOW, JOHN
- 105th Reg., 1830; 70th Reg., 1835.

BARLOW, JOSEPH
- Capt. Tilson's Company, 1st Batt., 70th Reg., 1803; Rifle Company, 1807; 1810; Capt. Preston's Company, 1811; 1815-1819.

BARLOW, SOLOMON
- 70th Reg., 1800-1802.

BARLOW, THOMAS
- 1st Batt., 70th Reg., 1798.

BARNETT, FREDERICK
- 1st Batt., 70th Reg., 1798, 1799, 1800.

BARNETT, NICHOLAS
- 105th Reg., 1822, 1824.

BARNETT, WILLIAM
- 105th Reg., 1831.

BARNS, ISAIH
- 105th Reg., 1817, 1819.

BARNS, JOSIAH
- 105th Reg., 1818.

BARR, GEORGE R.
- 105th Reg., 1834, 1835.

BARRAGER, FREDERICK
- 2nd Batt., 70th Reg., 1798. 2nd Batt., 105th Reg., 1799.

BARROW, HUGH
- Troop of Cavalry, 1st Batt., 70th Reg., 1809.

BARSON, HUGH
- 1st Batt., 105th Reg., 1804.

BATES, JOHN
- 70th Reg., 1809, 1810; Capt. Tate's Company, 2nd Batt., 1811, 1813.

BATTEY, J. W. P.
- 105th Reg., 1835.

BAUGH, ADAM
- 70th Reg., 1801; Capt. Campbell's Company, 1805, 1809, 1812, 1815.

BAUGH, MICHAEL
- 105th Reg., 1825.

BAUGH, VALENTINE
- Capt. Jones' Artillery Company, 105th Reg., 1808, 1814.

BAUGH, WILLIAM
- 105th Reg., 1830.

BAYS, PETER
- 70th Reg., 1835.

BEACHBOARD, LEVI
- Capt. Goodson's Company, 105th Reg., 1808.

BEAN, CHARLES
- Artillery Company, 105th Reg., 1815.

BEARD, BLODGET
- 1st Batt., 70th Reg., 1798.

BEARD, THOMAS
- Capt. Fulkerson's Company, 2nd Batt., 105th Reg., 1810, 1811.

BEATIE, ALEXANDER
- 70th Reg., 1823.

BEATIE, FOUNTAIN
- 105th Reg., 1825, 1826.

BEATIE, ISAAC
- 1st Batt., 105th Reg., 1800, 1801, 1806.

BEATIE, JOHN B.
- 70th Reg., 1833.

****

****

BIRD, OSTEN
- 70th Reg., 1818.

BISHOP, ELIAS
- 1st Batt., 70th Reg., 1798.

BISHOP, ENOS
- 70th Reg., 1814.

BISHOP, HENRY
- 1st Batt., 70th Reg., 1798.

BISHOP, JOHN
- 70th Reg., 1802; Capt. Tilson's Company, 1st Batt., 1803-1807.

BISHOP, JOSHUA
- 1st Batt., 70th Reg., 1798.

BISHOP, LEWIS
- Capt. Lyon's Company, 70th Reg., 1804.

BISHOP, NOAH
- 1st Batt., 70th Reg., 1798.

BISHOP, THOMAS
- 1st Batt., 70th Reg., 1798.

BISHOP, WILLIAM
- 70th Reg., 1817-1819, 1826.

BITTLE, GEORGE
- 2nd Batt., 105th Reg., 1802.

BITTLE, JACOB
- Capt. Fulkerson's Company, 2nd Batt., 105th Reg., 1808.

BLACK, HENRY
- 105th Reg., 1818, 1819.

BLACK, JAMES C.
- Rifle Company, 1st Batt., 105th Reg., 1829.

BLACK, JOHN
- 1st Batt., 70th Reg., 1798.

BLACK, STEPHEN (?)
- 2nd Batt., 70th Reg., 1798.

BLACK, WILLIAM
- 1st Batt., 105th Reg., 1803.

BLACKWELL, JOSEPH
- 105th Reg., 1813, 1816, 1824, 1825; 70th Reg., 1827.

BLACKWELL, JULIAS
- 105th Reg., 1817.

BLACKWELL, WILLIAM
- 2nd Batt., 70th Reg., 1798; Capt. Jones' Light Infantry Company, 1st Batt., 105th Reg., 1807; Capt. Jones' Artillery Company, 1808; Capt. Dixon's Rifle Company, 1810, 1811; 70th Reg., 1820.

BLACKWELL, WILLIAM, JR.
- 105th Reg., 1818.

BLAIR, JOHN
- 2nd Batt., 70th Reg., 1798.

BLAIR, RICHARD
- 105th Reg., 1817, 1823.

BLAKELY, JAMES
- Capt. Tilson's Company, 1st Batt., 70th Reg., 1807, 1825, 1826.

BLANKS, THOMPSON
- 105th Reg., 1824.

BLANSET, JARED
- 105th Reg., 1834.

BLEDSOE (BLADSOE), ABRAHAM
- 2nd Batt., 105th Reg., 1804.

BLEDSOE, AMBROSE
- 2nd Batt., 105th Reg., 1812.

BLEDSOE, ANTHONY
- 2nd Batt., 70th Reg., 1798; 2nd Batt., 105th Reg., 1799, 1813.

BLEDSOE, AUSTINE (AUSTIN)
- 2nd Batt., 105th Reg., 1802; Capt. Fulkerson's Company, 1808, 1811, 1812.

BLEDSOE, BARNY S. (OR L.)
- Capt. Tate's Company, 2nd Batt., 70th Reg., 1811, 1812.

BLEDSOE, ISAAC
- 2nd Batt., 105th Reg., 1799.

BLEDSOE, PINCKNEY T.
- Capt. Tate's Company, 2nd Batt., 70th Reg., 1811.

BLEDSOE, THOMAS
- 2nd Batt., 105th Reg., 1799.

BLEDSOE, VALENTINE
- 2nd Batt., 105th Reg., 1802; Capt. Larkey's Company, 1806; Capt. Fulkerson's Company, 1808, 1811.

****

BLEDSOE, WILLIAM
- 2nd Batt., 105th Reg., 1812.

BLESSING, ABRAM
- 70th Reg., 1812-1815, 1817, 1829.

BLESSING, HENRY
- 1st Batt., 70th Reg., 1798.

BLESSING, ISAAC
- 70th Reg., 1820.

BLESSING, JACOB
- 70th Reg., 1830.

BLESSING, SAMUEL
- 70th Reg., 1817.

BLEVINS, DANIEL
- 105th Reg., 1835.

BLEVINS, DAVID
- Capt. Edmondson's Company, 1st Batt., 105th Reg., 1810.

BLEVINS, JOHN
- 105th Reg., 1834.

BLOOMER, SAMUEL
- Capt. Talbert's Company, 2nd Batt., 70th Reg., 1803.

BLUMER, DANIEL
- 1st Batt., 70th Reg., 1798.

BOATWRIGHT, JAMES
- Capt. Bradley's Company, 1st Batt., 105th Reg., 1806.

BOATWRIGHT, WILLIAM
- Capt. Bradley's Company, 1st Batt., 105th Reg., 1806.

BOLES, JAMES
- 70th Reg., 1830.

BOLES, JOHN
- 70th Reg., 1801.

BOLES, JOHN D.
- 70th Reg., 1822.

BOLES, JOSEPH
- 70th Reg., 1830.

BOLES, ROBERT
- 70th Reg., 1830.

BOLES, SAMUEL
- 70th Reg., 1830.

BOLES, THOMAS
- Rifle Company, 1st Batt., 70th Reg., 1807.

BOLINGER, GEORGE W.
- 105th Reg., 1833, 1834.

BOLTON, BENJAMIN
- 1st Batt., 105th Reg., 1812.

BOLTON, NOAH
- Troop of Cavalry, 105th Reg., 1812, 1813.

BOMAN, JOHN
- 1st Batt., 105th Reg., 1803.

BOND, WILLIAM
- 2nd Batt., 105th Reg., 1803; Capt. Gillenwaters' Company, 1807.

BONHAM, HEZEKIAH
- 70th Reg., 1820.

BONHAM, JOHN
- 70th Reg., 1821.

BONNELL, DOUGLASS
- 105th Reg., 1834.

BONNEN, JAMES
- 105th Reg., 1831.

BONNER, THOMAS
- Capt. Fulkerson's Company, 2nd Batt., 105th Reg., 1809.

BOSSLEY, JAMES
- 70th Reg., 1801.

BOSTON, ISAAC
- 70th Reg., 1819-1821, 1823-1825.

BOTNER, ELIAS
- 105th Reg., 1832, 1833.

BOVILLE, JAMES
- 1st Batt., 105th Reg., 1803; Light Infantry Company, 1808, 1811.

BOW, JOEL
- 105th Reg., 1815, 1819, 1821-1823, 1829, 1831-1833.

BOWEN, ARTHUR
- 70th Reg., 1819.

BOWEN, GEORGE
- 105th Reg., 1817.

****

BOWEN, JOHN
- 1st Batt., 105th Reg., 1800, 1811.

BOWEN, JOSEPH
- 70th Reg., 1812, 1813.

BOWEN, THOMAS
- 70th Reg., 1814, 1815, 1817; 105th Reg., 1817.

BOWEN, WILLIAM
- 70th Reg., 1812.

BOWLIN, ISAAC
- 105th Reg., 1817.

BOWMAN, AARON
- 70th Reg., 1830, 1835.

BOWMAN, BENJAMIN
- 105th Reg., 1818, 1820.

BOWMAN, ESEIAS
- 70th Reg., 1830, 1835.

BOWMAN, ISAM
- 1st Batt., 70th Reg., 1798, 1827.

BOWNINE, MOSES
- Capt. Hayter's Company, 2nd Batt., 70th Reg., 1806, 1810.

BOWSER, EMANUEL
- 105th Reg., 1835.

BOYD, BARTLEY (BARTLETT)
- Capt. Irby's Company, 2nd Batt., 70th Reg., 1805, 1809.

BOYD, DANIEL
- 70th Reg., 1817.

BOYD, ELISHA
- 105th Reg., 1815, 1816.

BOYD, HENRY
- Capt. Jones' Artillery Company, 105th Reg., 1808; Light Infantry Company, 1st Batt., 1809.

BOYD, JAMES
- 105th Reg., 1825.

BOYD, JOHN
- 70th Reg., 1815, 1818.

BOYD, ROBERT
- Light Infantry Company, 1st Batt., 105th Reg., 1809.

BOYD, WILLIAM
- 2nd Batt., 70th Reg., 1798, 1802.

BOYS, DANIEL (OR DAVID)
- Capt. Meek's Company, 70th Reg., 1805.

BOYS, MICHAEL
- Capt. Meek's Company, 1st Batt., 70th Reg., 1806.

BOZWELL, LEWIS
- 105th Reg., 1811.

BOZWELL, WILLIAM
- 105th Reg., 1811.

BRADFULE (BRADFUTE), ARCHIBALD
- 105th Reg., 1831-1833.

BRADLEY, ANDREW
- 1st Batt., 70th Reg., 1798; Capt. Lyon's Company, 70th Reg., 1804.

BRADLEY, DANIEL
- 70th Reg., 1800.

BRADLEY, JAMES, JR.
- 105th Reg., 1815-1817.

BRADLEY, JOHN
- 70th Reg., 1800, 1802; Capt. Smyth's Company, 2nd Batt., 1803; 105th Reg., 1819, 1822.

BRADLEY, MERIDETH
- 105th Reg., 1835.

BRADLEY, REUBEN
- 2nd Batt., 70th Reg., 1798.

BRADLEY, WILLIAM
- 70th Reg., 1809, 1810.

BRADON, JOHN
- 70th Reg., 1801.

BRADON, SAMUEL
- 70th Reg., 1801, 1802.

BRADSHAW, MOSES
- 105th Reg., 1817.

BRADY (?), JOSIAH
- 1st Batt., 105th Reg., 1812.

BRANCH, PETER
- 70th Reg., 1815.

BRANCH, PETER J.
- 105th Reg., 1820-1824, 1826, 1827.

****

BRANSON, BRISCO
- 105th Reg., 1811.

BRANSON, DAVID
- 105th Reg., 1811.

BRANSON, HENRY
- Capt. Fulkerson's Company, 2nd Batt., 105th Reg., 1810.

BRANSON (OR BRANDON), SAMUEL
- Capt. Houston's Troop of Cavalry, 2nd Batt., 105th Reg., 1807, 1808.

BRAWLEY, JAMES B.
- 105th Reg., 1834.

BRAWN, WALKER
- 70th Reg., 1813.

BREADY, JOHN
- 2nd Batt., 70th Reg., 1798; 2nd Batt., 105th Reg., 1799.

BREDIN (BREADON), SAMUEL
- 2nd Batt., 70th Reg., 1798; 2nd Batt., 105th Reg., 1799; 70th Reg., 1800; Capt. Talbert's Company, 2nd Batt., 1803.

BRETON, WILLIAM
- Capt. Martin's Company, 1st Batt., 105th Reg., 1807.

BRICHET, JAMES
- 70th Reg., 1833.

BRIDGEWATER, WILLIAM
- 1st Batt., 70th Reg., 1798.

BRIDGES (BRIGES), JAMES B.
- 105th Reg., 1824, 1827, 1833.

BRONOUGH, AUSTIN S.
- 105th Reg., 1829, 1830, 1834, 1835.

BRONOUGH, JEREMIAH
- 105th Reg., 1824-1831, 1833-1835.

BRONOUGH, MALCOM
- 105th Reg., 1835.

BROOKS, GEORGE
- 105th Reg., 1814.

BROOKS, LUDWIN
- 1st Batt., 105th Reg., 1812, 1813.

BROOKSHIRE, JOSEPH
- 70th Reg., 1802.

BROWN, ALEXANDER
- 105th Reg., 1817.

BROWN, DANIEL
- 105th Reg., 1817.

BROWN, GEORGE
- Capt. Fulkerson's Company, 2nd Batt., 105th Reg., 1808.

BROWN, ISAAC
- Capt. George Byar's Company, 1st Batt., 70th Reg., 1811.

BROWN, JAMES
- 2nd Batt., 105th Reg., 1802; Capt. Fulkerson's Company, 1808.

BROWN, JOHN
- Capt. Larkey's Company, 2nd Batt., 105th Reg., 1806, 1813-1815.

BROWN, JOHN, JR.
- Capt. Fulkerson's Company, 2nd Batt., 105th Reg., 1808.

BROWN, SAMUEL
- Capt. Houston's Troop of Cavalry, 105th Reg., 1808, 1809.

BROWN, STEPEN (sic)
- 2nd Batt., 70th Reg., 1798, 1812.

BROWN, THOMAS
- Capt. Goodson's Company, 2nd Batt., 105th Reg., 1807; Light Infantry Company, 1st Batt., 1809.

BROWN, WILLIAM
- Capt. Campbell's Company, 1st Batt., 70th Reg., 1804; Capt. Martin's Company, 1st Batt., 105th Reg., 1806; Capt. Edmondson's Company, 1809; 70th Reg., 1819.

BROWNEN, EDMOND
- 70th Reg., 1813.

BROWNEN, JAMES
- 70th Reg., 1817.

BROWNEN, JOHN
- 70th Reg., 1812.

BROWNING, EDMOND
- 70th Reg., 1815, 1816, 1819.

BROWNING, JACOB
- 70th Reg., 1818, 1819.

****

BROWNING, JAMES
- 70th Reg., 1812.

BROWNLOW, JOSEPH A.
- 105th Reg., 1834.

BROWNLOW, SAMUEL
- 1st Batt., 105th Reg., 1806.

BROWNLOW, WILLIAM
- 105th Reg., 1824.

BRUCE, THOMAS
- 2nd Batt., 105th Reg., 1812.

BRUNDIGE, NATHANIEL
- 1st Batt., 70th Reg., 1798.

BRYAN, JAMES, SR.
- 70th Reg., 1800; Capt. Lyon's Company, 2nd Batt., 1804; Capt. Beatie's Company, 2nd Batt., 1805; Artillery Company, 105th Reg., 1815; 70th Reg., 1817, 1819.

BRYAN, JAMES, JR.
- 3rd Corporal, Artillery Company, 105th Reg., 1815.

BRYAN, JAMES
- 70th Reg., 1820, 1821, 1823, 1833.

BRYAN, JOHN
- 1st Batt., 70th Reg., 1798, 1800; Capt. Lyon's Company, 1805, 1806.

BRYAN, WILLIAM
- 70th Reg., 1833, 1834.

BRYANT, ABNER
- Capt. Craig's Company, 1st Batt., 70th Reg., 1803; Rifle Company, 1807.

BRYANT, ALEXANDER
- 70th Reg., 1822.

BRYANT, JAMES
- 70th Reg., 1802; Capt. Smyth's Company, 2nd Batt., 1803, 1810; 105th Reg., 1813; 70th Reg., 1822.

BRYANT, JAMES, SR.
- 70th Reg., 1810; 105th Reg., 1813; 70th Reg., 1817.

BRYANT, JOHN
- 70th Reg., 1801, 1802; Capt. Beatie's Company, 2nd Batt., 1803, 1804; Capt. William Byars' Company, 1st Batt., 1807; Capt. James Scott's Company, 2nd Batt., 1811, 1812.

BUCHANAN, ALEXANDER
- Capt. Tate's Company, 2nd Batt., 70th Reg., 1803.

BUCHANAN, ANDREW
- Capt. Edmiston's Company, 1st Batt., 70th Reg., 1803; Rifle Company, 1807, 1810, 1818, 1829.

BUCHANAN, BENJAMIN
- 105th Reg., 1835.

BUCHANAN, DAVID
- 70th Reg., 1813, 1819, 1824, 1826; 105th Reg., 1827.

BUCHANAN, JAMES
- Capt. Meek's Company, 1st Batt., 70th Reg., 1806, 1815, 1816, 1824.

BUCHANAN, JESSE
- 70th Reg., 1826, 1827.

BUCHANAN, JOHN
- 70th Reg., 1814, 1816, 1830, 1835.

BUCHANAN, MATTHEW
- 70th Reg., 1813.

BUCHANAN, PATRICK
- 70th Reg., 1821, 1826.

BUCHANAN, SAMUEL
- Rifle Company, 1st Batt., 105th Reg., 1829.

BUCHANAN, SOLEN
- 70th Reg., 1825.

BUCHANAN, WILLIAM (WILL)
- 70th Reg., 1802; 105th Reg., 1819; 70th Reg., 1824.

BUCHANAN, WILLIAM E.
- Capt. Smyth's Company, 2nd Batt., 70th Reg., 1803.

BUCHANAN, WILSON
- 70th Reg., 1817.

BUCKLY, ABRAHAM
- 2nd Batt., 105th Reg., 1802; Capt. Fulkerson's Company, 1808.

BULLEN, SAMUEL
- 1st Batt., 70th Reg., 1798.

BUNCH, JAMES
- 70th Reg., 1825.

****

BUNCH, JOHN
- 70th Reg., 1830.

BURCH, JOSEPH
- 70th Reg., 1816.

BURGER, GEORGE
- 70th Reg., 1814.

BURGER, MICHAEL
- 70th Reg., 1801, 1812, 1814, 1816.

BURGIS, DAVID
- 70th Reg., 1819.

BURGIS, GEORGE
- 70th Reg., 1830.

BURGIS, LORENS D.
- 70th Reg., 1824.

BURGIS, ROBERT
- 70th Reg., 1816-1819, 1823, 1824, 1831, 1832.

BURGIS, SAMUEL
- 70th Reg., 1816.

BURGIS, WILLIAM
- 1st Batt., 70th Reg., 1798, 1809, 1810, 1825, 1830 (?).

BURGIT, GEORGE
- 70th Reg., 1822.

BURKE, JAMES
- 2nd Batt., 105th Reg., 1801, 1802; 3rd Sergeant, Rifle Company, 1809; 70th Reg., 1819.

BURKE, JAMES D.
- 70th Reg., 1823.

BURKE, JOHN
- 2nd Batt., 70th Reg., 1798, 1800; 1st Batt., 105th Reg., 1800-1802.

BURKE, THOMAS
- 70th Reg., 1800, 1809, 1811-1813, 1815, 1817, 1818.

BURKETT, JOHN
- 70th Reg., 1817, 1818.

BURR, JOHN
- Light Infantry Company, 1st Batt., 105th Reg., 1809.

BURT, CLEMENT W.
- 105th Reg., 1816, 1817.

BUSEAL, RICHARD
- 70th Reg., 1833.

BUTLER, ENOCK
- 105th Reg., 1818.

BUTTERY (BUTERY), ABRAM
- 105th Reg., 1819.

BUTTERY, ROBERT
- 70th Reg., 1801.

BUTTERY, THOMAS
- Capt. Bradley's Company, 1st Batt., 105th Reg., 1809.

BYARS, JOHN
- 1st Batt., 105th Reg., 1800; 70th Reg., 1802.

BYARS, WILLIAM, JR.
- 105th Reg., 1835.

C----, WILLIAM
- Capt. Byars' Company, 1st Batt., 70th Reg., 1806.

CAGER, WILLIAM
- 70th Reg., 1830.

CAHOON, WILLIAM
- Capt. Tate's Company, 70th Reg., 1804.

CAITEO (?), SECRETARY
- 105th Reg., 1834.

CALDWELL, ANDREW
- Capt. Jones' Light Infantry Company, 1st Batt., 105th Reg., 1807; Capt. Dixon's Company, 1808.

CALDWELL, JOHN
- 105th Reg., 1811.

CALDWELL, JOHN S. (OR L.)
- 105th Reg., 1826; Rifle Company, 1st Batt., 1829.

CALDWELL, ROBERT
- 105th Reg., 1819.

CALDWELL, WILLIAM
- 2nd Batt., 70th Reg., 1798.

CALL, JOHN
- 70th Reg., 1830.

****

CALLAHAM, DANIEL
- 70th Reg., 1835.

CALLAHAM, DAVID
- 70th Reg., 1825, 1829, 1830.

CALLAHAM, JOHN
- 70th Reg., 1814.

CALLAHAM, WILLIAM
- 2nd Batt., 70th Reg., 1798. 2nd Batt., 105th Reg., 1799.

CALLEY, JOHN
- 70th Reg., 1825.

CALLISON, ANDREW
- 70th Reg., 1830, 1831.

CALLISON, DAVID
- 70th Reg., 1824.

CALLISON, JESSEE
- Capt. Bazil Scott's Company, 2nd Batt., 70th Reg., 1811.

CALVIN, ROBERT C.
- Troop of Cavalry, 1st Batt., 105th Reg., 1809.

CAMPBELL, ALEXANDER
- 70th Reg., 1830.

CAMPBELL, ALLEN
- Capt. Campbell's Company, 70th Reg., 1804, 1805.

CAMPBELL, ARTHUR
- Capt. Davis' Company, 2nd Batt., 105th Reg., 1807, 1810, 1815, 1817, 1819, 1821.

CAMPBELL, AUDLEY
- 70th Reg., 1802; Capt. Tate's Company, 2nd Batt., 1803.

CAMPBELL, DAVID
- Capt. Bradley's Company, 1st Batt., 105th Reg., 1810.

CAMPBELL, DAVID, JR.
- Capt. Bradley's Company, 1st Batt., 105th Reg., 1810.

CAMPBELL, EDWARD
- Light Infantry Company, 1st Batt., 105th Reg., 1809, 1812.

CAMPBELL, GEORGE
- 70th Reg., 1830.

CAMPBELL, JACOB
- 105th Reg., 1822.

CAMPBELL, JAMES
- 70th Reg., 1802; Capt. Tate's Company, 2nd Batt., 1803; Capt. Campbell's Company, 1805, 1812.

CAMPBELL, JAMES
- 105th Reg., 1805; Light Infantry Company, 1st Batt., 1809.

CAMPBELL, JOHN
- 70th Reg., 1799, 1802; Capt. Tate's Company, 2nd Batt., 1803; Capt. Campbell's Company, 1805.

CAMPBELL, JOHN
- Light Infantry Company, 1st Batt., 105th Reg., 1809, 1824, 1829.

CAMPBELL, JOHN S. M.
- 70th Reg., 1821, 1825, 1826.

CAMPBELL, JOHN T.
- 70th Reg., 1817.

CAMPBELL, JOSEPH
- 1st Batt., 70th Reg., 1798, 1800.

CAMPBELL, LYSANDER
- 105th Reg., 1830, 1832.

CAMPBELL, ROBERT, JR.
- Light Infantry Company, 1st Batt., 105th Reg., 1809, 1822.

CAMPBELL, SAMUEL Y.
- Troop of Cavalry, 1st Batt., 105th Reg., 1809, 1813.

CAMPBELL, WILLIAM
- 2nd Batt., 105th Reg., 1802.

CAMPBELL, WILLIAM
- Capt. Tate's Company, 2nd Batt., 70th Reg., 1805, 1820.

CAMPBELL, WILLIAM S.
- 70th Reg., 1822, 1827.

CANNADY, ANDREW
- 105th Reg., 1826, 1829.

CANNADY, CHARLES
- 2nd Batt., 70th Reg., 1798.

CANNADY, ELIJAH
- 105th Reg., 1826, 1829.

****

CANTER, LEVI
- 105th Reg., 1823, 1826.

CANTER, TRUEMAN
- 2nd Batt., 105th Reg., 1803.

CARMACK, CORNELIUS
- 2nd Batt., 105th Reg., 1799, 1800.

CARMACK, ENOCH
- Rifle Company, 2nd Batt., 105th Reg., 1809, 1811.

CARMACK, JOHN
- 2nd Batt., 70th Reg., 1798.

CARMACK, WILLIAM
- 2nd Batt., 105th Reg., 1799, 1800; Capt. Goodson's Company, 1806, 1808. (2nd Batt., 70th Reg., 1798.)

CARPENTER, ELIJAH
- 70th Reg., 1802; Capt. Lyon's Company, 1804, 1809, 1813, 1816.

CARPENTER, JOHN
- 70th Reg., 1820.

CARR, JOHN
- 70th Reg., 1814.

CARR, JOSEPH
- 105th Reg., 1829, 1830.

CARRELL, ISAAC
- 105th Reg., 1827, 1831.

CARRELL, MICHAEL
- 70th Reg., 1822, 1823.

CARROL, TIMOTHY
- Capt. Martin's Company, 1st Batt., 105th Reg., 1806, 1807.

CARSON, ALEXANDER
- 2nd Batt., 105th Reg., 1802, 1804.

CARSON, CHARLES S.
- 1st Batt., 105th Reg., 1800; "Member of Rifle Company ... died ... 22 Jan 1815 ... native of Ireland ... in business with the late William King ..." (Obituary in the "Political Prospect", 31 Jan 1815.)

CARSON, DAVID
- 70th Reg., 1813.

CARSON, SAMUEL
- Capt. Edmiston's Company, 1st Batt., 70th Reg., 1806.

CARTER, DAVID
- 70th Reg., 1801, 1802; Capt. Beatie's Company, 2nd Batt., 1803, 1809, 1810; Capt Tate's Company, 1811, 1812.

CARTER, ELIJAH
- 70th Reg., 1813, 1816, 1820, 1821, 1824, 1826, 1827, 1830.

CARTER, HENRY
- 70th Reg., 1820, 1821, 1824, 1827.

CARTER, JOHN
- Capt. Bradley's Company, 1st Batt., 105th Reg., 1806, 1807; Capt. Tate's Comapny, 2nd Batt., 70th Reg., 1811, 1821.

CARTER, PLODGE
- 105th Reg., 1817.

CARTER, SOLOMAN
- 70th Reg., 1809.

CARTWRIGHT, DAVID
- 105th Reg., 1819.

CARTY, DANIEL
- Capt. Martin's Company, 1st Batt., 105th Reg., 1809.

CASEY, JAMES
- 105th Reg., Reg., 1819, 1820; 70th Reg., 1833.

CASNOR, HENRY
- 1st Batt., 70th Reg., 1798; 1st Batt., 105th Reg., 1800, 1803.

CASNOR, JOHN M.
- 105th Reg., 1815.

CASNOR, JACOB M.
- 105th Reg., 1815.

CASNOR, JONAS
- 70th Reg., 1802.

CASNOR, LEN (?)
- 1st Batt., 70th Reg., 1798.

CASNOR, LEONARD
- 1st Batt., 70th Reg., 1798.

CASNOR, PHILIP
- 2nd Batt., 70th Reg., 1798.

CASNOR, WILLIAM
- 105th Reg., 1815, 1816.

****

CASSELL, MICHAEL
- Rifle Company, 2nd Batt., 105th Reg., 1809.

CATCHAN, JACOB
- 70th Reg., 1833.

CATCHEM, JAMES
- Rifle Company, 1st Batt., 70th Reg., 1807.

CATHARINE, CHRISTIAN
- Capt. Fulkerson's Company, 2nd Batt., 105th Reg., 1810, 1811.

CATHARINE, CHRISTOPHER
- Capt. Martin's Company, 1st Batt., 105th Reg., 1806; 2nd Batt., 1812.

CATHARINE, STOFFLE
- Capt. Martin's Company, 1st Batt., 105th Reg., 1807.

CATHARINE, VALENTINE
- Capt. Fulkerson's Company, 2nd Batt., 105th Reg., 1810, 1811.

CATLET, JOHN
- 105th Reg., 1835.

CATLET, GEORGE
- 105th Reg., 1829.

CATRON, CHRISTOPHER
- 105th Reg., 1818.

CATRON, FRANCIS
- 105th Reg., 1820, 1824.

CATTERING (CATTERN), FRANCIS
- Capt. Fulton's Company, 1st Batt., 70th Reg., 1811; 105th Reg., 1814, 1816, 1817.

CAYLOR, JOHN
- 105th Reg., 1821.

CENTER, DRURY
- 70th Reg., 1817.

CERTAIN, CHRISTOPHER
- Capt. Bradley's Company, 1st Batt., 105th Reg., 1806.

CHADWELL, WILLIAM
- 70th Reg., 1812.

CHAFIN, OMEGA
- Capt. Tate's Company, 2nd Batt., 70th Reg., 1807.

CHAMBERS, HUGH
- Capt. Meek's Company, 70th Reg., 1804.

CHAMMAN, WILLIAM
- 70th Reg., 1811.

CHANDLER, GEORGE
- 1st Batt., 105th Reg., 1806.

CHANDLER, JACOB
- Light Infantry Company, 105th Reg., 1808

CHANEY, CHRISTOPHER
- Artillery Company, 105th Reg., 1815.

CHANEY, JACOB
- 105th Reg., 1820.

CHAPHEN, CHRISTOPHER
- 70th Reg., 1809.

CHAPMAN, ISIAH
- 70th Reg., 1817.

CHAPMAN, JAMES
- 70th Reg., 1812; 105th Reg., 1833-1835.

CHAPMAN, JOB
- 70th Reg., 1802.

CHAPMAN, NATHANIEL (NATHAN)
- 70th Reg., 1811, 1815, 1816, 1820.

CHAPMAN, WILLIAM
- 70th Reg., 1814, 1825.

CHARLOTTE, WESLEY
- 105th Reg., 1825, 1826.

CHARLTON, JAMES
- Capt. George Byars' Company, 1st Batt., 70th Reg., 1807.

CHASTAIN, SAMUEL
- 70th Reg., 1823, 1835.

CHASTAIN, SAMUEL S.
- 105th Reg., 1835.

CHETSY (CHELSEY), ISAAC
- 70th Reg., 1802; Capt. Talbert's Company, 2nd Batt., 1803.

CHILDS, WILLIAM
- 70th Reg., 1802.

CHILDERS, GIDEON
- 2nd Batt., 70th Reg., 1798; 2nd Batt., 105th Reg., 1799, 1803.

****

CHILDERS, ISAAC
- 2nd Batt., 105th Reg., 1804; Capt. Fulkerson's Company, 1808.

CHITTIX (CHITTICKS), ELI
- Capt. Miller's Company, 2nd Batt., 70th Reg., 1811, 1812, 1814, 1815, 1816.

CHRISTY, JOHN W.
- 70th Reg., 1829.

CHRISTY, WYAT
- 70th Reg., 1829.

CHURCH, JONATHAN M.
- Capt. Martin's Company, 1st Batt., 105th Reg., 1805-1808, 1814, 1815.

CHURCH, ROBERT
- Capt. Bradley's Company, 1st Batt., 105th Reg., 1807, 1808, 1811, 1812.

CLAIBOURNE, NATHANIEL H.
- 1st Batt., 105th Reg., 1800.

CLAIR, JOHN
- 70th Reg., 1812.

CLAIR, MARTIN
- 70th Reg., 1813.

CLAPP, EARL B.
- 105th Reg., 1815.

CLAPP, THEOPHILUS C.
- 105th Reg., 1825, 1826, ("P.") 1835.

CLARE, JOHN
- 70th Reg., 1830.

CLARK, ALLEN
- 70th Reg., 1818-1820, 1822, 1823, 1825-1827.

CLARK, ARMSTRONG
- 70th Reg., 1814; Artillery Company, 105th Reg., 1815; 70th Reg., 1819.

CLARK, BENJAMIN
- 1st Batt., 105th Reg., 1799, 1800, 1805.

CLARK, BENJAMIN
- Capt. Fulkerson's Company, 2nd Batt., 105th Reg., 1809.

CLARK, DAVID
- 1st Batt., 70th Reg., 1798, 1802; Capt. Beatie's Company, 2nd Batt., 1803, 1807.

CLARK, DAVID
- Artillery Company, 105th Reg., 1815, 1816.

CLARK, GEORGE
- 70th Reg., 1802, 1809; 3rd Sergeant, Artillery Company, 105th Reg., 1815, 1817.

CLARK, JACOB
- Artillery Company, 105th Reg., 1815, 1816, 1817; 70th Reg., 1818; 105th Reg., 1820, 1822-1826, 1828, 1829.

CLARK, JAMES
- 105th Reg., 1813; Artillery Company, 1815, 1819, 1821.

CLARK, JESSE
- Capt. Edmiston's Company, 1st Batt., 70th Reg., 1806.

CLARK, JOB
- 105th Reg., 1821.

CLARK, JOHN "Son of George"
- 105th Reg., 1818-1820, 1823.

CLARK, JOHN
- 1st Sergeant, Artillery Company, 105th Reg., 1815, 1819, 1820, 1822; 70th Reg., 1827.

CLARK, JOHN, JR.
- Artillery Company, 105th Reg., 1815.

CLARK, JOHN J.
- 70th Reg., 1829.

CLARK, JOSEPH
- Capt. Hayter's Company, 2nd Batt., 70th Reg., 1803, 1814.

CLARK, PETER
- 70th Reg., 1833.

CLARK, ROBERT
- 70th Reg., 1831.

CLARK, SAMUEL
- Artillery Company, 105th Reg., 1815.

CLARK, WILLIAM, SR.
- 1st Batt., 105th Reg., 1799.

CLARK, WILLIAM ("North Folk")
- 105th Reg., 1820, 1825, 1830, 1831.

CLARK, WILLIAM ("of Ben")
- 105th Reg., 1825.

CLAWSON, JAMES

****

- Capt. Craig's Company, 1st Batt., 70th Reg., 1803, 1809, 1810, 1812-1814.

CLAWSON, JAMES W.
- 70th Reg., 1815, 1816.

CLAWSON, JOHN
- Capt. Craig's Company, 70th Reg., 1804.

CLAWSON, WILLIAM
- 70th Reg., 1802; Capt. Craig's Company, 1st Batt., 1803, 1804.

CLAYMON, JOHN
- 2nd Batt., 70th Reg., 1798; 2nd Batt., 105th Reg., 1799, 1800.

CLAYTON, WILLIAM J.
- 105th Reg., 1815.

CLAYTON, WILLIAM W.
- 105th Reg., 1820, 1824, 1832, 1835.

CLEEK, GEORGE
- Capt. Fulkerson's Company, 2nd Batt., 105th Reg., 1808.

CLEEK, MATHIAS
- Capt. Fulkerson's Company, 2nd Batt., 105th Reg., 1809, 1810, 1811.

CLEEK, MATHIAS, JR.
- Capt. Fulkerson's Company, 2nd Batt., 105th Reg., 1808.

CLEEK, MICHAEL
- Capt. Larkey's Company, 2nd Batt., 105th Reg., 1806.

CLEGHORN, JAMES
- Capt. Meek's Company, 1st Batt., 70th Reg., 1811, 1814, 1816-1820, 1823-1827.

CLEGHORN, JOHN
- 70th Reg., 1816, 1817.

CLEGHORN, ROBERT
- Capt. Meek's Company, 1st Batt., 70th Reg., 1811, 1815-1817.

CLEM, HEZEKIAH
- 70th Reg., 1800, 1801.

CLEM, WILLIAM
- 1st Batt., 70th Reg., 1798, 1800; Capt. Talbert's Company, 2nd Batt., 1807, 1809, 1814-1816, 1818-1820.

CLEMINGS, JOHN
- 70th Reg., 1800.

CLEMINGS, WILLIAM
- 70th Reg., 1799, 1812-1814.

CLENDENNAN, WILLIAM
- 1st Batt., 70th Reg., 1798.

CLENNAS (?), WILLIAM
- Capt. Talbert's Company, 2nd Batt., 70th Reg., 1803.

CLEVELAND, EZRA
- Capt. Tilson's Company, 70th Reg., 1805.

CLEVELAND, MAREENA
- 70th Reg., 1800.

CLEVELAND, MERES OR MERIS
- 1st Batt., 70th Reg., 1798, 1799.

CLEVELAND, WARREN
- 70th Reg., 1825.

CLEVELAND, ZAT (?)
- Capt. Edmiston's Company, 1st Batt., 70th Reg., 1806.

CLEVENGER, GEORGE
- 105th Reg., 1831, 1833, 1834; 70th Reg., 1835.

CLIMBS, VALENTINE
- 70th Reg., 1812.

CLINE, ANDREW
- 105th Reg., 1815, 1819.

CLINE, JOHN
- 2nd Batt., 105th Reg., 1804.

CLINER (CLYNARD), HENRY
- Capt. Berry's Company, 1st Batt., 105th Reg., 1806, 1807, 1812.

CLINES, HENRY
- 1st Batt., 105th Reg., 1801.

COATNEY, STEPHEN
- Capt. Edmiston's Company, 1st Batt., 70th Reg., 1807.

COCHRAN, CONNALLY
- 105th Reg., 1819, 1820.

COCHRAN, SAMUEL
- 70th Reg., 1810, 1812, 1814, 1815.

COGHRAN, JAMES
- 1st Batt., 70th Reg., 1798.

****

COLE, HUGH
- Rifle Company, 1st Batt., 70th Reg., 1807, 1827.

COLE, JACOB
- 70th Reg., 1814.

COLE, JAMES
- Capt. Tilson's Company, 70th Reg., Apr, 1804; Capt. Campbell's Company, Nov, 1804; Capt. Bishop's Company, 1st Batt., 1811, 1814, 1815, 1824.

COLE, JAMES ("Slitter" ?)
- 70th Reg., 1814.

COLE, JEREMIAH
- Capt. Byars' Company, 1st Batt., 70th Reg., 1807.

COLE, JOHN
- Capt. Preston's Company, 1st Batt., 70th Reg., 1811.

COLE, JOSEPH, JR.
- Capt. Campbell's Company, 70th Reg., 1805, 1819, 1820.

COLE, JOSEPH, SR.
- 70th Reg., 1799; Rifle Company, 1st Batt., 1807, 1818-1820.

COLE, JOSEPH S.
- 70th Reg., 1821.

COLE, JOSEPH ("Saluda" ?)
- Rifle Company, 1st Batt., 70th Reg., 1807.

COLE, NATHAN
- 70th Reg., 1830.

COLE, PELEG
- 70th Reg., 1816-1818.

COLE, SAMUEL
- 70th Reg., 1814, 1819, 1820.

COLE, THOMAS
- Rifle Company, 1st Batt., 70th Reg., 1807.

COLE, ZACHEUS
- 70th Reg., 1821, 1822.

COLEMAN, MOSES
- 70th Reg., 1816, 1818, 1819.

COLEMAN, RICHARD
- 70th Reg., 1813, 1814.

COLINGS, ISAAC
- 70th Reg., 1817, 1826.

COLLEY, DANIEL
- 2nd Batt., 105th Reg., 1812.

COLLEY, GEORGE
- 70th Reg., 1800, 1802.

COLLEY, SHADRACK
- Capt. Irby's Company, 2nd Batt., 70th Reg., 1805; 105th Reg., 1815, 1816.

COLLEY, THOMAS
- 70th Reg., 1802; Capt. Irby's Company, 2nd Batt., 1804, 1805; Capt. Hinds' Company, 1806; 1824, 1830.

COLLIER, JOHN
- 105th Reg., 1818, 1823.

COLLIN, JAMES
- 105th Reg., 1831.

COLLINS, JAMES
- 105th Reg., 1813.

COLLINS, JENSON
- 70th Reg., 1812.

COLLINS, JEREMIAH
- 105th Reg., 1826, 1831.

COLLINS, JILSON (GILSON)
- 105th Reg., 1819, 1820, 1826, 1828.

COLLINS, JOHN
- 1st Batt., 105th Reg., 1799; 1825.

COLLINS, LUKE
- Capt. Jones' Light Infantry Company, 1st Batt., 105th Reg., 1807; Capt. Jones' Artillery Company, 1808.

COLLINS, REES (RIECE)
- 105th Reg., 1813, 1816.

COLLINS, SAMUEL
- 105th Reg., 1813, 1819.

COLLAP, PETER
- 70th Reg., 1827.

COLVILL, ANDREW
- 1st Batt., 105th Reg., 1800.

COMBS, THOMAS

****

****

****

CRAWFORD, HUGH
- 105th Reg., 1811, 1815.

CRAWFORD, JAMES
- 70th Reg., 1819, 1820; 105th Reg., 1832.

CRAWFORD, JOHN
- Capt. Craig's Company, 1st Batt., 70th Reg., 1803; 1809, 1824.

CRAWFORD, JOHN
- Capt. Bradley's Company, 1st Batt., 105th Reg., 1810.

CREEKMORE, ROBERT
- 105th Reg., 1818, 1819.

CRESLY (?), GEORGE
- 70th Reg., 1816.

CRESSELL (?), GEORGE
- 70th Reg., 1818, 1833.

CREWEY, CHRISTOPHER
- 70th Reg., 1814, 1815, 1817, 1820, 1821, 1823, 1825-1827, 1830.

CRIST, DANIEL
- 105th Reg., 1831.

CROCKETT, GEORGE
- 105th Reg., 1805.

CROCKETT, SAMUEL
- 70th Reg., 1809.

CROSS, BENSON
- 105th Reg., 1822.

CROSS, MORDECAI
- 105th Reg., 1822.

CROUSE (CROWSE), FREDERICK
- Capt. Miller's Company, 2nd Batt., 70th Reg., 1811-1814, 1816, 1817.

CROW, JOHN
- 1st Batt., 70th Reg., 1798; 1st Batt., 105th Reg., 1800; Rifle Company, 1st Batt, 70th Reg., 1807.

CROW, LEWIS
- 1st Batt., 105th Reg., 1806.

CROW, ROBERT
- 70th Reg., 1802.

CROW, SAMUEL
- Capt. Campbell's Company, 70th Reg., 1805.

CROW, THOMAS
- 105th Reg., 1815.

CRUIT, CHRISTOPHER
- 105th Reg., 1811.

CRUMP, HENRY H.
- 1st Batt., 105th Reg., 1812.

CRUTCHFIELD, ROBERT, JR.
- 105th Reg., 1830.

CRYDER, JACOB
- Capt. Jones' Light Infantry Company, 1st Batt., 105th Reg., 1807.

CRYDER, JAMES
- 105th Reg., 1805; Capt. Bradley's Company, 1st Batt., 1807.

CRYDER, JOHN
- Artillery Company, 105th Reg., 1815; 1822, 1825.

CUBINE, PATRICK
- 105th Reg., 1831.

CULBERT, JOHN
- 70th Reg., 1826, 1827.

CULLOP, JOHN
- 70th Reg., 1809, 1810.

CUMMINGS, CHARLES C.
- 105th Reg., 1826, 1829.

CUMMINGS, JAMES
- 105th Reg., 1805.

CUMMINGS, JOHN C.
- 105th Reg., 1825.

CUMMINGS, ROBERT
- Capt. Bradley's Company, 1st Batt., 105th Reg., 1806.

CUMMINGS, ROBERT C.
- 105th Reg., 1830, 1832.

CUMMINGS, ROBERT E. (OR C.)
- Artillery Company, 105th Reg., 1815.

CUNNINGHAM, GEORGE
- 70th Reg., 1817, 1818.

CUNNINGHAM, JAMES
- Capt. Hayter's Company, 2nd Batt., 70th Reg., 1805; 1809.

****

CUNNINGHAM, JAMES
- 2nd Batt., 105th Reg., 1804; Capt. Goff's Company, 1808; 1811; 1st Batt., 1812; Artillery Company, 1815.

CUNNINGHAM, JOHN
- 70th Reg., 1824.

CUNNINGHAM, JOSEPH
- Capt. Hayter's Company, 2nd Batt.,70th Reg., 1807; 1812, 1813; Artillery Company, 105th Reg., 1815; 70th Reg., 1817, 1819.

CUNNINGHAM, SAMUEL
- Capt. Hayter's Company, 2nd Batt., 70th Reg., 1807; 1810; Capt. Logan's Company, 1811; 1812-1814.

CUNNINGHAM, THOMAS
- 70th Reg., 1815; Artillery Company, 105th Reg., 1815, 1816; 70th Reg., 1818, 1819.

CUNNINGHAM, WILLIAM
- Capt. Hayter's Company, 2nd Batt., 70th Reg., 1806, 1807.

CUNNINGHAM, WILLIAM
- 1st Batt., 105th Reg., 1800, 1810; 1811; 1812; Artillery Company, 1815.

CUPPENHEFFER (CUPENHAVER), DAVID
- 70th Reg., 1824.

CUPPENHEFFER, HENRY
- 70th Reg., 1814, 1817, 1826.

CURRIN, JONATHAN
- 70th Reg., 1809.

CURRIN, ROBERT ("P.", 1803)
- 70th Reg., 1801, 1802; Capt. Irby's Company, 2nd Batt., 1803.

CURRIN, WADDY T.
- 70th Reg., 1811-1816, 1818.

CUTLER, JOSEPH
- 105th Reg., 1822, 1823.

CUTLER, WALDO
- 105th Reg., 1820.

DAMRON, MICHAEL T.
- 70th Reg., 1830.

DANDRIDGE, WILLIAM D.
- 70th Reg., 1829.

DANIEL, OBADIAH
- 70th Reg., 1817.

DARNOLD, HENRY
- 105th Reg., 1811; 2nd Batt., 1812; 1813.

DAUGHERTY, CARSON
- 105th Reg., 1834.

DAUGHERTY, JAMES
- 70th Reg., 1827.

DAVENPORT, ABSOLOM
- 70th Reg., 1812.

DAVENPORT, JAMES
- 2nd Batt., 105th Reg., 1800.

DAVENPORT, JOHN
- 1st Batt., 105th Reg., 1799; Capt. Larkey's Company, 2nd Batt., 1806.

DAVENPORT, JULIUS
- Capt. Hayter's Company, 2nd Batt., 70th Reg., 1803.

DAVENPORT, JULIUS T.
- 70th Reg., 1814, 1815.

DAVENPORT, TERRY
- 70th Reg., 1800.

DAVENPORT, WILLIAM
- 70th Reg., 1820.

DAVENPORT, WILSON
- 70th Reg., 1820.

DAVIDSON, JAMES
- Capt. Bradley's Company, 1st Batt., 105th Reg., 1810.

DAVIDSON, JOHN
- Capt. Bradley's Company, 1st Batt., 105th Reg., 1810; 1819, 1820, 1823.

DAVIDSON, WILLIAM
- Troop of Cavalry, 1st Batt., 105th Reg., 1809.

DAVIS, ARCHIMEDES
- 105th Reg., 1833.

DAVIS, BENJAMIN

****

- Capt. Berry's Company, 1st Batt., 105th Reg., 1809.

DAVIS, CHARLES
- Light Infantry Company, 105th Reg., 1808

DAVIS, EDWARD
- Artillery Company, 1st Batt., 105th Reg., 1809, 1812.

DAVIS, GEORGE
- 105th Reg., 1834.

DAVIS, JAMES
- 70th Reg., 1818-1820, 1825, 1827.

DAVIS, JAMES
- 105th Reg., 1814, 1815.

DAVIS, JAMES, JR.
- 105th Reg., 1818-1822, 1824-1827; Rifle Company, 1st Batt., 105th Reg., 1829.

DAVIS, JOHN
- 105th Reg., 1818.

DAVIS, JOHN
- 1st Batt., 70th Reg., 1798, 1799, 1800; 1st Batt., 105th Reg., 1801; 2nd Batt., 1803, 1804; Capt. Jones' Light Infantry Company, 1807; Capt. Dixon's Rifle Company, 1808; Troop of Cavalry, 1st Batt., 1809; Troop of Cavalry, 2nd Batt., 1809; Capt. Duff's Troop of Cavalry, 1st Batt., 1810, 1811; Troop of Cavalry, 1812, 1813.

DAVIS, JONATHAN
- 1st Batt., 105th Reg., 1806; Light Infantry Company, 1808, 1811; 2nd Batt., 1812.

DAVIS, MOSEBY
- Capt. Jones' Company, 1st Batt., 105th Reg., 1810, 1818.

DAVIS, MOSES
- Capt. Davis' Company, 2nd Batt., 105th Reg., 1806, 1814.

DAVIS, NOAH
- 70th Reg., 1833.

DAVIS, ROBERT
- 105th Reg., 1819.

DAVIS, SAMUEL
- 105th Reg., 1820.

DAVIS, WILLIAM
- 105th Reg., 1814, 1825.

DAVIS, WILLIAM M.
- 105th Reg., 1829.

DAVISON, ANDREW
- 1st Batt., 105th Reg., 1812.

DAVISON, CALEB
- 70th Reg., 1821.

DAVISON, JAMES
- Capt. Fulkerson's Company, 2nd Batt., 105th Reg., 1809; Troop of Cavalry, 1812, 1813-1815.

DAVISON, JOHN
- 105th Reg., 1815, 1824-1827.

DAVISON, MOSEBY
- 105th Reg., 1814, 1815, 1819, 1821, 1822

DAVISON, ROBERT
- 70th Reg., 1815; 105th Reg., 1817; 70th Reg., 1821, 1823-1825.

DAVISON, WILLIAM
- 105th Reg., 1805; Capt. Houston's Troop of Cavalry, 2nd Batt., 1807.

DAVY, EDWARD
- Capt. Jones' Company, 1st Batt., 105th Reg., 1810.

DAWSON, JAMES
- Artillery Company, 105th Reg., 1815, 1816.

DEADMORE, JOHN
- Light Infantry Company, 1st Batt., 105th Reg., 1809, 1813.

DEAN, AARON
- Capt. Campbell's Company, 70th Reg., 1805; Capt. Byars' Company, 1st Batt., 1811, 1813, 1814.

DEAN, JEDIA
- Capt. Campbell's Company, 70th Reg., 1805.

DEAN, JOHN
- 105th Reg., 1820.

DEAN, JONATHAN
- 1st Batt., 70th Reg., 1798, 1800.

DEAN, MOSES
- Capt. Campbell's Company, 70th Reg., 1805; Capt. Tilson's Company, 1st Batt., 1807.

****

****

DERRINGER, JOHN
- 70th Reg., 1821.

DEVAULT, ADAM
- 105th Reg., 1816.

DEVAULT, DANIEL
- 2nd Batt., 105th Reg., 1812.

DEVAULT, JOHN
- Capt. Fulkerson's Company, 2nd Batt., 105th Reg., 1808.

DEVERS, JOSHUA
- 105th Reg., 1811.

DIAL, THOMAS
- 70th Reg., 1818, 1819, 1824.

DICKENSON (DICKASON, DICKERSON), CADWALLADER
- Capt. Beatie's Company, 2nd Batt., 70th Reg., 1805.

DICKENSON, HUMPHREY
- 70th Reg., 1802; Capt. Bradley's Company, 1st Batt., 105th Reg., 1808, 1810; Artillery Company, 1815, 1816.

DICKENSON, JAMES
- 1st Batt., 105th Reg., 1800, 1801.

DICKENSON, JOHN
- Capt. Dixon's Rifle Company, 1st Batt., 105th Reg., 1808, 1809; Capt. Logan's Company, 2nd Batt., 70th Reg., 1811.

DICKENSON, LEONARD
- Capt. Jones' Light Infantry Company, 1st Batt., 105th Reg., 1807; Artillery Company, 1808, 1809, 1810.

DICKENSON, LEWIS
- Artillery Company, 105th Reg., 1815, 1818.

DICKENSON, RICHMOND
- 70th Reg., 1800.

DICKENSON, RUSSELL
- 70th Reg., 1834, 1835.

DICKENSON, SAMUEL
- 70th Reg., 1835.

DICKENSON, W. L.
- 105th Reg., 1811; 1st Batt., 1812, 1813.

DICKSON, JAMES
- 70th Reg., 1815.

DICKSON, SAMUEL
- 70th Reg., 1802.

DILANE, JOHN
- 70th Reg., 1827.

DILWORTH, JAMES A.
- 105th Reg., 1817.

DINSMORE, SAMUEL
- 70th Reg., 1813, 1814.

DINSMORE, WILLIAM
- 105th Reg., 1834.

DISHNER, JOHN
- Rifle Company, 2nd Batt., 105th Reg., 1809.

DIXON, ARTHUR
- Capt. Meeks' Company, 70th Reg., 1804.

DIXON, ELISHA
- 105th Reg., 1826.

DIXON, JOHN
- 1st Batt., 105th Reg., 1800.

DIXON, REUBEN
- 1st Batt., 70th Reg., 1798.

DIXON, SAMUEL
- Capt. Houston's Troop of Cavalry, 2nd Batt., 105th Reg., 1807, 1808.

DODSON, JAMES
- 1st Batt., 70th Reg., 1798.

DOLAN, JAMES
- 70th Reg., 1814, 1816.

DOLLINGER, JOHN
- 70th Reg., 1833.

DOLLOSON, THOMAS
- 70th Reg., 1800, 1802.

DONAHEY, JOHN
- Light Infantry Company, 1st Batt., 105th Reg., 1809.

DONALDSON, THOMAS
- 1st Batt., 70th Reg., 1798.

DONE, HENRY
- 70th Reg., 1815, 1817.

DONE, JOHN

****

- Capt. Tilson's Company, 1st Batt., 70th Reg., 1806; Capt. Byars' Company, 1807, 1813, 1817, 1819, 1822-1824, 1827, 1829.

DONE, WILLIAM
- 70th Reg., 1824, 1830.

DONLY, RICHARD
- 70th Reg., 1814, 1816.

DONNAHOE, JOHN
- Light Infantry Company, 1st Batt., 105th Reg., 1807; Artillery Company, 1808, 1809.

DORAM, EDWARD
- 70th Reg., 1802.

DORAN, JAMES
- 4th Corporal, Rifle Company, 2nd Batt., 105th Reg., 1809, 1811.

DOSS, HENRY
- 70th Reg., 1831.

DOSTON, JAMES
- 1st Batt., 70th Reg., 1798.

DOUGLASS, JOHN
- 2nd Batt., 105th Reg., 1800.

DOUGLASS, WILLIAM
- 2nd Batt., 105th Reg., 1800.

DOWLAND, EDWARD
- Capt. Talbert's Company, 2nd Batt., 70th Reg., 1807.

DRAKE, ISAIAH
- 105th Reg., 1826.

DRISKILL, JESSE
- Capt. Fulkerson's Company, 2nd Batt., 105th Reg., 1808.

DRYDEN, JOEL
- 2nd Batt., 70th Reg., 1798.

DRYDEN, JONATHAN
- Capt. Berry's Company, 1st Batt., 105th Reg., 1808.

DUASON (?), LEWIS
- 70th Reg., 1810.

DUEL, CARTER
- 70th Reg., 1824.

DUFF, DAVID D.
- 105th Reg., 1823; Rifle Company, 1st Batt., 1829.

DUFF, JOHN
- 105th Reg., 1811, 1813, 1814.

DUFF, JOHN S.
- Troop of Cavalry, 1st Batt., 105th Reg., 1809, 1811, 1812, 1813, 1818.

DUFF, MATTHEW
- Capt. Edmondson's Company, 1st Batt., 105th Reg., 1809.

DUFF, SAMUEL
- Capt. Edmondson's Company, 1st Batt., 105th Reg., 1809, 1818.

DUFF, STEPHEN B.
- 105th Reg., 1834.

DUFF, THOMAS J.
- Rifle Company, 1st Batt., 105th Reg., 1829.

DUFF, WILLIAM
- 1st Batt., 105th Reg., 1802; Capt. Berry's Company, 1806.

DUKER, JOHN
- Capt. Campbell's Company, 70th Reg., 1805.

DUKES, WILLIAM
- 105th Reg., 1819; 70th Reg., 1820.

DUNCAN, JOHN
- Capt. Fulkerson's Company, 2nd Batt., 105th Reg., 1808.

DUNGANS, ELIJAH
- 70th Reg., 1814.

DUNGINGS, ELIJAH
- 70th Reg., 1815, 1822.

DUNGINGS, GEORGE
- 70th Reg., 1818, 1822.

DUNLAP, JAMES
- Capt. Edmiston's Company, 70th Reg., 1805.

DUNLAP, SAMUEL
- Capt. Meeks' Company, 70th Reg., 1805.

DUNN, BAKER
- 105th Reg., 1834.

DUNN, ISAAC B. (Baker Dunn above)
- 105th Reg., 1835.

****

DUNN, JOHN
- 70th Reg., 1814, 1815, 1818, 1819; 105th Reg., 1828, 1834.

DUNN, WILLIAM, SR.
- 70th Reg., 1819.

DUNN, WILLIAM
- 70th Reg., 1821.

DURHAM, ISAAC
- 70th Reg., 1809.

DURHAM, SAMUEL
- 70th Reg., 1825, 1826.

DUTTON, GEORGE
- 70th Reg., 1822.

DUTTON, JOHN
- 2nd Batt., 105th Reg., 1822.

DYER, GEORGE
- 70th Reg., 1809; Capt. William Byars' Company, 1st Batt., 1810, 1811, 1814, 1816, 1824.

DYER, THOMAS
- 70th Reg., 1802; Capt. Tate's Company, 2nd Batt., 1811, 1812, 1816.

EAGLETON, MOSSE
- Rifle Company, 1st Batt., 70th Reg., 1807

EAKIN, ABRAHAM
- 70th Reg., 1802.

EAKIN, JOHN
- 70th Reg., 1818; 105th Reg., 1824.

EAKIN, THOMAS, SR.
- 70th Reg., 1809, 1816, 1817.

EARLY, THOMAS
- Capt. Gillenwaters' Company, 2nd Batt., 105th Reg., 1806.

EASON, JOHN
- Capt. Dixon's Rifle Company, 105th Reg., 1808; 2nd Batt., 1812.

EATHERTON, THOMAS
- 70th Reg., 1801, 1802.

EATHY, JOHN
- 70th Reg., 1824, 1825.

EATHY, THOMAS
- 70th Reg., 1815, 1816.

ECOCKE, BURRIL
- 1st Batt., 70th Reg., 1798.

EDDS, WILLIAM
- 70th Reg., 1817.

EDES, ISAAC
- 105th Reg., 1820, 1824.

EDMOND, ROBERT
- Capt. Martin's Company, 105th Reg., 1808.

EDMONDS, DANIEL
- Capt. Bradley's Company, 1st Batt., 105th Reg., 1809.

EDMONDSON, ANDREW
- 70th Reg., 1813.

EDMONDSON, JOHN
- Rifle Company, 1st Batt., 105th Reg., 1829.

EDMONDSON, MOSES
- Capt. Edmiston's Company, 1st Batt., 70th Reg., 1807.

EDMONDSON, ROBERT
- Rifle Company, 1st Batt., 105th Reg., 1829.

****

EDMONDSON, SAMUEL (EDMISTON)
- 70th Reg., 1809, 1819.

EDMONDSON, THOMAS
- 70th Reg., 1815.

EDMONDSON, WILLIAM
- 70th Reg., 1818.

EDWARDS, EDWARD
- 70th Reg., 1815, 1819.

EDWARDS, HENRY
- 70th Reg., 1819.

EDWARDS, RICHARD
- 70th Reg., 1819.

EDWARDS, SYVANIS
- 70th Reg., 1815, 1819.

EGLEN, CORNELIUS
- Capt. Tilson's Company, 1st Batt., 70th Reg., 1807.

EGNOR, ANDREW
- 70th Reg., 1802.

ELDRIDGE, OBADIAH
- Rifle Company, 1st Batt., 70th Reg., 1807

ELINGER, GASPER
- Capt. Irby's Company, 2nd Batt., 70th Reg., 1803.

ELLIOT, EAVEL
- 70th Reg., 1801.

ELLIOT, JAMES
- 70th Reg., 1801, 1802.

ELLIOT, JOHN
- 70th Reg., 1802; Capt. Talbert's Company, 2nd Batt., 1803.

ELLIOT, WILLIAM
- 70th Reg., 1802.

ELLIS, JAMES
- 70th Reg., 1814; 105th Reg., 1835.

ELLIS, JOHN
- 70th Reg., 1802.

ELLISON, ARCHIBALD
- 1st Batt., 105th Reg., 1803.

ELLIT, BARTHOLOMEW
- 70th Reg., 1830.

ELLIT, BARTLEY
- 70th Reg., 1820.

ELLIT, JESU
- 70th Reg., 1812.

ELLIT, JOHN
- 70th Reg., 1818.

ELLIT, THOMAS
- Capt. Talbert's Company, 2nd Batt., 70th Reg., 1805.

ELMORE, ISAIAH
- 105th Reg., 1834, 1835.

ELSEY, CALVIN
- 105th Reg., 1826.

ELSEY, JOSEPH
- 70th Reg., 1825.

ELSEY, MARTIN
- 70th Reg., 1812, 1814, 1815.

ELSEY, THOMAS
- 105th Reg., 1819.

ENDSLEY, DAVID
- 70th Reg., 1832.

ENGLISH, JAMES
- 70th Reg., 1816, 1817, 1819.

ENGLISH, WILLIAM
- Capt. Edmiston's Company, 1st Batt., 70th Reg., 1809, 1815.

ENSER, JOSEPH
- Artillery Company, 105th Reg., 1815.

EPPERSON, GABRIEL
- 70th Reg., 1802.

EPPERSON, JOHN
- Capt. Tate's Company, 2nd Batt., 70th Reg., 1803.

EPPLER, JOHN
- 1st Batt., 105th Reg., 1800, 1803.

EREY (?), WILLIAM
- 70th Reg., 1820.

ERLE, JOHN
- 70th Reg., 1816, 1817.

ESTHER, ZACHARIAH
- 70th Reg., 1816.

****

EUEL, LATON
- 70th Reg., 1809.

EVANS, AKIN
- 105th Reg., 1828.

EVANS, BERRY
- 105th Reg., 1814.

EVANS, GREENBURY
- Capt. Campbell's Company, 70th Reg., 1805; Capt. George Byars' Company, 1st Batt., 1807.

EVANS, HESTIN
- Capt. Fulkerson's Company, 2nd Batt., 105th Reg., 1808.

EVANS, JEREMIAH
- 70th Reg., 1801; Capt. George Byars' Company, 1st Batt., 1806, 1807, 1810.

EVANS, JOHN
- Capt. William Byars' Company, 1st Batt., 70th Reg., 1807, 1816.

EVANS, OBADIAH
- 105th Reg., 1811.

EVANS, ROBERT
- Capt. Meek's Company, 1st Batt., 70th Reg., 1811.

EVANS, SHELTON
- 70th Reg., 1810; Capt. James Scott's Company, 2nd Batt., 1811.

EVANS, SIMON
- Rifle Company, 1st Batt., 105th Reg., 1829.

EVANS, TARLTON
- 105th Reg., 1811.

EVANS, WILKERSON
- Capt. Fulkerson's Company, 2nd Batt., 105th Reg., 1808, 1811.

EVANS, WILLIAM
- 70th Reg., 1815.

EVANS, WILLIAM W.
- 105th Reg., 1811.

EVITT, JOHN
- 70th Reg., 1799, 1800, 1802, 1813.

EVITT, THOMAS
- 70th Reg., 1799, 1801; Capt. Talbert's Company, 2nd Batt., 1803, 1809.

EVITT, TOBIAS
- 70th Reg., 1831.

EVITT, WILLIAM
- 70th Reg., 1802; Capt. Lyon's Company, 2nd Batt., 1805.

EWING, ROBERT
- Light Infantry Company, 1st Batt., 105th Reg., 1809.

FAIRCHILD, AARON
- 70th Reg., 1817, 1822, 1825; 105th Reg., 1830.

FAIRCHILD, BENJAMIN
- 70th Reg., 1818, 1819; 105th Reg., 1824, 1825; 70th Reg., 1826, 1827.

FAIRCHILD, HEZEKIAH
- Capt. Campbell's Company, 70th Reg., 1805; Capt. Byars' Company, 1st Batt., 1806

FAIRCHILD, JOSEPH
- 105th Reg., 1825, 1827, 1829, 1831.

FALKNER, HENRY
- Capt. Davis' Company, 105th Reg., 1808.

FALKNER, RICHARD
- Capt. Irby's Company, 2nd Batt., 70th Reg., 1803.

FARGESON, DOUGLAS
- 70th Reg., 1809.

FARGESON, JORDAN
- 70th Reg., 1812.

FARGESON, JOHN
- 70th Reg., 1809.

FARGESON, THOMAS
- 70th Reg., 1798.

FARGESON, WILLIAM
- 1st Batt., 70th Reg., 1798, 1800, 1801, 1815, 1817, 1818, 1820, 1824.

FARMER, RICHARD
- 105th Reg., 1834.

FARRIS (FAIRIS, FERIS, FARES), EDWARD
- Capt. Irby's Company, 2nd Batt., 70th Reg., 1803, 1823.

FARRIS, GIDION
- Capt. Martin's Company, 1st Batt., 105th

****

Reg., 1810.

FARRIS, ISAAC
- Capt. Talbert's Company, 2nd Batt., 70th Reg., 1805, 1813, 1815, 1816, 1818-1820.

FARRIS, JAMES
- 105th Reg., 1817.

FARRIS, LEVI
- 105th Reg., 1834.

FARRIS, MARTIN
- 105th Reg., 1814, 1817, 1822.

FARRIS, ROBERT
- 1st Batt., 105th Reg., 1801.

FARRIS, SAMUEL
- Troop of Cavalry, 1st Batt., 105th Reg., 1809.

FARRIS, THOMAS
- Capt. Talbert's Company, 2nd Batt., 70th Reg., 1805; Capt. Martin's Company, 1st Batt., 105th Reg., 1807; 70th Reg., 1813-1821, 1824, 1825.

FARRIS, WILLIAM, SR.
- 1st Batt., 70th Reg., 1798; 1st Batt., 105th Reg., 1799; 70th Reg., 1800; 1st Batt., 105th Reg., 1801; Capt. Martin's Company, 1808, 1814.

FELTY, MICHAEL
- 105th Reg., 1818, 1820, 1832.

FEMMING, CHARLES
- Capt. Houston's Troop of Cavalry, 2nd Batt., 105th Reg., 1807.

FERRIL, JOHN
- Capt. George Byars' Company, 1st Batt., 70th Reg., 1811.

FERRIL, ROBERT
- 1st Batt., 70th Reg., 1798; 1st Batt., 105th Reg., 1801, 1803.

FERRIN, HENRY
- 105th Reg., 1815.

FICKLE, ABRAM
- 105th Reg., 1816, 1817, 1819, 1835.

FICKLE, JACOB
- 105th Reg., 1822, 1826.

FIELDER, CHARLES
- Capt. Campbell's Company, 70th Reg., 1805; Capt. Byars' Company, 1st Batt., 1806, 1807; Rifle Company, 1st Batt., 1807.

FIELDS, JAMES
- Capt. Tate's Company, 70th Reg., 1804; 105th Reg., 1813.

FIELDS, JOHN
- 70th Reg., 1802; 105th Reg., 1817, 1818.

FIELDS, JOSEPH
- 70th Reg., 1825.

FIELDS, LAFAYETTE
- 105th Reg., 1827.

FIELDS, WILLIAM
- 105th Reg., 1811; 1st Batt., 1812, 1813, 1817, 1824. (Light Infantry Company, 1st Batt., 105th Reg., 1809.)

FINATEE, JAMES
- 105th Reg., 1816.

FINDLAY, ALEXANDER
- 105th Reg., 1816.

FINDLAY, CONNALLY
- 1st Batt., 105th Reg., 1800, 1803, 1804.

FINDLAY, JAMES
- 70th Reg., 1817.

FINDLAY, THOMAS
- 105th Reg., 1813, 1817-1819, 1821, 1822, 1825, 1827, 1829, 1832-1835.

FINK, DANIEL
- 70th Reg., 1801; Capt. Bradley's Company, 1st Batt., 105th Reg., 1807.

FINK, JAMES
- 105th Reg., 1815.

FINNERLY, JAMES
- 105th Reg., 1821, 1825.

FISHER, FREDERICK
- 70th Reg., 1820.

FITZGERALD, ALEXANDER
- 105th Reg., 1834, 1835.

FITZGERALD, JAMES
- Light Infantry Company, 1st Batt., 105th Reg., 1807; Artillery Company, 1808, 1809.

FITZGERALD, SAMUEL
- 105th Reg., 1834, 1835.

****

FITCHPATRICK, JAMES
- 70th Reg., 1823.

FLANAGAN, JAMES
- 105th Reg., 1825, 1827; Rifle Company, 1st Batt., 1829, 1830.

FLANAGAN, JOHN
- 70th Reg., 1826; Rifle Company, 1st Batt., 105th Reg., 1829.

FLEENOR, ADAM, SR.
- 2nd Batt., 105th Reg., 1803; Rifle Company, 1809.

FLEENOR, ALEXANDER B.
- 105th Reg., 1835.

FLEENOR, BENJAMIN
- Rifle Company, 2nd Batt., 105th Reg., 1809.

FLEENOR, CHRISTOPHER
- Rifle Company, 2nd Batt., 105th Reg., 1809.

FLEENOR, DANIEL
- Capt. Goff's Company, 2nd Batt., 105th Reg., 1807, 1811.

FLEENOR, DAVID
- 2nd Corporal, Rifle Company, 2nd Batt., 105th Reg., 1809.

FLEENOR, ISAAC
- Rifle Company, 2nd Batt., 105th Reg., 1809, 1820.

FLEENOR, JACOB
- Rifle Company, 2nd Batt., 105th Reg., 1809.

FLEENOR, JOHN
- 2nd Batt., 105th Reg., 1802; Rifle Company, 1809.

FLEENOR, MICHAEL
- 2nd Batt., 105th Reg., 1802.

FLEENOR, NICHOLAS
- 105th Reg., 1818.

FLEENOR, SOLOMON
- Rifle Company, 2nd Batt., 105th Reg., 1809.

FLEENOR, WESLEY
- 105th Reg., 1832.

FLEMING, JOHN R. A.
- 70th Reg., 1826.

FLEMING, WILLIAM
- 70th Reg., 1830.

FLESHMAN (?), ABRAM
- Capt. Byars' Company, 1st Batt., 70th Reg., 1806.

FLETCHER, JAMES
- 70th Reg., 1801.

FLETCHER, JOHN
- 70th Reg., 1799; 105th Reg., 1828.

FLETCHER, PATTERSON
- Capt. Bradley's Company, 1st Batt., 105th Reg., 1810; 1811, 1813-1815, 1825, 1826.

FLETCHER, WILLIAM
- 1st Batt., 70th Reg., 1798, 1802, 1820, 1821.

FLOYD, THOMAS
- 70th Reg., 1809.

FLUGER, MICHAEL
- 105th Reg., 1815.

FOBBER (FOBER), DAVID
- 1st Batt., 105th Reg., 1803.

FOBBER, DANIEL
- Capt. Bradley's Company, 1st Batt., 105th Reg., 1806; Light Infantry Company, 1807; Artillery Company, 1808.

FOLEY, MOSES
- 1st Batt., 70th Reg., 1798.

FOLEY, SPENSER
- Rifle Company, 2nd Batt., 105th Reg., 1809.

FOLEY, THOMAS
- Rifle Company, 2nd Batt., 105th Reg., 1809.

FORD, THOMAS F.
- 105th Reg., 1834.

FORD, WILLIAM
- 70th Reg., 1814, 1817.

FOREHAND, HENRY
- Capt. Logan's Company, 2nd Batt., 70th Reg., 1811.

FORREST, HENRY
- 105th Reg., 1835.

****

****

- 105th Reg., 1835.

FULCHER, JAMES
- 105th Reg., 1828, 1829.

FULCHER, THOMAS
- 70th Reg., 1821.

FULCHER, WILLIAM
- 70th Reg., 1813, 1830, 1832.

FULKERSON, JAMES L.
- 105th Reg., 1835.

FULKS, JACOB
- 70th Reg., 1817, 1821, 1825, 1827, 1830.

FULKS, JOHN
- 1st Batt., 105th Reg., 1804.

FULKS, WILLIAM
- 105th Reg., 1825.

FULLEN, ANDREW E.
- 70th Reg., 1814.

FULLEN, HIRAM
- 70th Reg., 1815.

FULLEN, JAMES
- 70th Reg., 1801, 1802; Capt. Talbert's Company, 2nd Batt., 1803, 1812, 1814, 1815, 1817.

FULLEN, JOHN
- 70th Reg., 1814.

FULLEN, WHITLEY
- 70th Reg., 1816, 1835.

FULLEN, WILLIAM
- 70th Reg., 1801, 1802, 1809; Capt. Talbert's Company, 2nd Batt., 1811, 1813.

FULLER, THOMAS
- Capt. Bradley's Company, 1st Batt., 105th Reg., 1806.

FULTON, ALLEN
- 70th Reg., 1835.

FULTON, ANTHONY
- 70th Reg., 1799.

FULTON, DAVID
- 70th Reg., 1799.

FULTON, JAMES
- Capt. Bradley's Company, 1st Batt., 105th Reg., 1806.

FULTON, JOHN
- Capt. Edmiston's Company, 1st Batt., 70th Reg., 1806.

FULTON, JOHN H.
- 105th Reg., 1819-1823, 1826-1830.

GABBERT, MICHAEL
- 105th Reg., 1813.

GAINS, HENRY B.
- 70th Reg., 1813; 105th Reg., 1814-1816.

GAINS, RICHARD
- 105th Reg., 1816.

GAINY, MATTHEW
- Artillery Company, 105th Reg., 1808.

GALBREATH, THOMAS
- Light Infantry Company, 1st Batt., 105th Reg., 1809; Capt. Bradley's Company, 1810.

GALLIHER, JAMES
- 105th Reg., 1822-1825, 1828-1831, 1835.

GALLIHER, JOEL
- 1st Batt., 105th Reg., 1799; Artillery Company, 1815, 1819.

GALLIHER, JOHN
- 1st Corporal, Artillery Company, 105th Reg., 1815.

GALLIHER, SAMUEL
- Artillery Company, 105th Reg., 1815, 1823-1825, 1829-1831, 1833, 1834.

GALLIHER, WILLIAM, SR.
- Capt. Duff's Troop of Cavalry, 1st Batt., 105th Reg., 1810, 1811; Artillery Company, 1815, 1816, 1817, 1822-1825.

GALLIHER, WILLIAM, JR.
- 105th Reg., 1823.

GALLION, JOSHUA
- 70th Reg., 1799.

GALLION, JOSIAH
- 70th Reg., 1799, 1800.

GALVIN, HUGH
- 105th Reg., 1811.

GANAWAY, MARTIN
- 70th Reg., 1816.

****

GANAWAY, WILLIAM
- 70th Reg., 1826.

GARLAND, JAMES
- Capt. Edmiston's Company, 1st Batt., 70th Reg., 1806, 1807.

GARDNER, CLARK
- 70th Reg., 1831.

GARLAND, JOHN
- 105th Reg., 1826.

GARNER, JEREMIAH
- 105th Reg., 1813-1815.

GARDNER, MORDECAI
- Artillery Company, 105th Reg., 1815, 1820-1822, 1829.

GARDNER, WILLIAM
- 70th Reg., 1812, 1814, 1815.

GARRET, JAMES
- 70th Reg., 1813-1815.

GARRET, JOHN
- Capt. Campbell's Company, 70th Reg., 1805.

GARRISON, HARVEY
- 105th Reg., 1827, 1829, 1834, 1835.

GASSETT, JOEL B.
- 105th Reg., 1828, 1832, 1835.

GEORGE, JOHN
- 70th Reg., 1825.

GIBSON, JACOB
- 2nd Batt., 105th Reg., 1812.

GIBSON, JAMES K.
- 105th Reg., 1830.

GIBSON, MARMADUKE
- 105th Reg., 1830.

GILBERT, WILLIAM
- Capt. Bradley's Company, 1st Batt., 105th Reg., 1810.

GILLENWATERS, JOHN
- 105th Reg., 1808.

GILLESPY, JAMES
- 70th Reg., 1824, 1827.

GILLESPY, ROBERT
- 70th Reg., 1800, 1820, 1821, 1827, 1830.

GILLILAND, DAVID
- 1st Batt., 105th Reg., 1800, 1803; Capt. Martin's Company, 1806-1808, 1810, 1812, 1813.

GILLILAND, JAMES
- Capt. Martin's Company, 1st Batt., 105th Reg., 1806; Capt. Houston's Troop of Cavalry, 1808, 1809; Capt. Duff's Troop, 1810.

GILLILAND, JOHN
- Capt. Martin's Company, 1st Batt., 105th Reg., 1806-1808.

GILLILAND, JOHN K.
- 105th Reg., 1825, 1827, 1831.

GILLILAND, JOSEPH
- 1st Batt., 105th Reg., 1799, 1801, 1803; Capt. Martin's Company, 1806-1808, 1810, 1812-1814, 1816, 1817.

GILLILAND, ROBERT
- Capt. Martin's Company, 1st Batt., 105th Reg., 1806, 1816-1818, 1826.

GILLILAND, SAMUEL
- 1st Batt., 70th Reg., 1798; Rifle Company, 1st Batt., 105th Reg., 1829.

GILLILAND, WILLIAM
- 1st Batt., 105th Reg., 1801; Capt. Martin's Company, 1806, 1808; Capt. Dixon's Company, 1808, 1809, 1824-1826; Rifle Company, 1829.

GILLUM (?), JOHN
- 105th Reg., 1818.

GILSON, ANDREW
- 1st Batt., 105th Reg., 1812.

GILSON, WILLIAM
- 105th Reg., 1814.

GILSWORTH, GEORGE
- 2nd Batt., 70th Reg., 1798; Capt. Goodson's Company, 2nd Batt., 105th Reg., 1808.

GLENN, DAVID
- 70th Reg., 1809; Capt. James Scott's Company, 2nd Batt., 1811, 1813.

GLENN, JOHN
- 70th Reg., 1813.

GOBBLE, ABRAHAM, SR.

****

- Capt. Hayter's Company, 2nd Batt., 70th Reg., 1803, 1805.

GOBBLE, ABRAHAM, JR.
- Capt. Hayter's Company, 2nd Batt., 70th Reg., 1803.

GOBBLE, ABRAHAM
- Capt. Bradley's Company, 1st Batt., 105th Reg., 1807, 1808, 1810, 1814.

GOBBLE, ABRAHAM ("Maryland")
- Capt. Bradley's Company, 105th Reg., 1808, 1815, 1816 (The designation "Maryland" dropped in 1816).

GOBBLE, ALEXANDER
- 105th Reg., 1829.

GOBBLE, ELIJAH
- 105th Reg., 1830.

GOBBLE, ISAAC
- Capt. Davis' Company, 2nd Batt., 105th Reg., 1810, 1820.

GOBBLE, JACOB ("of Christ.")
- 105th Reg., 1822, 1828, 1832.

GOBBLE, JOHN
- Capt. Duff's Troop of Cavalry, 1st Batt., 105th Reg., 1810, 1811.

GOBBLE, JOHN ("of George")
- 105th Reg., 1828.

GOBBLE, SAMUEL
- 105th Reg., 1828.

GOBBLE, WILLIAM, JR.
- 105th Reg., 1824.

GODDARD, JAMES M.
- 105th Reg., 1834, 1835.

GODSEY, BERRYMAN
- 2nd Batt., 70th Reg., 1798.
2nd Batt., 105th Reg., 1803.

GODSEY, JERRY
- 105th Reg., 1820.

GODSEY, JOEL
- 70th Reg., 1813.

GODSEY, MARTIN
- 105th Reg., 1823, 1834, 1835.

GODSEY, SOLOMON
- Capt. Goff's Company, 2nd Batt., 105th Reg., 1807.

GOFF, ELIJAH
- 105th Reg., 1833.

GOLD, JOHN
- 2nd Batt., 70th Reg., 1798.
1st Batt., 105th Reg., 1803; Light Infantry Company, 1808.

GOLLAHORN (GOLLIHON), GEORGE
- 1st Batt., 70th Reg., 1798, 1802.

GONES, MARTIN
- 70th Reg., 1810.

GOOD, JOHN
- 70th Reg., 1824, 1825.

GOOD, ROBERT
- 70th Reg., 1813-1820, 1823.

GOODIN, ROBERT B.
- 70th Reg., 1830.

GOODMAN, GEORGE
- Rifle Company, 2nd Batt., 105th Reg., 1809.

GOODMAN, HENRY
- Rifle Company, 1st Batt., 70th Reg., 1807.

GOODMAN, JACOB
- 2nd Batt., 70th Reg., 1798; 2nd Batt., 105th Reg., 1799; Capt. Goodson's Rifle Company, 1809.

GOODMAN, JOHN
- 70th Reg., 1809, 1810, 1812.

GOODMAN, JOSEPH
- 70th Reg., 1818; 105th Reg., 1820.

GOSS, ARMSTEAD
- 105th Reg., 1811.

GOSSAGE, DANIEL
- 105th Reg., 1817.

GOUGH, JOHN E.
- 105th Reg., 1818.

GOWEN (GOWAN), MARTIN
- Capt. Gibson's Rifle Company, 2nd Batt., 105th Reg., 1808, 1809.

GRACE, CALEB
- 70th Reg., 1812, 1814-1817, 1819, 1820, 1824.

****

GRACE, DAVID
- 70th Reg., 1801; Capt. Byars' Company, 1st Batt., 1806.

GRACE, GEORGE
- 70th Reg., 1809, 1832, 1835.

GRACE, WILLIAM
- 70th Reg., 1816, 1818, 1819.

GRADEY, WILLIAM
- 105th Reg., 1813.

GRAHAM, ANDREW
- 2nd Batt., 70th Reg., 1798.

GRAHAM, JAMES
- 1st Batt., 105th Reg., 1806; Light Infantry Company, 1809, 1811; 70th Reg., 1826.

GRAHAM, SAMUEL
- 70th Reg., 1815, 1816, 1826.

GRAHAM, THOMAS
- 105th Reg., 1813, 1815.

GRAHAM, WILLIAM
- 70th Reg., 1813, 1815; 105th Reg., 1817.

GRAHAM, WILLIAM A.
- 105th Reg., 1818.

GRAIL, WILLIAM
- 70th Reg., 1820.

GRANT, AARON
- 105th Reg., 1832, 1833, 1835.

GRANT, EDWIN
- Rifle Company, 1st Batt., 105th Reg., 1829.

GRANT, GARDNER
- 105th Reg., 1811.

GRANT, ISAAC
- 1st Batt., 105th Reg., 1799.

GRANT, ISAAC C. (?)
- 70th Reg., 1835.

GRANT, JAMES
- 105th Reg., 1816; Rifle Company, 1st Batt., 1829.

GRANT, JOHN
- 105th Reg., 1818.

GRANT, SAMUEL
- 70th Reg., 1827.

GRANT, WILLIAM
- 105th Reg., 1817, 1819, 1820, 1823.

GRASS, RICHARD
- 70th Reg., 1824.

GRATNER, HENRY
- 70th Reg., 1809.

GRATNER, JOHN
- 70th Reg., 1809.

GRAVES, HENRY W.
- 105th Reg., 1824, 1825, 1827, 1830, 1834, 1835.

GRAY, JAMES
- 105th Reg., 1821.

GRAY, JOSEPH, SR.
- 2nd Batt., 70th Reg., 1798.

GRAY, JOSEPH ("JR.")
- 2nd Batt., 70th Reg., 1798; 2nd Batt., 105th Reg., 1799, 1800; Rifle Company, 1809.

GRAY, ROBERT
- 1st Batt., 70th Reg., 1798, 1820.

GREEN, EDMOND
- 70th Reg., 1813, 1816, 1830.

GREEN, ELIJAH
- Capt. Goff's Company, 2nd Batt., 105th Reg., 1807; Capt. Gillenwaters' Company, 1808.

GREEN, FREDERICK
- 70th Reg., 1817.

GREEN, GEORGE
- 1st Batt., 105th Reg., 1810.

GREEN, HENRY
- 105th Reg., 1822-1826.

GREEN, JAMES
- 70th Reg., 1835.

GREEN, JOHN
- 2nd Batt., 105th Reg., 1802, 1st Batt., 1803, 1804; Capt. Davis' Company, 2nd Batt., 1807; 1st Corp., Rifle Company, 1809.

GREEN, THOMAS

****

- Capt. Fulkerson's Company, 2nd Batt., 105th Reg., 1808.

GREEN, WILLIAM
- Capt. Fulkerson's Company, 2nd Batt., 105th Reg., 1808; 70th Reg., 1813; 105th Reg., 1820.

GREENWAY, EDWARD M.
- 1st Batt., 105th Reg., 1812-1815.

GREENWAY, JAMES M.
- 105th Reg., 1818-1820, 1827, 1828.

GREENWAY, JOHN
- 105th Reg., 1813.

GREENWAY, JOHN C.
- 105th Reg., 1822-1835.

GREENWAY, WILLIAM
- 1st Batt., 105th Reg., 1800.

GREER, BENJAMIN
- 105th Reg., 1818; 70th Reg., 1823; Rifle Company, 1st Batt., 105th Reg., 1829; 70th Reg., 1834.

GREER, JAMES
- 70th Reg., 1812, 1815, 1816; 105th Reg., 1816.

GREER, JOHN
- 1st Batt., 105th Reg., 1801, 1802.

GREEVER (GRIEVER), PHELTY
- 70th Reg., 1802.

GREEVER, PHILIP
- 70th Reg., 1801.

GREEVER, WILLIAM
- 70th Reg., 1818.

GREGG, HENRY
- 105th Reg., 1818.

GREGORY, FLEMING
- 70th Reg., 1799, 1800.

GRIFFIN, EZRA
- 70th Reg., 1799.

GRIFFIN, PALMER
- 1st Batt., 70th Reg., 1798.

GRIFFIN, PERMOR (PERSNOR)
- 1st Batt., 70th Reg., 1798.

GRIFFIN, SOLOMON
- 1st Batt., 70th Reg., 1798, 1799; Capt. Craig's Company, 2ns Batt., 1806.

GRIFFIN, ZACHEUS
- 70th Reg., 1801.

GRIM, WILLIAM
- 105th Reg., 1820, 1831.

GRIM, WILLIAM M.
- 105th Reg., 1818, 1824, 1830.

GRIMES, HENRY
- 2nd Batt., 105th Reg., 1804.

GRIMES, JAMES
- 1st Batt., 105th Reg., 1799, 1801.

GRIMES, ROBERT
- 70th Reg., 1821, 1829.

GRISSELL, JESSE
- 105th Reg., 1813.

GROSS, DANIEL
- Capt. Gillenwater's Company, 2nd Batt., 105th Reg., 1806.

GROSSE, ISAAC
- 1st Batt., 70th Reg., 1798.

GROSSE, JACOB
- 1st Batt., 70th Reg., 1798.

GROW, JOHN
- Rifle Company, 1st Batt., 70th Reg., 1807.

GRUBB, ANDREW
- 105th Reg., 1824.

GRUBB, CURTIS
- 70th Reg., 1825, 1826.

GRUBB, NICHOLAS
- 105th Reg., 1805; Capt. Bradley's Company, 1st Batt., 1806.

GRUBB, WILLIAM
- 70th Reg., 1820, 1833, 1834.

GULLUM (?), JOHN
- 105th Reg., 1817.

GULLEY, JAMES
- 105th Reg., 1833.

GUMM (GUM), CLAIBOURNE
- 105th Reg., 1827, 1834.

****

GUMM, JOHN
- Capt. Berry's Company, 1st Batt., 105th Reg., 1806; Troop of Cavalry, 1809, 1810, 1811; Troop of Cavalry, 1812, 1813.

GUNN, JAMES
- 1st Batt., 70th Reg., 1798, 1800.

GUNN, WILLIAM
- 1st Batt., 70th Reg., 1798, 1799.

HACKLEY, LOTT
- 105th Reg., 1814.

HACOK, WILLIAM
- 105th Reg., 1834.

HAGEY (HAGY), GEORGE
- 1st Batt., 105th Reg., 1803.

HAGEY, HENRY
- 1st Batt., 105th Reg., 1812, 1816.

HAGEY, JACOB
- Light Infantry Company, 1st Batt., 105th Reg., 1809.

HAGEY, JOHN
- 1st Batt., 105th Reg., 1799, 1814.

HAGEY, MARTIN, JR.
- 105th Reg., 1825.

HAGEY, MARTIN ("of John")
- 105th Reg., 1833; 70th Reg., 1835.

HAGEY, JOSEPH
- 105th Reg., 1813.

HAGEY, MICHAEL
- Capt. Bradley's Company, 1st Batt., 105th Reg., 1810.

HAINES, AUSTIN
- 70th Reg., 1825-1827.

HAINES, JOHN
- 105th Reg., 1822, 1834.

HAISLEY, JONATHAN
- Capt. Hayter's Company, 2nd Batt., 70th Reg., 1805.

HALE, JOHN
- Capt. Beatie's Company, 2nd Batt., 70th Reg., 1805.

HALFACRE, CHARLES
- 70th Reg., 1830.

HALFACRE, CHRISTOPHER
- 1st Batt., 70th Reg., 1798.

HALFACRE, HENRY
- 70th Reg., 1814, 1815, 1819, 1820.

HALFACRE, ISAAC
- 1st Batt., 105th Reg., 1800.

HALFACRE, SAMPSON
- 70th Reg., 1814, 1818.

****

HALFACRE, SAMUEL
- 70th Reg., 1822.

HALLIARD (HILYARD), JAMES
- 1st Batt., 105th Reg., 1801, 1810; Artillery Company, 1815.

HALLIARD, THOMAS
- 105th Reg., 1834.

HALLIARD, WILLIAM
- 105th Reg., 1833.

HAM, EZEKIAL
- Capt. Edmiston's Company, 1st Batt., 70th Reg., 1806.

HAM, JESSEE
- 70th Reg., 1810.

HAM, JOSIAH
- Capt. James Scott's Company, 2nd Batt., 70th Reg., 1811.

HAMILTON, ALEXANDER
- Capt. Bradley's Company, 1st Batt., 105th Reg., 1806, 1808.

HAMILTON, B.
- 105th Reg., 1831.

HAMILTON, EDLEA
- 1st Batt., 70th Reg., 1798.

HAMILTON, FREDERICK
- 2nd Batt., 70th Reg., 1798.

HAMILTON, JAMES
- 70th Reg., 1800.

HAMILTON, WILLIAM
- Troop of Cavalry, 1st Batt., 105th Reg., 1809.

HAMMERSLEY, JOHN
- Capt. Beatie's Company, 2nd Batt., 70th Reg., 1805.

HAMMOND, ABSOLOM
- Capt. Larkey's Company, 2nd Batt., 105th Reg., 1806.

HAMMOND, BENJAMIN
- 105th Reg., 1817.

HANCOCK, LEWIS
- Capt. Campbell's Company, 70th Reg., 1805.

HAND, JAMES
- 70th Reg., 1800; 105th Reg., 1816, 1822.

HAND, JAMES, JR.
- 105th Reg., 1833; 70th Reg., 1834.

HAND, JOHN
- Rifle Company, 1st Batt., 70th Reg., 1807; Capt. Preston's Company, 1811.

HAND, THOMAS
- Capt. Preston's Company, 1st Batt., 70th Reg., 1811.

HANDELIGHT, BARKELEY
- 70th Reg., 1830.

HANNUM, HENRY
- 105th Reg., 1827, 1828.

HANSON, WILLIAM W.
- 105th Reg., 1828-1832.

HARDBARGER, JOHN
- 105th Reg., 1834.

HARDISTER, HENRY
- Capt. Meek's Company, 1st Batt., 70th Reg., 1803.

HARDY, CHARLES
- 2nd Batt., 70th Reg., 1798.

HARGIS, SAMUEL
- 70th Reg., 1802; Capt. Campbell's Company, 1804.

HARGIS, THOMAS
- 1st Batt., 70th Reg., 1798, 1801, 1802, 1809; Capt. Miller's Company, 2nd Batt., 1811.

HARKMAN, ABRAM
- Capt. Campbell's Company, 70th Reg., 1805.

HARLEY, DAVID
- 105th Reg., 1834.

HARLEY, JACOB
- 70th Reg., 1817.

HARLEY, JAMES
- 70th Reg., 1810, 1817.

HARLEY, JOHN
- Capt. James Scott's Company, 2nd Batt., 70th Reg., 1811.

HARLEY, WILLIAM

****

- 70th Reg., 1830.

HARLIS, JACOB
- 70th Reg., 1825.

HARLIS, WILLIAM
- 70th Reg., 1825.

HARLOW, ISIAH
- 70th Reg., 1812.

HARMON, HENRY
- 70th Reg., 1830.

HARMON, JAMES
- 105th Reg., 1826.

HAROLD, THOMAS
- 70th Reg., 1824.

HARR, DAVID
- Capt. Goodson's Company, 2nd Batt., 105th Reg., 1807; Capt. Goff's Company, 1809, 1812.

HARRINGTON, WILLIAM
- 70th Reg., 1814.

HARRIS, ABRAHAM
- 2nd Batt., 105th Reg., 1803.

HARRIS, ANDREW
- 70th Reg., 1824, 1826, 1830.

HARRIS, JOHN
- Rifle Company, 2nd Batt., 105th Reg., 1809, 1811.

HARRIS, JOHN E.
- Rifle Company, 1st Batt., 105th Reg., 1829.

HARRIS, PAYTON
- 1st Batt., 105th Reg., 1800; 70th Reg., 1802.

HARRIS, SAMUEL
- 70th Reg., 1802.

HARRISON, CHARLES E.
- 105th Reg., 1828, 1830, 1831, 1833.

HARRISON, WILLIAM
- 105th Reg., 1824.

HARROLD, JAMES H.
- 105th Reg., 1835.

HARROLD, JOHN
- 70th Reg., 1826.

HARTSOCK (HARTZOG), CHARLES
- Capt. Gibson's Rifle Company, 2nd Batt., 105th Reg., 1808, 1809.

HARTSOCK, DANIEL
- Capt. Goff's Company, 2nd Batt., 105th Reg., 1807.

HARTSOCK, JAMES
- 2nd Batt., 105th Reg., 1801; Capt. Gibson's Company, 1808, 1809.

HARTSOCK, SAMUEL
- Capt. Gibson's Rifle Company, 2nd Batt., 105th Reg., 1808, 1809.

HARVEY, NATHAN
- 2nd Batt., 105th Reg., 1812.

HARVEY, ZACHARIAH
- 105th Reg., 1817.

HASKETT, JOSEPH
- 105th Reg., 1811; 2nd Batt., 1812, 1813, 1814, 1818, 1819.

HASLING, WILLIAM
- 105th Reg., 1822.

HATHAWAY, GEORGE
- 105th Reg., 1831.

HAVELY, CHARLES B.
- 105th Reg., 1824.

HAVELY, ISAAC
- Artillery Company, 105th Reg., 1815.

HAWK, ANDREW
- Capt. Bradley's Company, 1st Batt., 105th Reg., 1806.

HAWKSMITH, GEORGE
- 1st Batt., 105th Reg., 1800.

HAWLEY, DAVID
- 70th Reg., 1812, 1813, 1815, 1816, 1818, 1819.

HAWLEY, ISAAC
- 105th Reg., 1818.

HAWLEY, JONATHAN
- 70th Reg., 1802.

HAWS, MILTON
- 70th Reg., 1827.

HAWTHORN (HATHORN), CHARLES

****

-70th Reg., 1814.

HAWTHORN, ROBERT
- 70th Reg., 1823.

HAWTHORN, SAMUEL
- 70th Reg., 1809, 1810; Capt. Byars' Company, 1st Batt., 1811.

HAYNES (HANES), BETHNEY
- 70th Reg., 1802.

HAYNES, JOHN
- Capt. Fulkerson's Company, 2nd Batt., 105th Reg., 1809, 1810.

HAYNES, MILTON
- 70th Reg., 1830.

HAYNES, RICHARD
- 1st Batt., 70th Reg., 1798.

HAYS, DAVID
- 2nd Batt., 70th Reg., 1798.

HAYS, HENRY
- Capt. Irby's Company, 2nd Batt., 70th Reg., 1805.

HAYTER (HAYTOR), ABSOLEM
- 70th Reg., 1824.

HAYTER, JOHN
- Capt. Hayter's Company, 2nd Batt., 70th Reg., 1807, 1813.

HAYTER, THOMAS
- 70th Reg., 1816.

HAYTER, WILLIAM
- 70th Reg., 1809, 1815, 1819.

HAYTON, ABRAM
- 70th Reg., 1821.

HAYTON, ISAIH
- 70th Reg., 1810, 1815.

HAYTON, ISAIAH R.
- 105th Reg., 1834.

HAYTON, JOHN
- 70th Reg., 1809, 1810, 1815.

HAYTON, ROBERT
- 70th Reg., 1825.

HAYTON, THOMAS
- 70th Reg., 1827.

HAYTON, WASHINGTON
- 70th Reg., 1816, 1817, 1824, 1825.

HAYTON, WILLIAM
- 1st Batt., 70th Reg., 1798, 1799, 1810, 1814, 1824.

HAZLE, HENSEL
- Capt. Tate's Company, 2nd Batt., 70th Reg., 1807.

HAZLE, JOHN
- Capt. Tate's Company, 2nd Batt., 70th Reg., 1807.

HAZLE, JUTSON
- 70th Reg., 1802; Capt. Tate's Company, 2nd Batt., 1803.

HAZLERIG, RICHARD
- 1st Batt., 105th Reg., 1801, 1806, 1812, 1813, 1814.

HAZLERIG, WILLIAM
- 105th Reg., 1821.

HEAD, GAVIN
- 2nd Batt., 105th Reg., 1799, 1802; Capt. Larkey's Company, 1806.

HEAD, JAMES
- Capt. Larkey's Company, 2nd Batt., 105th Reg., 1806.

HEAD, MOSES
- 2nd Batt., 105th Reg., 1803, 1811, 1812.

HEISKELL, WILLIAM K.
- 105th Reg., 1833.

HELBERT, GEORGE
- 105th Reg., 1813.

HELBERT, JACOB
- 105th Reg., 1826.

HELBERT, JOHN
- 105th Reg., 1811.

HELBERT, MICHAEL
- 105th Reg., 1819.

HELDRITH, REECE
- 70th Reg., 1809.

HELPERT, GEORGE
- 105th Reg., 1821, 1829.

HELPERT, MICHAEL
- 105th Reg., 1821.

****

HELTON, JOHN
- 105th Reg., 1830, 1832.

HELTON, JONATHAN
- 105th Reg., 1813.

HELVEY, JACOB
- 105th Reg., 1827.

HEMPHILL, JOSEPH
- 1st Batt., 105th Reg., 1799.

HENDERSON, ANDREW
- 70th Reg., 1814, 1817.

HENDERSON, ARTHUR
- 105th Reg., 1817, 1818.

HENDERSON, ISAAC
- 105th Reg., 1822.

HENDERSON, JAMES
- 70th Reg., 1802; Capt. Talbert's Company, 2nd Batt., 1806, 1807, 1809, 1812

HENDERSON, JOHN
- Capt. Campbell's Company, 70th Reg., 1805.

HENDERSON, JOHN
- 2nd Batt., 105th Reg., 1802, 1804; Capt. Davis' Company, 1806, 1811, 1813, 1817, 1827.

HENDERSON, LITTLETON
- 105th Reg., 1816-1819.

HENDERSON, ROBERT
- Capt. Davis' Company, 2nd Batt., 105th Reg., 1806.

HENDERSON, WILLIAM
- 70th Reg., 1819.

HENDRICK, WILLIAM
- 70th Reg., 1799.

HENEGAR (and variants), CHRISTIAN
- 70th Reg., 1809.

HENEGAR, CHRISTOPHER
- 70th Reg., 1799; Capt. William Byars' Company, 1st Batt., 1811.

HENEGAR, DAVID
- 70th Reg., 1814, 1819, 1820.

HENEGAR, JACOB
- 1st Batt., 70th Reg., 1798, 1800, 1809, 1819, 1821-1823.

HENEGAR, SAMUEL
- Capt. William Byars' Company, 1st Batt., 70th Reg., 1811; Capt. Talbert's Company, 2nd Batt., 1811, 1813-1815, 1817-1819, 1827.

HENEGAR, SAUL
- 70th Reg., 1824.

HENEGAR, SOLOMAN
- 70th Reg., 1825, 1826, 1830.

HENRITZIE, PETER
- Light Infantry Company, 1st Batt., 105th Reg., 1809, 1811; Artillery Company, 1815.

HENRITZIE, WILLIAM
- 105th Reg., 1820, 1825.

HENRY, EDMOND
- Capt. Dixon's Rifle Company, 1st Batt., 105th Reg., 1810, 1815; 70th Reg., 1818.

HENRY, HIRAM
- 105th Reg., 1828.

HENRY, JAMES
- 1st Batt., 105th Reg., 1804.

HENRY, ROBERT
- 1st Batt., 105th Reg., 1801; Capt. Fulton's Company, 1st Batt., 70th Reg., 1811; 105th Reg., 1814.

HENRY, SAMUEL
- 105th Reg., 1830.

HENSLEY, ANTHONY
- 105th Reg., 1813.

HENSLEY, FIELDING
- 2nd Batt., 70th Reg., 1798; Capt. Fulkerson's Company, 2nd Batt., 105th Reg., 1808.

HENSLEY, ICABOD
- 2nd Batt., 70th Reg., 1798; 2nd Batt., 105th Reg., 1804.

HENSLEY, JESSE
- Capt. Goff's Company, 2nd Batt., 105th Reg., 1807.

HENSLEY, JOHN
- 105th Reg., 1833.

HENSLEY, LARKAN
- 2nd Batt., 70th Reg., 1798.

****

HENSLEY, NICHOLAS
- 2nd Batt., 70th Reg., 1798; 2nd Batt., 105th Reg., 1804.

HENSLEY, ROBERT
- 105th Reg., 1801.

HENSLEY, ROBERT, JR.
- 2nd Batt., 105th Reg., 1801.

HENSLEY, SAMUEL, JR.
- 2nd Batt., 105th Reg., 1799.

HENSLEY, WILLIAM
- 2nd Batt., 70th Reg., 1798; Capt. Goff's Company, 2nd Batt., 105th Reg., 1807, 1832

HENSON, SAMUEL
- 1st Batt., 70th Reg., 1798.

HERRON, SAMUEL
- 70th Reg., 1814, 1825, 1832, 1833.

HERRON, JAMES
- 70th Reg., 1825.

HERRON, SAMUEL
- 70th Reg., 1830.

HERRALL (?), GEORGE
- 105th Reg., 1833.

HETHERBY, WILLIAM
- 105th Reg., 1834.

HIBBIN, JOHN
- Capt. Campbell's Company, 1st Batt., 70th Reg., 1803.

HICKAM, JOSEPH
- 2nd Batt., 70th Reg., 1798; 2nd Batt., 105th Reg., 1799, 1800; Capt. Fulkerson's Company, 1810, 1811, 1812.

HICKENBOTTOM, ADAM
- Capt. Martin's Company, 1st Batt., 105th Reg., 1806.

HICKENBOTTOM, JOSEPH
- Capt. Martin's Company, 1st Batt., 105th Reg., 1806.

HICKENBOTTOM, MOSES
- Capt. Martin's Company, 1st Batt., 105th Reg., 1807, 1808, 1809.

HICKENBOTTOM, WILLIAM
- Capt. Martin's Company, 1st Batt., 105th Reg., 1806.

HICKEY, DAVID
- Capt. Talbert's Company, 2nd Batt., 70th Reg., 1811-1815.

HICKEY, WILLIAM
- Capt. Berry's Company, 1st Batt., 105th Reg., 1810.

HICKMAN, ADAM
- 105th Reg., 1816, 1819, 1822-1828, 1831, 1833-1835.

HICKMAN, HICKMAN
- 105th Reg., 1832.

HICKMAN, JOHN
- 70th Reg., 1801; 105th Reg., 1811; 2nd Batt., 1812, 1819, 1822.

HICKMAN, MICHAEL
- 2nd Batt., 105th Reg., 1799, 1800; Capt. Goodson's Company, 1807.

HICKMAN, PETER
- 105th Reg., 1819, 1832.

HICKMAN, THOMAS
- 105th Reg., 1811.

HICKS, BERRY
- 70th Reg., 1825, 1827.

HICKS, CHARLES
- 70th Reg., 1817.

HICKS, JOSEPH
- 105th Reg., 1826.

HICKS, ROBERT
- 2nd Batt., 70th Reg., 1798.

HICKY, DAVID
- 70th Reg., 1816, 1818.

HICKY, ROBERT
- 70th Reg., 1827.

HILL, BENJAMIN B.
- 70th Reg., 1827.

HILL, DAVID
- 70th Reg., 1800.

HILL, JAMES
- 105th Reg., 1814, 1815.

****

****

****

- 70th Reg., 1801.

HOUSTEY, WILLIAM
- 70th Reg., 1827.

HOUSTON, JAMES
- 70th Reg., 1829.

HOUSTON, PAUL
- 70th Reg., 1812.

HOUSTON, PRESTON
- Capt. Gibson's Rifle Company, 105th Reg., 1808; 4th Sergeant, Rifle Company, 1st Batt., 1809, 1813.

HOUSTON, ROBERT
- 1st Batt., 105th Reg., 1800, 1811, 1812, 1823; 70th Reg., 1826.

HOUSTON, WALTER M.
- 105th Reg., 1825.

HOVARTER, JACOB
- 1st Batt., 105th Reg., 1803.

HOWARD, ZIBA
- 1st Batt., 70th Reg., 1798.

HOWSER, JOHN
- 105th Reg., 1816.

HUBBLE, DAVID
- 70th Reg., 1809.

HUBBLE, LIFLET (?)
- 1st Batt., 70th Reg., 1798.

HUDDLE, PETER
- 105th Reg., 1824.

HUDSON, ISAIAH
- 105th Reg., 1833-1835.

HUDSON, RICHARD
- 70th Reg., 1830.

HUFFAKER, JACOB
- 70th Reg., 1835.

HUFFMAN, CHRISTOPHER
- 70th Reg., 1830, 1835.

HUFFMAN, GEORGE
- 70th Reg., 1824.

HUFFMAN, JOSEPH
- 70th Reg., 1809, 1812.

HUFFMAN, MOSES
- 70th Reg., 1809; Capt. Logan's Company, 2nd Batt., 1811, 1812-1814, 1816.

HUGHES, ABNER
- 70th Reg., 1800.

HUGHES, ISAAC
- 70th Reg., 1810.

HUGHES, JAMES
- 2nd Batt., 105th Reg., 1804, 1819, 1820.

HUGHES, JOHN
- 1st Batt., 70th Reg., 1798, 1802; Capt. Meek's Company, 1803; Capt. Beatie's Company, 1804.

HUGHES, NIMROD
- 70th Reg., 1800; 1st Batt., 105th Reg., 1800, 1803; Capt. Bradley's Company, 1806, 1808; 70th Reg., 1809, 1810; Capt. James Scott's Company, 2nd Batt., 1811, 1812, 1813, 1815, 1816.

HUGHES, PRIOR
- 70th Reg., 1817.

HUGHES, WASHINGTON
- 70th Reg., 1830.

HUGHES, WILLIAM
- 105th Reg., 1818.

HULL, JAMES
- 2nd Batt., 70th Reg., 1798.

HULL, THOMAS
- 70th Reg., 1822.

HUMES, ANDREW
- 105th Reg., 1834.

HUMES, JOHN N.
- 105th Reg., 1829, 1830, 1832, 1833, 1835

HUMPHREY, ELIJAH
- Capt. Davis' Company, 105th Reg., 1808.

HUMPHREY, WILLIAM
- Capt. Meek's Company, 70th Reg., 1804.

HUNNEL, AARON
- Capt. Tate's Company, 2nd Batt., 70th Reg., 1811, 1814, 1820.

HUNNEL, ABRAM
- 70th Reg., 1814, 1820, 1826, 1830.

HUNNEL, MOSES
- 70th Reg., 1809; Capt. Tate's Company,

****

2nd Batt., 1811, 1812, 1813, 1815.

HUNT, JAMES
- 70th Reg., 1815, 1816.

HUNT, WILLIAM
- Capt. Berry's Company, 105th Reg., 1808.

HUNTER, GEORGE
- Capt. Gillenwaters' Company, 2nd Batt., 105th Reg., 1807.

HUNTER, THOMAS C.
- 105th Reg., 1833.

HUNTSUCKER, ABRAHAM
- Rifle Company, 2nd Batt., 105th Reg., 1809.

HURLEY, THOMAS
- 105th Reg., 1818, 1819.

HURT, HENRY
- 70th Reg., 1813, 1814.

HURT, JOHN
- Capt. Tilson's Company, 70th Reg., 1805.

HURT, MOSES
- 70th Reg., 1801.

HUTSON, ISAIAH (See HUDSON)
- 70th Reg., 1830, 1831.

HUTSON, MINERY
- 70th Reg., 1812.

HUTTON, ARTHUR
- 70th Reg., 1835.

HUTTON, JAMES
- 70th Reg., 1817, 1829.

HUTTON, JOHN
- 70th Reg., 1817, 1818.

HUTTON, LEONARD
- Capt. Lyon's Company, 2nd Batt., 70th Reg., 1805, 1813, 1814.

HUTTON, MOSES
- 70th Reg., 1818.

HUTTON, WILLIAM
- 70th Reg., 1814.

IGNOR, ANDREW
- Capt. Irby's Company, 2nd Batt., 70th Reg., 1803; Capt. Talbert's Company, 1805.

INGLE, WILLIS
- 105th Reg., 1833.

INGRIM, VALENTIN
- 70th Reg., 1823, 1829.

IRBY, FRANCIS W.
- 105th Reg., 1820.

IRESON, JAMES
- 105th Reg., 1813, 1817; 70th Reg., 1819, 1820, 1825-1827.

IRESON, WILLIAM
- Capt. Davis' Company, 105th Reg., 1808, 1813, 1819.

IRYCK, CONRAD
- 1st Batt., 105th Reg., 1801.

ISENOUR, JOHN
- Artillery Company, 105th Reg., 1815, 1816, 1817.

ISON, ARCHIBALD
- Capt. Larkey's Company, 2nd Batt., 105th Reg., 1806.

ISRAEL, JAMES
- 2nd Batt., 105th Reg., 1812.

IVY, WILLIAM
- Capt. Talbert's Company, 2nd Batt., 70th Reg., 1805; Capt. Irby's Company, 1805.

JACKAWAY, ARCHIBALD
- Capt. Campbell's Company, 1st Batt., 70th Reg., 1804.

JACKSON, ELSAPHON (ELSE)
- 1st Batt., 70th Reg., 1798, 1802.

JACKSON, GEORGE
- 1st Batt., 70th Reg., 1798; 1st Batt., 105th Reg., 1800; 2nd Batt., 1801.

JACKSON, HUGH
- Capt. Houston's Troop of Cavalry, 2nd Batt., 105th Reg., 1807; Troop of Cavalry, 1st Batt., 1809, 1811.

JACKSON, JOHN R. (?)
- 70th Reg., 1835.

JAMES, BARTLEY
- 70th Reg., 1817.

JAMES, JOHN

****

- 70th Reg., 1819, 1824.

JAMISON, EDWARD H.
- 70th Reg., 1835.

JAMISON, THOMAS
- 1st Batt., 105th Reg., 1799; Capt. Bradley's Company, 1806, 1811, 1814.

JANES (OR JONES), CALVIN
- Rifle Company, 1st Batt., 105th Reg., 1829.

JANES, FERNY
- Rifle Company, 1st Batt., 105th Reg., 1829.

JANES, JOHN
- Rifle Company, 1st Batt., 105th Reg., 1829.

JANE, STEPHEN
- 70th Reg., 1809.

JANE, WHEELER
- 70th Reg., 1818, 1827.

JEANES, JAMES
- 1st Batt., 70th Reg., 1798.

JENKINS, AUSTIN
- 1st Batt., 70th Reg., 1798.

JENT, JESSE
- 105th Reg., 1813.

JIMS (?), ELISHA
- Capt. Talbert's Company, 2nd Batt., 70th Reg., 1807.

JINGRIM, JOHN
- 70th Reg., 1821.

JININGS, JESSEE
- 70th Reg., 1825.

JININGS, WILLIAM
- 70th Reg., 1815, 1816, 1818.

JINKINS, DAVID
- 105th Reg., 1822.

JOHN, JESSE
- 1st Batt., 70th Reg., 1798.

JOHN, JOSEPH
- 1st Batt., 70th Reg., 1798, 1802.

JOHNSON, ELIJAH
- 70th Reg., 1825.

JOHNSON, JAMES
- 105th Reg., 1833, 1835.

JOHNSON, JOHN W.
- 1st Batt., 105th Reg., 1812.

JOHNSON, SAMUEL
- Capt. Davis' Company, 2nd Batt., 105th Reg., 1810.

JOHNSTON, ALGERNON S.
- 105th Reg., 1820-1826.

JOHNSTON, AMBROS
- 70th Reg., 1830.

JOHNSTON, BENJAMIN
- 70th Reg., 1814, 1820, 1821, 1823-1827, 1830.

JOHNSTON, BEVERLY R.
- 105th Reg., 1823, 1835.

JOHNSTON, CAMPBELL
- Capt. Davis' Company, 2nd Batt., 105th Reg., 1810.

JOHNSTON, CHARLES
- 105th Reg., 1814, 1816.

JOHNSTON, CHARLES C.
- 105th Reg., 1817-1820, 1823, 1825, 1826.

JOHNSTON, EGBERT
- 70th Reg., 1825.

JOHNSTON, ELIJAH
- Capt. Tate's Company, 2nd Batt., 70th Reg., 1811, 1812-1814, 1816, 1817, 1820, 1821, 1823, 1826, 1827, 1830.

JOHNSTON, EPHRAIM
- 2nd Batt., 105th Reg., 1803.

JOHNSTON, FRANCIS
- 70th Reg., 1809.

JOHNSTON, GEORGE
- 70th Reg., 1815, 1821, 1826, 1827, 1830.

JOHNSTON, HIRAM
- 70th Reg., 1819.

JOHNSTON, HUGH
- 70th Reg., 1816, 1818.

JOHNSTON, ISAAC
- 70th Reg., 1820, 1821.

****

****

- 105th Reg., 1828, 1834, 1835.

JONES, WILLIAM C.
- 70th Reg., 1835.

JONIKEN, ALEXANDER
- Capt. Martin's Company, 105th Reg., 1808.

JORDAN, THOMAS
- 70th Reg., 1819.

JORDAN, ZACKARIAH
- 105th Reg., 1823.

JOURDAN, JONAS
- 105th Reg., 1813.

JOURDAN, MOSES
- Light Infantry Company, 1st Batt., 105th Reg., 1809, 1823, 1825, 1827, 1828.

JOURDAN, THOMAS
- 105th Reg., 1813.

KAYHOE, JOHN
- Artillery Company, 105th Reg., 1815; 70th Reg., 1820, 1821; 105th Reg., 1823.

KAYHOE, THOMAS
- Capt. Bradley's Company, 1st Batt., 105th Reg., 1807; Artillery Company, 1808; Light Infantry Company, 1808, 1809, 1811.

KAYLOR, JACOB
- 105th Reg., 1813.

KAYLOR, JOHN
- 2nd Batt., 70th Reg., 1798.

KELLENGER, GEORGE
- Capt. Byars' Company, 1st Batt., 70th Reg., 1806.

KELLENGER, WILLIAM
- 105th Reg., 1823.

KELLER, CONRAD
- Capt. Houston's Troop of Cavalry, 2nd Batt., 105th Reg., 1807.

KELLER, JOHN
- 105th Reg., 1814-1816.

KELLER, JOHN F.
- Capt. Tate's Company, 2nd Batt., 70th Reg., 1811-1813, 1816.

KELLER, SAMUEL
- 70th Reg., 1813; 105th Reg., 1819.

KELLER, WILLIAM
- 105th Reg., 1831; 70th Reg., 1835.

KELLY (KELLEY), ANDERSON
- Capt. Talbert's Company, 2nd Batt., 70th Reg., 1805, 1816, 1819.

KELLY, JAMES
- Capt. Berry's Company, 1st Batt., 105th Reg., 1807; 70th Reg., 1809, 1813.

KELLY, JOHN
- 2nd Batt., 105th Reg., 1802; 70th Reg., 1809, 1810; Capt. William Byars' Company, 1st Batt., 1811.

KELLY, MILTON L.
- 105th Reg., 1835.

KELLY, SAMUEL
- 70th Reg., 1801, 1802; Capt. Tate's Company, 2nd Batt., 1807, 1815.

KELLY, THORNTON

****

- 105th Reg., 1811.

KELLY, WILLIAM
- 70th Reg., 1813.

KELSEY, JOEL
- 105th Reg., 1817.

KELSEY, JOHN C.
- 105th Reg., 1829.

KELSEY, MATHEW
- 70th Reg., 1802; Capt. Smyth's Company, 2nd Batt., 1803; Capt. Lyon's Company, 1804.

KENNEDY (and variants), ELISHA
- 105th Reg., 1815, 1819.

KENNEDY, ISAAC
- 105th Reg., 1822, 1823.

KENNEDY, JAMES
- 105th Reg., 1829.

KENNEDY, JOHN
- 1st Batt., 105th Reg., 1800.

KENNEDY, JOSEPH
- Troop of Cavalry, 1st Batt., 105th Reg., 1809, 1811.

KENNEDY, SAMUEL
- 105th Reg., 1820, 1822-1824.

KENNEDY, WILLIAM
- Capt. Houston's Troop of Cavalry, 2nd Batt., 105th Reg., 1807, 1810, 1815, 1816.

KERR, JOHN
- 2nd Batt., 105th Reg., 1799, 1800.

KERR, WILLIAM
- 2nd Batt., 105th Reg., 1799; 1811. ("William Kerr ... under age, you will therefore ... collect the fine off his father." 1799 not on list of muster fines)

KERREL, MICHAEL
- 70th Reg., 1820.

KESLER, JOHN
- 70th Reg., 1802.

KESNER, CHARLES H.
- 105th Reg., 1835.

KESNER, JACOB M.
- Light Infantry Company, 1st Batt., 105th Reg., 1807, 1813.

KESNER, JOHN
- 105th Reg., 1813; 70th Reg., 1835.

KESNER, WILLIAM
- Light Infantry Company, 1st Batt., 105th Reg., 1807; Artillery Company, 1809, 1812, 1815, 1825.

KETCHIM, JAMES
- 70th Reg., 1802.

KETTRING, GEORGE
- 70th Reg., 1823.

KEYS, BENJAMIN
- Rifle Company, 1st Batt., 105th Reg., 1829.

KEYS, FRANCIS
- 70th Reg., 1813, 1817.

KEYS, HARVEY
- 70th Reg., 1814, 1825.

KEYS, HENRY
- 1st Batt., 70th Reg., 1798; Capt. Houston's Troop of Cavalry, 2nd Batt., 105th Reg., 1807.

KEYS, JOHN
- Capt. Martin's Company, 1st Batt., 105th Reg., 1806; 70th Reg., 1816; 105th Reg., 1816, 1827.

KEYS, ROBERT
- Capt. Martin's Company, 1st Batt., 105th Reg., 1808-1810, 1818, 1827, 1831.

KEYS, ROBERT, JR.
- 105th Reg., 1817.

KEYS, ROGER
- Troop of Cavalry, 1st Batt., 105th Reg., 1809, 1810, 1811, 1815-1819, 1824.

KEYS, SAMUEL
- 105th Reg., 1813, 1818-1820.

KEYWOOD (CAYWOOD), BENJAMIN
- 70th Reg., 1799, 1809.

KEYWOOD, JOHN
- 1st Batt., 70th Reg., 1798, 1810, 1812.

KEYWOOD, JOSEPH
- Capt. Lyon's Company, 1st Batt., 70th Reg., 1806.

KEYWOOD, MOSES

****

- Capt. Lyon's Company, 1st Batt., 70th Reg., 1806; Capt. Logan's Company, 2nd Batt., 1811, 1816.

KEYWOOD, STEPHEN
- 70th Reg., 1827.

KEYWOOD, THOMAS
- 1st Batt., 70th Reg., 1798, 1799.

KEYWOOD, WILLIAM
- 70th Reg., 1835.

KILBURN, ELIJAH
- 1st Batt., 70th Reg., 1798, 1799, 1800.

KILBURN, MARTIN
- Capt. Hayter's Company, 2nd Batt., 70th Reg., 1807.

KILKANNON, GEORGE
- 70th Reg., 1802.

KILLINGER, GEORGE
- 1st Batt., 70th Reg., 1798, 1799, 1800.

KILLINGER, JACOB
- 70th Reg., 1817, 1818, 1821, 1823.

KILLINGER, JACOB W.
- 70th Reg., 1825-1827.

KILLINGER, JOHN
- 70th Reg., 1817.

KILLINGER, PETER
- 70th Reg., 1829.

KIMES, ABRAM
- 70th Reg., 1825.

KIMES, HIRAM
- 70th Reg., 1825.

KINCADE, ROBERT
- Capt. Bradley's Company, 1st Batt., 105th Reg., 1806.

KINCANNON, ANDREW
- 70th Reg., 1817.

KINCANNON, DAVID
- 1st Batt., 70th Reg., 1798; 1st Batt., 105th Reg., 1801, 1803.

KINCANNON, FRANCIS
- 70th Reg., 1816-1827, 1829, 1830.

KINCANNON, JAMES
- 70th Reg., 1813.

KINCANNON, SAMUEL
- 70th Reg., 1812, 1813, 1819, 1820, 1823-1827, 1829, 1830.

KINCANNON, WALTER
- Capt. Hayter's Company, 2nd Batt., 70th Reg., 1803.

KINCANNON, WILLIAM
- 70th Reg., 1813, 1815, 1817-1825.

KINCANNON, ZACHERIAH
- Capt. Hayter's Company, 2nd Batt., 70th Reg., 1803.

KINDER, JOHN
- 70th Reg., 1820, 1822, 1827.

KING, JAMES, JR.
- 105th Reg., 1820-1824, 1826.

KING, JONATHAN
- 105th Reg., 1817.

KING, WILLIAM
- 1st Batt., 105th Reg., 1803; Light Infantry Company, 1807; Artillery Company, 1808.

KINGSOLVEN, CHARLES
- Capt. Bradley's Company, 1st Batt., 105th Reg., 1806.

KINSOLVER, JAMES
- 105th Reg., 1828, 1829.

KINNAMON, PHILIP
- 70th Reg., 1817.

KINNAMON, RICHARD
- Capt. George Byars' Company, 1st Batt., 70th Reg., 1811, 1813, 1816, 1817.

KINEANAN, JAMES
- Capt. Campbell's Company, 70th Reg., 1805.

KIRK, ANDREW
- 70th Reg., 1833.

KLINE, DAVID
- Capt. Tate's Company, 2nd Batt., 70th Reg., 1811, 1812.

KLINE, GEORGE
- 70th Reg., 1817-1819.

KLINE, JOHN
- 70th Reg., 1814.

****

KNAVE, HENRY
- 70th Reg., 1826.

KNAVE, MICHAEL
- Capt. William Byars' Company, 1st Batt., 70th Reg., 1811.

KNIGHT, AMBROSE
- 105th Reg., 1816.

KNIGHT, JOSHUA
- 105th Reg., 1830.

KNOTT, ANDREW
- 105th Reg., 1827.

KNOTT, EMMET
- 105th Reg., 1835.

KNOTT, SAMUEL
- 105th Reg., 1811; 1st Batt., 1812, 1813, 1815.

KNOWLES, WILLIAM
- 105th Reg., 1822.

KNOX, JOHN
- 70th Reg., 1802.

KREGAR, PETER
- 105th Reg., 1825.

KURTZ, HENRY
- 105th Reg., 1811.

KUTCH, ROSIN
- 70th Reg., 1813.

LACHER, JACOB
- Light Infantry Company, 1st Batt., 105th Reg., 1809.

LADDS, EZEKIEL
- Light Infantry Company, 1st Batt., 105th Reg., 1807.

LAMERMAN, WASHINGTON
- 70th Reg., 1821.

LAMMY, JOHN
- 70th Reg., 1802.

LAMPHIN, JOHN W.
- 105th Reg., 1834.

LANE, BENJAMIN
- 70th Reg., 1815-1817.

LANGFORD, THOMPSON
- Capt. Fulkerson's Company, 2nd Batt., 105th Reg., 1808.

LANKFORD, JESSE
- 70th Reg., 1813.

LANKFORD, THOMAS
- 70th Reg., 1816.

LANGLY, JOHN
- 105th Reg., 1825.

LANTERN, DAVID
- 70th Reg., 1819.

LANTERN, REUBEN
- 70th Reg., 1819.

LARGE, SOLOMON
- 105th Reg., 1832.

LARIMORE, ROBERT E.
- Rifle Company, 1st Batt., 105th Reg., 1829.

LARIMORE, VANCE
- Rifle Company, 1st Batt., 105th Reg., 1829.

LARKEY, JAMES
- Capt. Fulkerson's Company, 2nd Batt., 105th Reg., 1808-1810, 1811-1813.

LARKEY, JOHN
- Capt. Fulkerson's Company, 2nd Batt., 105th Reg., 1808-1810, 1811-1813.

LAZWELL, ISAAC
- 70th Reg., 1818-1820.

LAZWELL, JOHN
- 70th Reg., 1801; Capt. Talbert's Company, 2nd Batt., 1803, 1807, 1811.

LAZWELL, WILLIAM
- 70th Reg., 1801, 1802; Capt. Irby's Company, 2nd Batt., 1803, 1804; Capt. Hinds' Company, 1806.

LATHIM, EDWARD
- Capt. Goodson's Company, 105th Reg., 1808, 1818.

LATHIM, JACOB H.
- 105th Reg., 1829.

LATHIM, JOHN
- Capt. Goodson's Company, 2nd Batt., 105th Reg., 1808.

****

LATHIM, MOSES
- 105th Reg., 1816.

LAUDIBACK, DANIEL
- 2nd Batt., 70th Reg., 1798; 2nd Batt., 105th Reg., 1799.

LAUGLIN, ALEXANDER D.
- Capt. Houston's Troop of Cavalry, 2nd Batt., 105th Reg., 1807-1809, 1811.

LAUGHLIN, CLINTON
- 105th Reg., 1820.

LAUGHLIN, JOHN
- 2nd Batt., 70th Reg., 1798; 2nd Batt., 105th Reg., 1799, 1800; Capt. Berry's Company, 1st Batt., 1810.

LAUGHLIN, HARVEY C.
- 105th Reg., 1817.

LAUGHLIN, NATHAN M.
- 105th Reg., 1813.

LAURENCE, JOHN
- 70th Reg., 1800.

LAURMEY (?), JOHN
- 1st Batt., 70th Reg., 1798.

LAWDER, JAMES
- 70th Reg., 1809.

LAWLESS, ABRAM
- 70th Reg., 1833.

LAWLESS, JAMES
- 105th Reg., 1817.

LAWLESS, JESSEE
- 70th Reg., 1833.

LAWLESS, JOHN
- 105th Reg., 1814.

LAWSON, PRESTON
- 105th Reg., 1829.

LEA, WARREN M.
- 105th Reg., 1818.

LEACH, JONATHAN
- 70th Reg., 1833, 1835.

LEACHER, BENJAMINE
- 105th Reg., 1811.

LECKIE, JOHN W.
- 105th Reg., 1834, 1835.

LEE, ABNER
- 70th Reg., 1800.

LEE, ARCHER
- 70th Reg., 1813, 1815-1821.

LEE, BENJAMIN
- 1st Batt., 70th Reg., 1798.

LEE, CAMPBELL
- 70th Reg., 1831.

LEE, CHESLY
- 70th Reg., 1800.

LEE, EVAN
- 1st Batt., 70th Reg., 1798; Capt. Hayter's Company, 2nd Batt., 1803; Capt. Talbert's Company, 1807.

LEE, GRISOM (GRISIM)
- 70th Reg., 1815, 1816, 1825.

LEE, JEHU
- 70th Reg., 1800.

LEE, JESSE
- 70th Reg., 1817.

LEE, JOHN
- 70th Reg., 1800.

LEE, MILLER
- 70th Reg., 1820.

LEE, RICHARD
- 70th Reg., 1801; Capt. Talbert's Company, 2nd Batt., 1803; Capt. Lyon's Company, 1805. (70th Reg., 1799.)

LEE, STEPHEN
- 70th Reg., 1802; Capt. Lyon's Company, 1804, 1809, 1810; Capt. Talbert's Company, 2nd Batt., 1811.

LEE, WILLIAM
- 70th Reg., 1800, 1815.

LEEDY, JAMES
- 105th Reg., 1834.

LEEDY, LORENZ V. (?)
- 105th Reg., 1835.

LEEDY, MADISON
- 105th Reg., 1834.

LEEPER, SAMUEL

****

- 70th Reg., 1824.

LEFEBVRE, ALEXANDER
- 1st Batt., 105th Reg., 1803.

LEGARD, JOSEPH H.
- 70th Reg., 1835.

LEGARD, ROBERT
- 105th Reg., 1816.

LEGARD, ROBERT L.
- 105th Reg., 1822, 1823, 1825, 1829, 1830

LEMMON, JOHN
- 1st Batt., 105th Reg., 1799.

LEONARD, FREDERICK
- 3nd Corporal, Rifle Company, 2nd Batt., 105th Reg., 1809, 1821, 1832.

LEONARD, GEORGE
- 105th Reg., 1817.

LEONARD, JOHN
- 105th Reg., 1819.

LEONARD, MICHAEL
- 105th Reg., 1821, 1835.

LESTER, WOODFIN
- 70th Reg., 1826.

LETHCO, JAMES
- 70th Reg., 1815, 1816.

LEWARK (LUARK), JOHN
- Light Infantry Company, 1st Batt., 105th Reg., 1807; Artillery Company, 1808, 1810.

LEWARK, JOSEPH
- 105th Reg., 1815-1819, 1825, 1834.

LEWELLEN, JOHN
- 105th Reg., 1816.

LEWIS, CHARLES
- 70th Reg., 1831.

LEWIS, EPHRAIM
- Capt. Berry's Company, 1st Batt., 105th Reg., 1806.

LEWIS, HARVEY
- 105th Reg., 1820.

LEWIS, JAMES
- 105th Reg., 1835.

LEWIS, JAMES H.
- 105th Reg., 1813.

LEWIS, JEWEL
- 105th Reg., 1835.

LEWIS, JOHN
- 2nd Batt., 105th Reg., 1799; Rifle Company, 1809.

LEWIS, JOHN
- Capt. Miller's Company, 2nd Batt., 70th Reg., 1811, 1815, 1816.

LEWIS, NATHANIEL
- Capt. Dixon's Company, 105th Reg., 1808.

LEWIS, PETER
- 2nd Batt., 105th Reg., 1799, 1803; Capt. Houston's Troop of Cavalry, 1807-1809, 1814.

LEWIS, SAMUEL
- 70th Reg., 1819, 1827.

LIGHT, JAMES
- 70th Reg., 1817.

LIGHT, SAMUEL
- 70th Reg., 1802; Capt. Tate's Company, 1804; Capt. Hayter's Company, 2nd Batt., 1805, 1809, 1810; Capt. Tate's Company, 1811, 1812-1814.

LILES (?), JACOB
- 105th Reg., 1820.

LILLEY (LILLY), BIRD
- 105th Reg., 1832.

LILLEY, DAVID
- 105th Reg., 1811; 1st Batt., 1812; Artillery Company, 1815.

LILLEY, JAMES
- 70th Reg., 1829; 105th Reg., 1829, 1832-1835.

LILLEY, WINSTON
- 105th Reg., 1829.

LINDER, ISAAC
- Capt. Bradley's Company, 105th Reg., 1808.

LINDER, JOHN
- 105th Reg., 1818.

LINDER, WILLIAM
- Capt. Bradley's Company, 1st Batt., 105th Reg., 1806.

****

LINSAY, JAMES
- Light Infantry Company, 1st Batt., 105th Reg., 1807; Artillery Company, 1808, 1811.

LINSAY, JOHN
- Capt. Martin's Company, 1st Batt., 105th Reg., 1806.

LINSAY, ROBERT
- Light Infantry Company, 1st Batt., 105th Reg., 1807.

LINTACUM, JOHN
- 70th Reg., 1812, 1813, 1816.

LINTACUM, THOMAS
- 70th Reg., 1823, 1824, 1826.

LITCHFIELD, GEORGE
- 105th Reg., 1817.

LITCHFIELD, GEORGE V.
- 105th Reg., 1819, 1820, 1823-1830, 1835.

LITS, JOHN
- 70th Reg., 1819, 1822.

LITTS, STEVEN (STEPHAN)
- 105th Reg., 1826, 1827.

LITTERAL, WINSTEAD
- 105th Reg., 1834.

LITTLE, ABEL
- 70th Reg., 1820, 1826.

LITTLE, ALEXANDER
- 70th Reg., 1830.

LITTLE, EDMUND
- 70th Reg., 1825, 1826.

LITTLE, GEORGE
- 105th Reg., 1813.

LITTLE, HARRINGTON
- 70th Reg., 1830.

LITTLE, JAMES
- 70th Reg., 1817.

LITTLE, PETER
- Capt. Campbell's Company, 70th Reg., 1805.

LITTLE, THOMAS
- 70th Reg., 1830.

LITTLE, WILLIAM
- 70th Reg., 1814, 1817, 1820, 1821.

LITTON, HIRAM V.
- 70th Reg., 1833.

LITTON, JOHN
- Capt. Talbert's Company, 2nd Batt., 70th Reg., 1811.

LITTON, MILTON
- 105th Reg., 1835.

LIVINGSTON (LEVINGSTON), ELIJAH
- Capt. Goff's Company, 2nd Batt., 105th Reg., 1807.

LIVINGSTON, HENRY
- 2nd Batt., 105th Reg., 1800.

LIVINGSTON, JAMES
- 2nd Batt., 105th Reg., 1804.

LIVINGSTON, JESSE
- 2nd Batt., 105th Reg., 1804.

LOCK, JACOB
- 70th Reg., 1822, 1823.

LOCK, JOHN
- 105th Reg., 1805; Capt. Berry's Company, 1st Batt., 1808.

LOCKET, FORREST
- 70th Reg., 1825.

LOGAN, JOHN
- 1st Batt., 70th Reg., 1798; 1st Batt., 105th Reg., 1800; Capt. Hayter's Company, 2nd Batt., 70th Reg., 1807, 1819.

LOGAN, SAMUEL
- 105th Reg., 1827-1832, 1834, 1835.

LOGAN, WILLIAM B.
- 105th Reg., 1827-1832, 1834.

LOGAN, WILLIAM S.
- 1st Batt., 70th Reg., 1798; Capt. Hayter's Company, 2nd Batt., 1803.

LOHR, DANIEL
- 70th Reg., 1831.

LONG, JACOB
- Capt. Bradley's Company, 1st Batt., 105th Reg., 1806; Capt. Houston's Troop of

****

Cavalry, 2nd Batt., 1807, 1809; Capt. Duff's Company of Cavalry, 1st Batt., 1810

LONG, JOSEPH
- Artillery Company, 105th Reg., 1808.

LONG, PETER
- 105th Reg., 1814.

LONG, WILLIAM, JR.
- Capt. Edmiston's Company, 1st Batt., 70th Reg., 1806.

LONGLEY, BENJAMIN
- 1st Batt., 105th Reg., 1800.

LONGLEY, GEORGE
- 1st Batt., 105th Reg., 1800.

LONGLEY, JAMES
- Light Infantry Company, 1st Batt., 105th Reg., 1809.

LONGLEY, JAMES, JR.
- 105th Reg., 1815.

LONGLEY, JOHN
- 105th Reg., 1813.

LONGLEY, PETER
- 70th Reg., 1800; 1st Batt., 105th Reg., 1802.

LONGLEY, WILLIAM
- 1st Batt., 70th Reg., 1798; 1st Batt., 105th Reg., 1799; 70th Reg., 1800.

LOVE, ANDREW
- 70th Reg., 1817.

LOVE, ANDREW K.
- 70th Reg., 1809.

LOVE, ISAAC
- Capt. Talbert's Company, 70th Reg., 1804

LOVE, JOHN
- 1st Batt., 105th Reg., 1800; 70th Reg., 1815, 1816, 1819.

LOVE, JOSEPH
- Capt. Bishop's Company, 1st Batt., 70th Reg., 1811.

LOVE, LEONIDAS
- 70th Reg., 1833.

LOVE, WILLIAM, SR.
- 70th Reg., 1818.

LOVE, WILLIAM
- 70th Reg., 1817-1819.

LOVELESS, PERMANUS
- 105th Reg., 1830, 1831.

LOVELESS, THOMAS
- 105th Reg., 1824.

LOVLIS, JOHN
- 70th Reg., 1820.

LOWE (LOW), HENRY
- Light Infantry Company, 1st Batt., 105th Reg., 1807; Artillery Company, 1808.

LOWE, JAMES
- 105th Reg., 1817.

LOWE, JOHN
- 105th Reg., 1826.

LOWE, VINCENT
- 105th Reg., 1832.

LOWE, WILLIAM
- Capt. Gibson's Rifle Company, 105th Reg., 1808.

LOWRY (LOWREY), DAVID, JR.
- 105th Reg., 1824.

LOWRY, JAMES
- 70th Reg., 1812, 1814.

LOWRY, JOHN
- Capt. Bradley's Company, 1st Batt., 105th Reg., 1810.

LOWRY, JOHN, (JR.)
- Capt. Fulton's Company, 1st Batt., 70th Reg., 1811, 1812-1815.

LOWRY, JOHN M.
- 70th Reg., 1834.

LOWRY, WILLIAM
- 105th Reg., 1834.

LOYD, BENJAMIN
- 2nd Batt., 105th Reg., 1802.

LOYD, JOHN
- 2nd Batt., 105th Reg., 1802; Capt. Byars' Company, 1st Batt., 70th Reg., 1806.

LOYD, LEWIS
- 105th Reg., 1824.

****

LOYD, STEPHEN
- 70th Reg., 1830.

LOYD, WILLIAM
- 70th Reg., 1830.

LUCKER (OR LUCKEN), KINCHEN
- Rifle Company, 1st Batt., 105th Reg., 1829.

LUNCEFORD, MOSES
- Rifle Company, 1st Batt., 70th Reg., 1807; Capt. Edmiston's Company, 1807.

LUTRALL, RICHARD
- 2nd Batt., 70th Reg., 1798.

LYNCH, DANIEL
- Light Infantry Company, 1st Batt., 105th Reg., 1809, 1812, 1813, 1815, 1819.

LYNCH, EDWARD
- 2nd Batt., 105th Reg., 1804.

LYNCH, JAMES
- 105th Reg., 1818, 1820.

LYNCH, JOHN
- 105th Reg., 1835.

LYNCH, PATRICK
- 1st Batt., 105th Reg., 1801.

LYNN, JAMES
- 70th Reg., 1821, 1825.

LYON, HUMBERSON
- 70th Reg., 1831.

LYON, JACOB
- 70th Reg., 1813, 1835.

LYON, JAMES
- 70th Reg., 1802, 1815, 1816.

LYON, STEPHEN
- 70th Reg., 1825.

LYON, WILLIAM
- Capt. Hayter's Company, 2nd Batt., 70th Reg., 1803, 1815, 1816.

McALLISTER, CHARLES
- 70th Reg., 1816.

McALLISTER, SAMUEL
- 1st Batt., 105th Reg., 1801.

McBATH, RUSSELL
- 105th Reg., 1811.

McCALL, JAMES
- Capt. Houston's Troop of Cavalry, 2nd Batt., 105th Reg., 1807.

McCALL, JOHN
- 70th Reg., 1799.

McCALL, SAMUEL
- Capt. Houston's Troop of Cavalry, 2nd Batt., 105th Reg., 1807; Capt. Martin's Company, 1st Batt., 1810.

McCAMPBELL, ANDREW
- 105th Reg., 1816, 1817.

McCARLE, WILLIAM
- 70th Reg., 1802.

McCARTY, BENJAMINE
- Capt. Tate's Company, 2nd Batt., 70th Reg., 1807, 1811, 1812, 1820, 1821, 1823.

McCARTY, CALVIN
- 70th Reg., 1830.

McCARTY, ENOCH
- 70th Reg., 1816, 1817, 1820, 1821, 1823-1826.

McCAULEY, MICHAEL
- 105th Reg., 1828.

McCEWEN, ISAAC
- Capt. Bradley's Company, 1st Batt., 105th Reg., 1806; Light Infantry Company, 1807.

McCHESNEY, JOHN
- Capt. Duff's Troop of Cavalry, 1st Batt., 105th Reg., 1810, 1811.

McCHESNEY, THOMAS
- 105th Reg., 1811.

McCLELLAN, HUGH
- Troop of Cavalry, 105th Reg., 1812.

McCLELLAN, JAMES
- Light Infantry Company, 1st Batt., 105th Reg., 1809.

****

McCLELLAN, SAMUEL
- Light Infantry Company, 1st Batt., 105th Reg., 1809.

McCLELLAN, WILLIAM
- Rifle Company, 2nd Batt., 105th Reg., 1809, 1817.

McCLINTER, JOHN
- Capt. Irby's Company, 2nd Batt., 70th Reg., 1803; Capt. Talbert's Company, 1804.

McCLOUD, DANIEL
- Capt. Hayter's Company, 2nd Batt., 70th Reg., 1806.

McCLOUD, JAMES
- 70th Reg., 1812, 1813, 1816.

McCLOUD, WILLIAM
- Capt. Hayter's Company, 2nd Batt., 70th Reg., 1806, 1812.

McCLURE, HALBERT
- 1st Batt., 70th Reg., 1798, 1799, 1800.

McCLURE, JAMES
- 1st Batt., 105th Reg., 1800; 70th Reg., 1813.

McCLURE, WILLIAM
- 1st Batt., 70th Reg., 1798, 1800, 1802; Capt. Tilson's Company, 1803.

McCOLLUM, WILLIAM
- 105th Reg., 1835.

McCONKEY, JOHN
- 2nd Batt., 70th Reg., 1798; 2nd Batt., 105th Reg., 1799, 1800, 1826.

McCONKEY, SAMUEL
- 105th Reg., 1817, 1819.

McCONNELL, ABRAM
- 105th Reg., 1817.

McCONNELL, MOSES
- Capt. Berry's Company, 1st Batt., 105th Reg., 1806; Troop of Cavalry, 1808, 1809.

McCONNELL, SAMUEL
- Light Infantry Company, 1st Batt., 105th Reg., 1807; Artillery Company, 1809. (2nd Batt., 105th Reg., 1803.)

McCONNELL, WILLIAM
- Artillery Company, 105th Reg., 1815.

McCORD, ALEXANDER
- 1st Batt., 70th Reg., 1798, 1800, 1801, 1802, 1809.

McCORD, JOHN
- Capt. Edmiston's Company, 1st Batt., 105th Reg., 1809, 1815; 70th Reg., 1819, 1823, 1824.

McCORD, ROBERT
- 70th Reg., 1801, 1802; Capt. Campbell's Company, 1st Batt., 1804, 1809, 1823, 1824. (70th Reg., 1799.)

McCORD, THOMAS
- 70th Reg., 1827.

McCORD, WILLIAM
- 70th Reg., 1822, 1823, 1827.

McCORMACK, CAGGY (McCAGGY)
- Capt. Beatie's Company, 70th Reg., 1804, 1813, 1819, 1835.

McCORMACK, CLAIBOURNE
- Capt. Bradley's Company, 1st Batt., 105th Reg., 1808, 1811, 1812.

McCORMACK, SAMUEL
- Capt. Houston's Troop of Cavalry, 2nd Batt., 105th Reg., 1807; Capt. Talbert's Company, 2nd Batt., 70th Reg., 1811, 1812-1816.

McCORMACK, THOMAS
- 2nd Batt., 105th Reg., 1801.

McCORMACK, WASHINGTON
- 105th Reg., 1825, 1827, 1833.

McCRABB, JOSEPH
- 105th Reg., 1818, 1819.

McCRABB, MATTHEW
- 2nd Batt., 105th Reg., 1800.

McCRACKEN, HUGH, JR.
- Rifle Company, 1st Batt., 105th Reg., 1829.

McCRACKEN, ISOM
- 70th Reg., 1829.

McCRACKEN, JOHN
- Capt. Martin's Company, 1st Batt., 105th Reg., 1806, 1808.

McCREARY, WILLIAM
- 105th Reg., 1822-1824.

****

****

****

MADDEN (MADEN), JAMES
- 2nd Batt., 70th Reg., 1798; 2nd Batt., 105th Reg., 1799, 1801.

MADDEN, STEPHEN
- 1st Batt., 70th Reg., 1798, 1802; Capt. Smyth's Company, 2nd Batt., 1803.

MADDISON, SAMUEL
- Capt. Bradley's Company, 1st Batt., 105th Reg., 1810, 1811.

MAHAFFEY, JAMES S.
- 105th Reg., 1835.

MAHAFFEY, JOSEPH
- 105th Reg., 1818.

MAHAFFEY, JOSEPH L.
- 105th Reg., 1835.

MAIDEN, BENJAMIN
- 2nd Batt., 105th Reg., 1802.

MAIDEN, ELIJAH
- 2nd Batt., 105th Reg., 1812.

MAIDEN, JAMES
- 2nd Batt., 105th Reg., 1802.

MAIDEN, JOHN
- Capt. Goff's Company, 2nd Batt., 105th Reg., 1807.

MAIN, LAWLESS
- Capt. Byars' Company, 1st Batt., 70th Reg., 1806.

MALONE, JOHN
- Capt. Goodson's Company, 2nd Batt., 105th Reg., 1806; 2nd Sergeant, Rifle Company, 1809, 1819, 1824.

MALTER, PETER
- 1st Batt., 70th Reg., 1798.

MANAFEE, JOHN
- Capt. Hayter's Company, 2nd Batt., 70th Reg., 1806, 1823, 1826.

MANNING, PETER
- Capt. Duff's Troop of Cavalry, 1st Batt., 105th Reg., 1810.

MANNOR, WILLIAM
- 70th Reg., 1812, 1814, 1816, 1817.

MARGRAVE, WILLIAM
- Artillery Company, 105th Reg., 1815.

MARKLAND, WILLIAM
- Capt. Beatie's Company, 70th Reg., 1804.

MARKS, DAVID
- 105th Reg., 1834.

MARKS, FREEMAN
- 70th Reg., 1821.

MARKS, TRUMAN
- 70th Reg., 1822.

MARLOW, ALLIN
- 70th Reg., 1799.

MARLOW, THOMAS
- 70th Reg., 1799.

MARSHAL, JOHN
- Capt. Tate's Company, 2nd Batt., 70th Reg., 1803.

MARSHAL, WILLIAM
- Capt. Tate's Company, 2nd Batt., 70th Reg., 1807, 1811, 1813.

MARTIN, ABRAHAM
- 105th Reg., 1805.

MARTIN, BENJAMIN
- 70th Reg., 1801; Capt. Craig's Company, 1st Batt., 1803; 1st Batt., 105th Reg., 1804; Capt. Bradley's Company, 1807; Capt. Martin's Company, 1808, 1827.

MARTIN, BLACKSTON W.
- 105th Reg., 1829.

MARTIN, JAMES
- Capt. Beatie's Company, 2nd Batt., 70th Reg., 1806, 1807.

MARTIN, JEREMIAH
- 105th Reg., 1828, 1829.

MARTIN, JOHN G.
- 105th Reg., 1811; Troop of Cavalry, 1812; 70th Reg., 1815, 1817, 1822, 1825-1827.

MARTIN, JOSEPH
- 2nd Batt., 70th Reg., 1798.

MARTIN, TARLTON
- 70th Reg., 1809; Capt. Bazil Scott's Company, 2nd Batt., 1811, 1812-1815.

MASH, DAVID
- 105th Reg., 1821.

MASH, JOHN
- 105th Reg., 1820.

MASON, JOHN
- Capt. Bradley's Company, 105th Reg., 1808; 70th Reg., 1827.

****

MASON, JOHN P.
- 70th Reg., 1825, 1826.

MASTON, RICHARD
- 70th Reg., 1810.

MATHENA, JOHN
- 70th Reg., 1819-1827.

MATHEWS, JAMES
- 70th Reg., 1812.

MATHEWS, JOHN
- 105th Reg., 1822.

MATHEWS, RANDOLPH
- 105th Reg., 1818.

MATHIS, JAMES
- Capt. Bradley's Company, 1st Batt., 105th Reg., 1809, 1811.

MATNEY, JOHN
- Capt. Davis' Company, 2nd Batt., 105th Reg., 1810.

MATTINGLEY, BROOKS
- 1st Batt., 70th Reg., 1798.

MATTINGLEY, CHARLES
- 1st Batt., 70th Reg., 1798.

MATTINGLEY, WALTER
- 70th Reg., 1799, 1800.

MAULTER, PETER
- 1st Batt., 70th Reg., 1798.

MAXWELL, JAMES
- 105th Reg., 1801; Capt. Bradley's Company, 1st Batt., 1806.

MAXWELL, MOSES
- Capt. Berry's Company, 1st Batt., 105th Reg., 1809, 1816, 1817.

MAYO, ALEXANDER
- 105th Reg., 1834.

MAYO, JOHN
- 70th Reg., 1827.

MAYO, PETER
- 105th Reg., 1814, 1818, 1819, 1825, 1828, 1830, 1831, 1833, 1834.

MAYO, RICHARD
- 70th Reg., 1827.

MAYS, JOHN
- 105th Reg., 1827.

MAZINGO, THOMAS
- 105th Reg., 1819.

MEADE, SAMUEL B.
- 105th Reg., 1818, 1819.

MEADOWS, JOEL
- 70th Reg., 1800; Capt. Talbert's Company, 2nd Batt., 1807, 1809, 1819, 1815, 1818.

MEADOWS, JOSEPH
- 70th Reg., 1800.

MEADOWS, MILES H.
- 70th Reg., 1835.

MECE, PETER
- Capt. George Byars' Company, 1st Batt., 70th Reg., 1807.

MEEK, ARCHIBALD
- 70th Reg., 1817, 1819, 1827, 1833.

MEEK, JESSE
- 70th Reg., 1818, 1825, 1826.

MEEK, JOSEPH
- Capt. Meek's Company, 1st Batt., 70th Reg., 1811, 1817, 1819.

MEEK, SAMUEL
- Capt. Meek's Company, 70th Reg., 1805, 1826.

MEEK, THOMAS
- 70th Reg., 1810.

MEEM (?), JOHN
- 105th Reg., 1815.

MELSON, JOHN
- 1st Batt., 70th Reg., 1798.

MELTON, JAMES
- Artillery Company, 105th Reg., 1815, 1823.

MELTON, THOMAS
- Capt. Duff's Troop of Cavalry, 1st Batt., 105th Reg., 1810, 1811.

MERCER, ADAM
- Capt. Byars' Company, 1st Batt., 70th Reg., 1806.

MERCHANT, JACOB
- 105th Reg., 1830, 1833.

****

****

- 105th Reg., 1817, 1824, 1832.

MINICK (MINOCK), ADAM
- Capt. Davis' Company, 2nd Batt., 105th Reg., 1806; Capt. Bradley's Company, 1st Batt., 1810, 1811-1814.

MINICK, HENRY
- 1st Batt., 105th Reg., 1803; Capt. Berry's Company, 1806; Capt. Bradley's Company, 1810, 1816.

MINICK, ISAAC
- 1st Batt., 105th Reg., 1802, 1806.

MINICK, JACOB
- 105th Reg., 1826.

MINICK, JOHN
- Capt. Berry's Company, 1st Batt., 105th Reg., 1806, 1826, 1835.

MINICK, MICHAEL
- 70th Reg., 1827.

MINOCH, GEORGE
- 105th Reg., 1832.

MINOCH, JOHN ("son of Samuel")
- 105th Reg., 1832.

MINOCH, MICHAEL
- 105th Reg., 1824.

MINOCH, SAMUEL
- 105th Reg., 1822.

MINKS, DAVID
- 70th Reg., 1827.

MINKS, JOHN
- Rifle Company, 1st Batt., 70th Reg., 1807.

MINKS, PETER
- 1st Batt., 70th Reg., 1798, 1801; Capt. Campbell's Company, 1805.

MINTON, EBENEZER
- 1st Batt., 70th Reg., 1798.

MINTON, JACOB
- 70th Reg., 1823.

MINTON, JAMES
- 70th Reg., 1827.

MINTON, PHILIP
- 1st Batt., 70th Reg., 1798, 1801; Capt. Campbell's Company, 1st Batt., 1803, 1812.

MINTON, RICHARD
- 70th Reg., 1812, 1817, 1821-1824, 1827, 1830.

MIRES, JACOB
- Capt. Larkey's Company, 2nd Batt., 105th Reg., 1806.

MIRES, LEWIS
- Capt. Goodson's Company, 2nd Batt., 105th Reg., 1806, 1807.

MITCHAM, JAMES
- 2nd Batt., 105th Reg., 1801.

MITCHELL, CHARLES
- 1st Batt., 70th Reg., 1798; Capt. Talbert's Company, 2nd Batt., 1807.

MITCHELL, CHARTER
- 70th Reg., 1802; Capt. Talbert's Company, 2nd Batt., 1803.

MITCHELL, JOHN
- 70th Reg., 1800-1802; Capt. Irby's Company, 2nd Batt., 1803-1805; Capt. Byars' Company, 1st Batt., 1806; Capt. Bradley's Company, 1st Batt., 105th Reg., 1810.

****

MITCHELL, JOHN D.
- 105th Reg., 1819, 1822-1829.

MITCHELL, ROBERT
- 1st Batt., 70th Reg., 1798, 1800, 1801, 1810, 1814, 1815, 1817, 1822; 105th Reg., 1830.

MITCHELL, WILLIAM
- 70th Reg., 1799, 1802; Capt. Talbert's Company, 2nd Batt., 1803, 1807, 1809; Capt. Talbert's Company, 1811, 1812, 1819-1821.

MOBLEY, JAMES
- 70th Reg., 1813; Artillery Company, 105th Reg., 1815, 1820-1822; 70th Reg., 1823; 105th Reg., 1824.

MOBLEY, JOHN
- 70th Reg., 1799.

MOBLEY, SAMUEL
- 70th Reg., 1825, 1826, 1830, 1835.

MOBLEY, THOMAS
- 70th Reg., 1799.

MOBLEY, THOMSON
- 70th Reg., 1799.

MOBLEY, WILLIAM
- 70th Reg., 1800.

MOCK (MAUCK), PETER
- 105th Reg., 1826, 1828.

MOFFETT, JOHN
- 1st Batt., 105th Reg., 1799, 1800.

MOFFETT, THOMAS
- 2nd Batt., 70th Reg., 1798.

MONGLE (AND VARIANTS), CYRUS
- Light Infantry Company, 1st Batt., 105th Reg., 1807; 70th Reg., 1814.

MONGLE, JOHN
- 105th Reg., 1811, 1816, 1825.

MONGLE, ROBERT
- Light Infantry Company, 1st Batt., 105th Reg., 1807.

MONGLE, WILLIAM
- Light Infantry Company, 1st Batt., 105th Reg., 1809.

MONTGOMERY, CHESSA P.
- 105th Reg., 1824.

MONTGOMERY, HENRY
- 70th Reg., 1802; Capt. Smyth's Company, 2nd Batt., 1803, 1820, 1822.

MONTGOMERY, JAMES
- Capt. Edmiston's Company, 1st Batt., 70th Reg., 1806, 1809, 1810.

MONTGOMERY, JOHN
- Capt. Edmiston's Company, 1st Batt., 70th Reg., 1807, 1814, 1816-1820, 1825. (105th Reg., 1818.)

MONTGOMERY, JOHN G.
- Rifle Company, 1st Batt., 105th Reg., 1829.

MONTGOMERY, JOSEPH
- 105th Reg., 1805.

MONTGOMERY, PRESTON
- 105th Reg., 1816, 1817.

MONTGOMERY, THOMAS
- 105th Reg., 1805; Troop of Cavalry, 1st Batt., 1809, 1811.

MOORE, ARTHUR
- 2nd Batt., 105th Reg., 1803; Capt. Rhea's Company, 1810, 1811.

MOORE, DAVID
- 1st Batt., 105th Reg., 1800.

MOORE, ELIJAH
- Capt. Logan's Company, 2nd Batt., 70th Reg., 1811, 1814, 1815.

MOORE, ESA
- 70th Reg., 1835.

MOORE, FRANCIS
- 105th Reg., 1819, 1820, 1826.

MOORE, HAMILTON
- 70th Reg., 1825.

MOORE, HENRY
- 2nd Batt., 70th Reg., 1798; 2nd Batt., 105th Reg., 1799, 1802, 1811, 1812.

MOORE, JAMES
- 70th Reg., 1821-1827.

MOORE, JOHN
- 70th Reg., 1800; Light Infantry Company, 105th Reg., 1808; Capt. Fulkerson's Company, 2nd Batt., 1810, 1811-1813; 70th Reg., 1819, 1829; 105th Reg., 1832.

****

MOORE, JOHN W.
- Capt. Dixon's Rifle Company, 105th Reg., 1808, 1813.

MOORE, JOSEPH
- 70th Reg., 1821, 1825, 1827.

MOORE, LEWIS
- 105th Reg., 1811.

MOORE, MARTIN
- 2nd Batt., 105th Reg., 1799; Capt. Rhea's Company, 1810.

MOORE, NIMROD
- Light Infantry Company, 1st Batt., 105th Reg., 1807; Artillery Company, 1808.

MOORE, SAMUEL
- 70th Reg., 1816-1818, 1823.

MOORE, THOMAS
- Capt. Fulkerson's Company, 2nd Batt., 105th Reg., 1808-1819, 1811, 1812.

MOORE, WILLIAM
- 70th Reg., 1834, 1835.

MOORE, ZACHARIAH
- 105th Reg., 1817.

MOPPIN, GEORGE
- 70th Reg., 1809, 1810.

MOPPIN, MORGAN
- 70th Reg., 1814, 1815, 1817, 1819, 1820.

MORELL, JACOB
- 1st Batt., 105th Reg., 1800; 70th Reg., 1815, 1822, 1824, 1827.

MORELL, JOHN
- 70th Reg., 1813, 1814; 105th Reg., 1822, 1823, 1826.

MORELL, LEWIS
- 105th Reg., 1822, 1823, 1827, 1828.

MORFORD, JOHN
- 2nd Bat., 70th Reg., 1798.

MORGAN, BENJAMIN
- Capt. Davis' Company, 2nd Batt., 105th Reg., 1809.

MORGAN, CHARLES
- 2nd Batt., 105th Reg., 1804.

MORGAN, ROBERT
- 105th Reg., 1817.

MORRIS, EPHRAIM
- Capt. Fulkerson's Compny, 2nd Batt., 105th Reg., 1810.

MORRIS, FAIRIS (FARIS)
- 70th Reg., 1814, 1817, 1827.

MORRIS, JAMES
- 105th Reg., 1817.

MORRIS, JOHN
- 70th Reg., 1801; Capt. Hayter's Company, 2nd Batt., 1803; Capt. Meek's Company, 1805.

MORRISON, DAVID
- 70th Reg., 1835.

MORRISON, JOHN
- 70th Reg., 1830-1832, 1835.

MORROW, DANIEL
- Capt. Fulkerson's Company, 2nd Batt., 105th Reg., 1808, 1809.

MOSS, WILLIAM
- 105th Reg., 1827.

MOUNTAIN, JAMES
- 105th Reg., 1817.

MULLINS, AUSTIN
- 70th Reg., 1822, 1823.

MULLINS, JOSEPH
- 70th Reg., 1812.

MULLINS, ROGER (RODDY)
- Light Infantry Company, 1st Batt., 105th Reg., 1809, 1812.

MULLINS, WILLIAM
- 105th Reg., 1811; 2nd Batt., 1812.

MULLIS, AMBROSE
- Capt. Larkey's Company, 2nd Batt., 105th Reg., 1806; Capt. Fulkerson's Company, 1808, 1809, 1810.

MUMPOWER, PETER
- Capt. Fulkerson's Company, 2nd Batt., 105th Reg., 1808.

MURPHEY, BAZEL
- 105th Reg., 1811.

MURPHEY, GEORGE
- 70th Reg., 1815-1819.

****

****

1820, 1822.

NELSON, REASON
- Capt. Bishop's Company, 1st Batt., 70th Reg., 1811.

NEWCOME, JOHN
- 105th Reg., 1826.

NEWCOME, RICHARD
- 70th Reg., 1819.

NEWHOUSE, ISAAC
- 70th Reg., 1799-1802.

NEWHOUSE, JAMES
- 70th Reg., 1801, 1802; Capt. Hayter's Company, 2nd Batt., 1803, 1805.

NEWHOUSE, JOHN
- 70th Reg., 1801; Capt. Hayter's Company, 2nd Batt., 1805, 1806. (1st Batt., 105th Reg., 1800.)

NEWLAND, JAMES
- 105th Reg., 1815, 1817, 1818.

NEWLIN, JAMES
- 1st Batt., 105th Reg., 1812, 1813.

NEWMAN, WILLIAM
- 70th Reg., 1814-1816.

NEWTON, GEORGE
- 105th Reg., 1833.

NEWTON, JOSEPH
- 70th Reg., 1824.

NEWTON, RICHARD
- 70th Reg., 1820.

NICELY, GEORGE
- 2nd Batt., 70th Reg., 1798; 2nd Batt., 105th Reg., 1799.

NICELY, JACOB
- 1st Sergeant, Rifle Company, 2nd Batt., 105th Reg., 1809.

NICELY, MARTIN
- 2nd Batt., 70th Reg., 1798; 2nd Batt., 105th Reg., 1799.

NICKLES (NICHOLS), JOHN
- 105th Reg., 1821.

NICKLES, MATHIAS
- Capt.George Byars' Company, 1st Batt., 70th Reg., 1811, 1813, 1814, 1816-1827, 1829, 1830.

NICKELSON, ESAU
- 70th Reg., 1809.

NICHOL, JOSIAH
- 1st Batt., 70th Reg., 1798.

NOBLE, WILLIAM
- 1st Batt., 105th Reg., 1812.

NORDYKE, BENAJA
- Rifle Company, 2nd Batt., 105th Reg., 1809.

NORMAN, JOSEPH
- Troop of Cavalry, 1st Batt., 105th Reg., 1809.

NORMAN, THOMAS
- 105th Reg., 1811.

NORRIS, WILLIAM
- Capt. Bradley's Company, 1st Batt., 105th Reg., 1808.

NORTHERN, REUBEN
- 70th Reg., 1798, 1801.

NORTON, NELSOM
- Capt. Campbell's Company, 70th Reg., 1805.

NOSEBALM, GEORGE
- 70th Reg., 1809.

NOVIS, WILLIAM
- Capt. Bradley's Company, 1st Batt., 105th Reg., 1807.

NUSOM, HARRISON
- 105th Reg., 1813.

NUTTY, JOHN
- 2nd Batt., 70th Reg., 1798; 1st Batt., 105th Reg., 1802; Capt. Hayter's Company, 2nd Batt., 70th Reg., 1803; Light Infantry Company, 105th Reg., 1807; Artillery Company, 1808, 1809.

OAK, LEVI
- 70th Reg., 1816.

O'BRYAN (O'BRIAN), CHARLES
- 105th Reg., 1834, 1835.

O'BRYAN, HALCOM
- 70th Reg., 1809.

****

PAFFORD, JOHN
- 70th Reg., 1821.

PAGE, JAMES H.
- 105th Reg., 1832.

PAINTER, GEORGE
- Rifle Company, 1st Batt., 105th Reg., 1829.

PAINTER, JACOB P.
- 105th Reg., 1820.

PAINTER, THOMAS
- 1st Batt., 105th Reg., 1803; Capt. Hayter's Company, 2nd Batt., 70th Reg., 1807.

PALMER, DAVID
- 105th Reg., 1832.

PALMER, JOSEPH
- 105th Reg., 1827.

PALMER, SAMUEL
- 1st Batt., 105th Reg., 1800.

PALMER, WILLIAM
- 1st Batt., 105th Reg., 1804.

PANDERGRASS, AARON
- 105th Reg., 1830.

PARKER, JOEL
- 70th Reg., 1802.

PARKER, JOHN
- 2nd Batt., 105th Reg., 1799.

PARKS, DAVID
- Capt. Berry's Company, 2nd Batt., 105th Reg., 1810.

PARMER, DAVID
- 105th Reg., 1811; 2nd Batt., 1812, 1813.

PARMER, WILLIAM
- 105th Reg., 1816.

PARSLEY, JAMES
- 70th Reg., 1818.

PARSLEY, JESSE
- 70th Reg., 1812-1814, 1816, 1820, 1821.

PARSLEY, JOSEPH
- 70th Reg., 1814.

PARSLEY, MOSES
- 70th Reg., 1816.

PARSLEY, SAMUEL
- 70th Reg., 1814, 1816.

PARSONS, JAMES
- 105th Reg., 1826.

PATRICK (PATERICK), HUGH
- 70th Reg., 1825-1827.

PATRICK, WILLIAM
- 70th Reg., 1826.

PATON, WILLIAM
- 70th Reg., 1817, 1819.

PATTERSON, ANDREW
- Capt. Edmiston's Company, 1st Batt., 70th Reg., 1807.

PATTERSON, WILLIAM
- 1st Batt., 105th Reg., 1806.

PEARSON, WALTER
- Troop of Cavalry, 1st Batt., 105th Reg., 1809.

PECK, JACOB
- 70th Reg., 1825, 1827.

PECK, MARTIN
- 70th Reg., 1818, 1820.

PECTOL, PETER
- 70th Reg., 1800; Capt. Talbert's Company, 2nd Batt., 1803.

PEEDLER, CHRISTOPHER
- Capt. Fulkerson's Company, 2nd Batt., 105th Reg., 1808.

PEMBERTON, WILLIAM C.
- 105th Reg., 1830.

PENDLETON, JOSEPH
- 70th Reg., 1801.

PENNINGTON, JAMES
- 70th Reg., 1821.

PEOPLES, HANCE
- 105th Reg., 1811.

PERKEBILE, FRANKLIN
- 70th Reg., 1835.

PERKINS, SAMUEL
- 70th Reg., 1799.

****

PERNELL, JAMES
- 70th Reg., 1810.

PERRIGEN, JACOB
- 70th Reg., 1812-1814.

PERRIGEN, JOHN
- Capt. Goodson's Company, 2nd Batt., 105th Reg., 1808, 1818, 1819.

PERRIGEN, THOMAS
- Capt. Goodson's Company, 2nd Batt., 105th Reg., 1806.

PERSON, THEODORE G.
- 70th Reg., 1824.

PETERS, HENRY
- Capt. Larkey's Company, 2nd Batt., 105th Reg., 1806.

PETERS, JACOB
- 2nd Batt., 105th Reg., 1799, 1802.

PETERS, JOHN
- 2nd Batt., 70th Reg., 1798; 2nd Batt., 105th Reg., 1799.

PETRIE, ALEXANDER
- Capt. Fulton's Company, 1st Batt., 70th Reg., 1811.

PHAUP, JOHN
- Capt. Duff's Troop of Cavalry, 1st Batt., 105th Reg., 1810; 70th Reg., 1813.

PHELPS, JAMES
- 70th Reg., 1821.

PHELPS, JOHN
- Capt. Bradley's Company, 1st Batt., 105th Reg., 1808.

PHELPS, MARTIN
- Artillery Company, 105th Reg., 1815.

PHELPS, ROBERT
- 105th Reg., 1811.

PHELPS, SAMUEL
- 1st Batt., 105th Reg., 1804; Capt. Bradley's Company, 1808.

PHELPS, VALENTIN
- Rifle Company, 2nd Batt., 105th Reg., 1809.

PHELTY, MICHAEL
- 105th Reg., 1813.

PHILLIPS, GEORGE
- 70th Reg., 1827, 1830.

PHILLIPS, JAMES
- 70th Reg., 1800.

PHILLIPS, JOHN
- Capt. Talbert's Company, 2nd Batt., 70th Reg., 1803.

PHILLIPS, JONATHAN
- 70th Reg., 1813.

PHILLIPS, MARTIN
- 70th Reg., 1816.

PHILLIPS, MOSES
- Capt. Gillenwaters' Company, 2nd Batt., 105th Reg., 1806.

PHILLIPS, WILLIAM
- 1st Batt., 70th Reg., 1798, 1799; Capt. Campbell's Company, 1805; Rifle Company, 2nd Batt., 105th Reg., 1809; 70th Reg., 1820.

PHIPPS, ALFRED
- 105th Reg., 1831.

PHIPPS, DAVID
- 70th Reg., 1801.

PHIPPS, GASPER
- 70th Reg., 1818.

PHIPPS, HIRIAM
- 70th Reg., 1829.

PHIPPS, ISAAC
- 105th Reg., 1817, 1818.

PICKLE, CHRISTOPHER
- 70th Reg., 1822.

PICKLE, HENRY
- 70th Reg., 1822.

PICKLE, JACOB
- 1st Batt., 105th Reg., 1801, 1803; Capt. Martin's Company, 1806; Rifle Company, 1829.

PICKLE, JOHN
- Capt. Campbell's Company, 70th Reg., 1805, 1809, 1820, 1822.

PICKLE, JONAS
- 70th Reg., 1827.

PICKLE, JOSEPH

****

- 70th Reg., 1822.

PICKLE, SOLOMON
- 70th Reg., 1826, 1827.

PIERCE, EDWARD
- 105th Reg., 1811.

PIERCE, JOHN
- Capt. Talbert's Company, 2nd Batt., 70th Reg., 1803.

PIERCELY, JOSEPH
- Capt. Lyon's Compny, 70th Reg., 1804.

PIERSAY, ISHAM
- Capt. Martin's Company, 105th Reg., 1808

PEIRSON, WALTER
- Capt. Bradley's Company, 1st Batt., 105th Reg., 1807; Capt. Houston's Troop of Cavalry, 1808, 1809.

PILLAR, WILLIAM E.
- Capt. Hinds' Company, 2nd Batt., 70th Reg., 1806.

PIPER, DAVID
- 70th Reg., 1830.

PIPER, DUDLEY
- 70th Reg., 1802.

PIPER, DUDLEY C.
- Capt. Lyon's Company, 70th Reg., 1804; 2nd Batt., 1805; Capt. Beatie's Company, 1807, 1809.

PIPER, JAMES
- 105th Reg., 1811; 1st Batt., 1812, 1813, 1817, 1821, 1825, 1827.

PIPER, SAMUEL
- 70th Reg., 1824, 1829.

PIPER, THOMAS
- 70th Reg., 1818.

PIPER, WILLIAM
- 70th Reg., 1820, 1822, 1830.

PIPPIN, WILLIAM
- 105th Reg., 1832.

PIPPIN, ZACHARIAH
- 105th Reg., 1829.

PITTS, ELIJAH (ABIJAH)
- 2nd Batt., 105th Reg., 1812, 1813, 1821, 1823.

PLUMMER, JAMES
- 70th Reg., 1825-1827, 1829.

POE, JOHN
- 105th Reg., 1833.

POFF, HENRY
- Capt. Goff's Company, 2nd Batt., 105th Reg., 1809, 1811-1813.

POINTS, JAMES
- 105th Reg., 1822.

POLLY, WILLIAM
- 70th Reg., 1799.

POOL, JOHN
- 105th Reg., 1816.

POQUE, JOHN
- 105th Reg., 1805.

PORCH, EZEKIEL
- 105th Reg., 1818.

PORTERFIELD, CHARLES
- Troop of Cavalry, 1st Batt., 105th Reg., 1809.

PORTERFIELD, JOHN
- 1st Batt., 105th Reg., 1801.

PORTERFIELD, ROBERT
- 70th Reg., 1824, 1824, 1829, 1830.

POSTON, ALEXANDER B.
- 70th Reg., 1817, 1826.

POSTON, ELIAS
- 70th Reg., 1800, 1802; Capt. Talbert's Company, 1804; Capt. Hinds' Company, 2nd Batt., 1806, 1825.

POSTON, FIELDER
- Capt. Houston's Troop of Cavalry, 2nd Batt., 105th Reg., 1807.

POSTON, HATCH D.
- 70th Reg., 1820, 1821, 1823, 1826, 1830.

POSTON, ISAAC
- 70th Reg, 1815-1817, 1823-1826, 1830.

POSTON, JAMES
- 70th Reg., 1835.

POSTON, JOHN W.
- Capt. Irby's Company, 2nd Batt., 70th Reg., 1803.

****

****

RADER (READER), CHARLES
- 70th Reg., 1813-1815.

RADER, HENRY
- Capt. Miller's Company, 2nd Batt., 70th Reg., 1811.

RADER, JOHN
- 70th Reg., 1814, 1815.

RAEBOURNE, JOHN
- Capt. Martin's Company, 1st Batt., 105th Reg., 1810.

RAIMY (RAINEY), OWEN
- Capt. George Byars' Company, 1st Batt., 70th Reg., 1811, 1812.

RAMBOUGH, JOHN
- Capt. Martin's Company, 1st Batt., 105th Reg., 1806.

RAMSEY, BUTLER
- 105th Reg., 1815.

RAMSEY, HIRAM
- Rifle Company, 1st Batt., 105th Reg., 1829.

RAMSEY, JESSEE
- Rifle Company, 1st Batt., 105th Reg., 1829, 1832.

RAMSEY, JOHN
- Capt. Martin's Company, 105th Reg., 1808, 1813, 1815, 1817, 1818.

RAMSEY, MARTIN
- Capt. Martin's Company, 1st Batt., 105th Reg., 1809, 1814.

RAMSEY, WILLIAM
- 105th Reg., 1827, 1828, 1830, 1831, 1834.

RANDSHAW, JAMES
- Artillery Company, 105th Reg., 1809.

RATHBONES, HENRY A.
- 105th Reg., 1824.

REAGAL, JOHN
- Capt. Bradley's Company, 105th Reg., 1808

REAGAN, NICHOLAS
- 70th Reg., 1799, 1802, 1809.

REAGAN, WILLIAM
- Capt. Bradley's Company, 1st Batt., 105th Reg., 1807; Light Infantry Company, 1808, 1809; Capt. Edmondson's Company, 1809.

REAMY, BUTLER
- Capt. Fulkerson's Company, 2nd Batt., 105th Reg., 1809; 1st Batt., 1812.

REAMY, JAMES
- 1st Batt., 70th Reg., 1798, 1799.

REAMY, JEREMIAH
- 2nd Batt., 70th Reg., 1798; 2nd Batt., 105th Reg., 1799, 1802, 1804; Capt. Fulkerson's Company, 1808, 1809.

REAMY, JOHN
- 1st Batt., 70th Reg., 1798.

REAMY, WILLIAM
- 1st Batt., 70th Reg., 1798, 1800.

REBECK (?), MICHAEL
- 70th Reg., 1816.

REDPATH, JAMES
- 2nd Batt., 70th Reg., 1798.

REDSHAW, WILLIAM
- 70th Reg., 1802; Capt. Edmiston's Company, 1st Batt., 1803.

REDWINE, ROLAN R. (?)
- 70th Reg., 1833.

REECE, JESSE
- Capt. Meek's Company, 1st Batt., 70th Reg., 1806.

REED, ARTHUR
- 70th Reg., 1818.

REED, BENJAMIN
- 70th Reg., 1833.

REED, JAMES
- Troop of Cavalry, 1st Batt., 105th Reg., 1809, 1810, 1811; 70th Reg., 1824.

REED, LAMBERT
- 1st Batt., 70th Reg., 1798.

REES, DAVID
- Artillery Company, 105th Reg., 1808; 1st Batt., 1810.

REES, JORDAN
- 105th Reg., 1811.

REESE, WILLIAM
- 105th Reg., 1834.

REID, DRURY

****

- Capt. George Byars' Company, 1st Batt., 70th Reg., 1807.

REID, HARVEY
- 70th Reg., 1827.

REID, JAMES
- 70th Reg., 1809.

REMINE, HIRAM
- 105th Reg., 1831.

RENSHAW, JAMES
- 1st Batt., 105th Reg., 1812; 70th Reg., 1835.

RENSHAW, ROBERT
- 70th Reg., 1834.

RENSHAW, WILLIAM
- 70th Reg., 1823.

REYNOLDS, ADIBIAH
- 70th Reg., 1834.

REYNOLDS, ANSON
- Capt. Campbell's Company, 1st Batt., 70th Reg., 1804.

REYNOLDS, DRAKE
- Capt. Lyon's Company, 70th Reg., 1804.

REYNOLDS, ELIAS
- Capt. Larkey's Company, 2nd Batt., 105th Reg., 1806.

REYNOLDS, HENRY
- 70th Reg., 1814, 1815.

RHEA, GEORGE G.
- Rifle Company, 1st Batt., 105th Reg., 1829.

RHEA, JAMES
- 105th Reg., 1824; Rifle Company, 1st Batt., 1829.

RHEA, JOHN
- Capt. Edmiston's Company, 1st Batt., 105th Reg., 1810.

RHEA, JOSEPH
- 2nd Batt., 105th Reg., 1800, 1828

RHEA, JOSEPH C.
- Rifle Company, 1st Batt., 105th Reg., 1829.

RHEA, WILLIAM
- Capt. Goodson's Company, 2nd Batt., 105th Reg., 1808.

RHOR (ROHR), PHILIP
- 105th Reg., 1825-1827, 1833, 1834.

RICE, AUGUSTUS
- 70th Reg., 1819.

RICE, JAMES
- Capt. Bradley's Company, 1st Batt., 105th Reg., 1809.

RICE, LEMUEL
- 70th Reg., 1814.

RICE, MOSES
- 70th Reg., 1819.

RICE, ORVILLE
- 70th Reg., 1818.

RICE, PRESLEY
- 70th Reg., 1809.

RICHARDS, AMOS
- 105th Reg., 1813.

RICHARDS, BAZEL
- Capt. Davis' Company, 2nd Batt., 105th Reg., 1809, 1810, 1812.

RICHARDS, DANIEL
- Capt. Bradley's Company, 105th Reg., 1808, 1813, 1815, 1818, 1826, 1827.

RICHARDS, ELIJAH
- 105th Reg., 1816.

RICHARDS, MATHEW
- 105th Reg., 1815.

RICHARDS, NATHAN
- Capt. Talbert's Company, 2nd Batt., 70th Reg., 1803.

RICHARDSON, BENJAMIN
- 70th Reg., 1809.

RICHARDSON, ISAAC
- 70th Reg., 1809, 1810; Capt. Tate's Company, 2nd Batt., 1811, 1812.

RICHARDSON, JESSEE
- Capt. Tate's Company, 2nd Batt., 70th Reg., 1811, 1812, 1814.

RICHARDSON, JOHN
- 70th Reg., 1813; 105th Reg., 1818; Rifle Company, 1st Batt., 1829; 70th Reg., 1835; 105th Reg., 1835.

****

RICHARDSON, NATHAN
- 70th Reg., 1802, 1809.

RICHMOND, DAVID
- 2nd Batt., 70th Reg., 1798.

RICKERT, JACOB
- 1st Batt., 105th Reg., 1806.

RICKERT, LEONARD
- Capt. Larkey's Company, 2nd Batt., 105th Reg., 1806.

RIDDLE, ANTHONY
- 70th Reg., 1815.

RIGGS, CHARLES
- 70th Reg., 1801.

RILEY, ABRAM
- 70th Reg., 1809.

RILEY, ANDREW
- 70th Reg., 1815.

RILEY, CHARLES
- 70th Reg., 1819.

RILEY, WILLIAM
- 70th Reg., 1809, 1812.

RINEY, ANDREW
- 70th Reg., 1835.

RINGLEY, ELIJAH
- 105th Reg., 1832.

RINGLEY, LEWIS
- 105th Reg., 1832.

RIPPY (?), HENRY
- 70th Reg., 1801.

RITZY, PETER
- 1st Batt., 105th Reg., 1801-1803.

ROACH, JAMES
- 105th Reg., 1815, 1819.

ROACH, WILLIAM
- 2nd Batt., 70th Reg., 1798.

ROADY, ELIAS
- Rifle Company, 1st Batt., 105th Reg., 1829.

ROAPER, THOMAS E.
- 105th Reg., 1833.

ROARK, JAMES W.
- 70th Reg., 1830.

ROBERTS, AARON
- 2nd Batt., 70th Reg., 1798.

ROBERTS, AUSWELL
- 70th Reg., 1824, 1830.

ROBERTS, BAZIL
- 70th Reg., 1809.

ROBERTS, BENJAMIN
- 105th Reg., 1832.

ROBERTS, BILLINGS
- 70th Reg., 1817.

ROBERTS, BILLINGSBY
- 70th Reg., 1820, 1825-1827, 1830.

ROBERTS, ISAAC
- Capt. Tate's Company, 2nd Batt., 70th Reg., 1811.

ROBERTS, JAMES
- 70th Reg., 1835.

ROBERTS, JOHN
- 70th Reg., 1799, 1802; 105th Reg., 1816; 70th Reg., 1819, 1821; 105th Reg., 1834.

ROBERTS, PAWL
- 2nd Sergeant, Artillery Company, 105th Reg., 1815.

ROBERTS, SAMUEL
- 105th Reg., 1815, 1828.

ROBERTS, WILLIAM
- Capt. Beatie's Company, 2nd Batt., 70th Reg., 1806.

ROBERTSON, MAJOR
- 2nd Batt., 105th Reg., 1812.

ROBERTSON, WILLIAM
- 2nd Batt., 105th Reg., 1812.

ROBESON, ALEXANDER, SR.
- Capt. Edmiston's Company, 1st Batt., 70th Reg., 1807, 1830.

ROBINSON (ROBISON), JOHN
- 2nd Batt., 70th Reg., 1798; 1st Batt., 105th Reg., 1799.

ROBINSON, MARK
- Rifle Company, 1st Batt., 70th Reg., 1807, 1817.

****

ROBINSON, MITCHEL
- 70th Reg., 1819, 1820.

ROBINSON, MOOR (MOAR)
- 70th Reg., 1824-1827, 1830.

ROBINSON, SAMUEL
- Rifle Company, 1st Batt., 70th Reg., 1807, 1812, 1813.

REDEFER, SAMUEL
- 105th Reg., 1834, 1835.

REDEFER, WILLIAM
- 105th Reg., 1830.

RODGERS, JOHN
- 1st Batt., 105th Reg., 1800.

RODGERS, JOSEPH
- 105th Reg., 1811.

RODGERS, WILLIAM
- 105th Reg., 1811.

ROE (OR ROC), BENJAMIN
- 1st Batt., 70th Reg., 1798.

ROE, EDMOND
- Rifle Company, 1st Batt., 70th Reg., 1807

ROE, JOHN
- Rifle Company, 1st Bat., 70th Reg., 1809, 1827, 1835.

ROGAN, GRIFFITH
- 105th Reg., 1819, 1820.

ROGERS, ACHILLES
- 105th Reg., 1820, 1821.

ROGERS, BENJAMIN
- 70th Reg., 1802.

ROGERS, DAVID
- 105th Reg., 1829.

ROGERS, GILBERT
- 105th Reg., 1825.

ROGERS, JOHN A.
- Light Infantry Company, 1st Batt., 105th Reg., 1809.

ROLAND (ROLAN), ARMSTRONG
- 70th Reg., 1829.

ROLAND, JOHN
- 70th Reg., 1826, 1829.

ROLAND, MICHAEL
- 70th Reg., 1822.

ROLAND, RILEY
- 70th Reg., 1820.

ROLAND, WILLIAM
- 70th Reg., 1802.

ROLLINS, HARRISON
- 105th Reg., 1819.

ROMANS, JACOB
- 70th Reg., 1816.

ROMANS, JOHN
- Capt. Byars' Company, 1st Batt., 70th Reg., 1807.

ROMANS, JOSEPH
- 70th Reg., 1802; Capt. Campbell's Company, 1st Batt., 1803.

ROMANS, JOSHUA, JR.
- Capt. Campbell's Company, 70th Reg., 1805; Capt. Byars' Company, 1st Batt., 1807, 1809, 1810.

ROMINE (?), HIRAM
- 70th Reg., 1835.

ROPER, THOMAS E.
- 105th Reg., 1830.

ROSE, GEORGE
- 105th Reg., 1835.

ROSE, JOHN E.
- Capt. Bradley's Company, 1st Batt., 105th Reg., 1810, 1811, 1812.

ROSENBUM, ANTHONY
- 1st Batt., 105th Reg., 1800, 1801.

ROSENBUM, JOHN
- 2nd Batt., 70th Reg., 1798.

ROSEBALM, DAVID
- 70th Reg., 1831.

ROSEBALM, JOHN
- Rifle Company, 1st Batt., 105th Reg., 1829.

ROSS, ANDREW
- 105th Reg., 1833.

ROSS, JAMES
- 105th Reg., 1835.

****

ROSS, JOHN
- 105th Reg., 1811; 1st Batt., 1812.

ROSS, JOSHUA
- 70th Reg., 1827.

ROULAND, JOHN
- Capt. Byars' Company, 1st Batt., 70th Reg., 1807.

ROUSE, EBAZER
- 70th Reg., 1823, 1830.

ROUSE, GEORGE
- Rifle Company, 1st Batt., 70th Reg., 1807

ROUSE, HENRY
- 70th Reg., 1829.

ROUSE, JACOB
- Rifle Company, 1st Batt., 70th Reg., 1807

ROUSE, JOHN
- Rifle Company, 1st Batt., 70th Reg., 1807

ROUSE, PAULSER
- Rifle Company, 1st Batt., 70th Reg., 1807, 1814, 1816, 1818.

ROUSE, PHILIP
- 70th Reg., 1815.

ROWAN, JAMES
- Artillery Company, 105th Reg., 1809, 1811

ROWAN, SAMUEL
- 70th Reg., 1809, 1815.

ROWAN, WILLIAM, JR.
- Capt. Meek's Company, 1st Batt., 70th Reg., 1805, 1806.

ROWE, GEORGE
- 2nd Batt., 105th Reg., 1799.

ROWLAND, JOHN
- 70th Reg., 1799.

ROWLAND, THOMAS
- 105th Reg., 1805; Capt. Houston's Troop of Cavalry, 2nd Batt., 1807, 1815.

ROWLAND, WILLIAM
- 70th Reg., 1800; Capt. Meek's Company, 1st Batt., 1803.

ROWMAN, JACOB
- 1st Batt., 70th Reg., 1798.

RUDDY, JOHN
- Capt. Martin's Company, 1st Batt., 105th Reg., 1807-1809.

RULEY, NICHOLAS H.
- 105th Reg., 1834, 1835.

RULEY, WILLIAM
- 105th Reg., 1827.

RUMUGE, DANIEL
- Artillery Company, 105th Reg., 1815.

RUNNELS, JOHN
- 70th Reg., 1819-1822.

RUSH, DAVID
- 105th Reg., 1819.

RUSH, JEREMIAH
- 1st Batt., 105th Reg., 1806; Capt. Dixon's Rifle Companyk, 1808, 1813.

RUSH, JOHN
- 105th Reg., 1822.

RUSSELL, CALAHAM
- 70th Reg., 1833.

RUSSELL, JAMES
- Capt. Gillenwaters' Company, 2nd Batt., 105th Reg., 1806, 1807.

RUSSELL, JOHN
- 2nd Batt., 70th Reg., 1798; 2nd Batt., 105th Reg., 1799; 70th Reg., 1826.

RUSSELL, JOSEPH
- 105th Reg., 1811; 2nd Batt., 1812, 1813.

RUSSELL, MICHAEL
- Capt. Irby's Company, 2nd Batt., 70th Reg., 1803.

RUST, JOHN
- 2nd Batt., 105th Reg., 1804.

RUTHERFORD, ROBERT
- 70th Reg., 1801.

RUTHERFORD, WILLIAM
- Rifle Company, 2nd Batt., 105th Reg., 1809, 1823.

RUTLEDGE, PETER
- 105th Reg., 1825.

RYAN, JAMES
- 105th Reg., 1820.

****

RYBURN, JAMES
- Rifle Company, 1st Batt., 105th Reg., 1829.

SACKETT, BENJAMIN F.
- 105th Reg., 1830.

SADDLER (SADLER), JAMES
- Capt. Talbert's Company, 2nd Batt., 70th Reg., 1803.

SADDLER, THOMAS
- 1st Batt., 70th Reg., 1798, 1800, 1801, 1802; 1st Batt., 105th Reg., 1803, 1804; Capt. Bradley's Company, 1806.

SAMPSON, RICHARD
- 70th Reg., 1802.

SANDERS, FREDERICK
- Capt. Fulkerson's Company, 2nd Batt., 105th Reg., 1810.

SANDERS, HAROLD
- 70th Reg., 1821, 1830.

SANDERS, JAMES
- 70th Reg., 1822.

SANDERS, JOHN
- 70th Reg., 1813, 1814, 1821-1823, 1825, 1826.

SANDERS, MOSES
- 70th Reg., 1809.

SANDERS, ROBERT
- 70th Reg., 1821, 1824, 1825.

SANDERS, WILLIAM
- 70th Reg., 1830.

SANDOE, GEORGE B.
- 105th Reg., 1827, 1829, 1830, 1833, 1834.

SANNS (?), JOHN
- 70th Reg., 1830.

SANTER, JOHN
- 1st Batt., 70th Reg., 1798.

SAUL, EDMOND
- 105th Reg., 1827, 1830.

SAUL, JAMES
- 105th Reg., 1835.

SAUL, SAMUEL
- 70th Reg., 1815, 1816, 1821.

SAWYERS, HARTWELL
- 105th Reg., 1813.

SAWYERS, ISAAC
- 70th Reg., 1825, 1826.

SAWYERS, JOHN
- 105th Reg., 1834.

SAWYERS, LEWIS
- 105th Reg., 1822, 1824.

SAYWELL, ABRAM
- 2nd Batt., 70th Reg., 1798.

SCANADY (?), ABRAM
- 105th Reg., 1815.

SCHOOLCRAFT, MICHAEL
- Capt. Tate's Company, 2nd Batt., 70th Reg., 1811; 105th Reg., 1820.

SCHOOLFIELD, DANIEL S.
- 105th Reg., 1829-1831.

SCHOOLFIELD, ENOCH
- 1st Batt., 105th Reg., 1803.

SCHOOLFIELD, SHEFFY
- 105th Reg., 1828.

SCOTT, AARON
- Capt. Bradley's Company, 1st Batt., 105th Reg., 1807, 1808.

SCOTT, ABIDIAH
- 70th Reg., 1815, 1835.

SCOTT, ALEXANDER
- 70th Reg., 1817, 1823, 1831.

SCOTT, ANDREW
- Capt. Beatie's Company, 2nd Batt., 70th Reg., 1807.

SCOTT, DANIEL
- 105th Reg., 1811.

SCOTT, HUGH
- Capt. Beatie's Company, 2nd Batt., 70th Reg., 1803, 1816.

SCOTT, JERIMIAH
- Troop of Cavalry, 105th Reg., 1812.

****

****

****

SHUFF, PAD
- 70th Reg., 1825, 1826.

SHUFFIELD, WHITNEY
- 105th Reg., 1831.

SHUGART, HENRY
- Capt. Berry's Company, 1st Batt., 105th Reg., 1806; Light Infantry Company, 1807; 70th Reg., 1827.

SHUGART, HENRY F.
- 70th Reg., 1821, 1823-1826.

SHUGART, MICHAEL
- 2nd Batt., 70th Reg., 1798; 1st Batt., 105th Reg., 1802; Capt. Berry's Company, 1806, 1807, 1810, 1814.

SHUGART, SAMUEL
- 70th Reg., 1819, 1824.

SHUTTERS, HENRY
- 2nd Batt., 105th Reg., 1812, 1818, 1819.

SHUTTERS, JACOB
- 2nd Batt., 105th Reg., 1802.

SILCOCK, RICHARD
- 70th Reg., 1829.

SIMERLY, WILLIAM
- 105th Reg., 1826.

SIMON, ANDREW F.
- 70th Reg., 1835.

SIMS, ELISHA
- 105th Reg., 1832, 1833.

SIMS, FRANCIS
- Capt. Campbell's Company, 1st Batt., 70th Reg., 1804.

SIMS, WILLIAM
- 105th Reg., 1831.

SIMPSON, BENJAMIN
- 2nd Batt., 105th Reg., 1801, 1802.

SIMPSON, FRANCIS C.
- 2nd Batt., 70th Reg., 1798.

SISK, ANSIL
- 70th Reg., 1812-1815, 1817-1820, 1830-1832.

SISK, JOHN
- 70th Reg., 1816.

SKENADY, ISAAC (see ISAAC SCANADY)
- 105th Reg., 1818, 1819.

SKIDMORE, JOHN (SR.)
- Light Infantry Company, 1st Batt., 105th Reg., 1807; Artillery Company, 1808.

SKINNER, SAMUEL
- 105th Reg., 1835.

SLAGLE, L.
- 105th Reg., 1833.

SLATON, WILLIAM
- 105th Reg., 1832.

SLEGAL, WILLIAM
- Capt. Gibson's Compan, 2nd Batt., 105th Reg., 1810.

SLUSHER, PHILIP
- Capt. Larkey's Company, 2nd Batt., 105th Reg., 1806.

SMALLWOOD, ZADDOCK
- Rifle Company, 1st Batt., 70th Reg., 1807.

SMEATHERS, JOHN
- 2nd Batt., 105th Reg., 1804, 1805.

SMILEY, JAMES
- 70th Reg., 1809; Capt. Bradley's Company, 1st Batt., 105th Reg., 1810; Capt. Tate's Company, 2nd Batt., 70th Reg., 1811, 1812, 1813, 1816, 1817.

SMILEY, JOHN
- 70th Reg., 1809, 1812.

SMITH (SMYTH), ALEXANDER
- 70th Reg., 1801; Capt. Campbell's Company, 1st Batt., 1803-1805; Capt. Byars' company, 1806, 1815.

SMITH, ALEXANDER
- 105th Reg., 1811, 1813, 1816, 1826.

SMITH, ANDREW
- Capt. Martin's Company, 105th Reg., 1808, 1820.

SMITH, ANTHONY
- Artillery Company, 105th Reg., 1815.

SMITH, BENJAMIN
- 1st Batt., 70th Reg., 1798, 1802; Capt. Talbert's Company, 2nd Batt., 1803; Capt. Campbell's Company, 1st Batt., 1804; Capt.

****

****

SMITH, PLEASANT
- 70th Reg., 1813, 1820, 1823, 1824.

SMITH, SAMUEL
- 70th Reg., 1802; Capt. Tate's Company, 2nd Batt., 1803.

SMITH, SAMUEL
- 105th Reg., 1818.

SMITH, THOMAS
- Capt. Fulkerson's Company, 2nd Batt., 105th Reg., 1810, 1811, 1812, 1813, 1818.

SMITH, THOMAS, JR.
- 105th Reg., 1819.

SMITH, THOMAS J.
- 105th Reg., 1824, 1828, 1833, 1834, 1835

SMITH, THOMAS W.
- 70th Reg., 1815.

SMITH, TOBIAS
- 105th Reg., 1818, 1821, 1823, 1824.

SMITH, TOBIAS
- 70th Reg., 1809; Capt. William Byars' Company, 1st Batt., 1811, 1813.

SMITH, WILLIAM
- Capt. Irby's Company, 2nd Batt., 70th Reg., 1801, 1805; Capt. Hayter's Company, 1806; Capt. James Scott's Company, 1811, 1813, 1820, 1826.

SMITH, WILLIAM
- 70th Reg., 1799, 1800, 1802; Capt. Tate's Company, 2nd Batt., 1805; Capt. Irby's Company, 1805.

SMITH, WILLIAM
- Capt. Fulkerson's Company, 2nd Batt., 105th Reg., 1808; Troop of Cavalry, 1st Batt., 1809; 2nd Batt., 1812, 1813, 1814, 1816, 1817.

SMITH, WILLIAM, JR.
- Capt. Hayter's Company, 2nd Batt., 70th Reg., 1807.

SMITH, WILLIAM A.
- 70th Reg., 1818.

SMITH, WILLIAM E.
- 70th Reg., 1833.

SMITH, WINDEL
- 105th Reg., 1826.

SMITH, WYAT
- 105th Reg., 1805; Capt. Jones' Company, 1st Batt., 1810, 1811.

SMOCK, JAMES
- Capt. Craig's Company, 70th Reg., 1805.

SMOCK, JAMES, JR.
- Rifle Company, 1st Batt., 70th Reg., 1807.

SMOCK, MATHIAS
- 70th Reg., 1799.

SMOTHERS, THOMAS
- 70th Reg., 1800.

SNEED (SNEAD), ADAM
- 70th Reg., 1831, 1832.

SNEED, BOLEN
- 70th Reg., 1820.

SNEED, HENRY
- 70th Reg., 1819-1821, 1823.

SNEED, JOHN
- Capt. Hinds' Company, 2nd Batt., 70th Reg., 1806.

SNEED, NICKERSON
- 105th Reg., 1820, 1821.

SNIDER, HENRY
- 2nd Batt., 105th Reg., 1804.

SNIDER, SOLOMON
- 2nd Batt., 105th Reg., 1803; 70th Reg., 1809.

SNIDER, THOMAS
- Capt. Campbell's Company, 70th Reg., 1805, 1809, 1810, 1814, 1816.

SNIDER, WILLIAM
- 105th Reg., 1834.

SNODDY, SAMUEL
- 105th Reg., 1823.

SNODGRASS, BENJAMIN
- 70th Reg., 1814.

SNODGRASS, DAVID
- 70th Reg., 1830, 1831.

SNODGRASS, FRANCIS
- 70th Reg., 1833.

SNODGRASS, HUGH

****

- 70th Reg., 1812.

SNODGRASS, JAMES M.
- 70th Reg., 1835.

SNODGRASS, JOSEPH
- Capt. Edmiston's Company, 1st Batt., 70th Reg., 1803, 1812, 1833.

SNODGRASS, ROBERT
- 70th Reg., 1816, 1817.

SNODGRASS, WILLIAM
- 70th Reg., 1818.

SOULE, RUFUS
- Light Infantry Company, 1st Batt., 105th Reg., 1809; Capt. Dixon's Rifle Company, 1811, 1812, 1813, 1815-1818.

SOURBEER, GEORGE
- 105th Reg., 1818.

SOURBEER, ISAAC
- 105th Reg., 1817, 1819, 1829.

SOURBEER, JACOB
- 105th Reg., 1821.

SOURBEER, JOHN
- 105th Reg., 1814-1816, 1819.

SPAHR, ISAAC
- 105th Reg., 1832.

SPARKS, ABSALOM
- Capt. Edmiston's Company, 1st Batt., 70th Reg., 1805-1807; Capt. Martin's Company, 105th Reg., 1808.

SPARKS, REUBEN H.
- 1st Batt., 105th Reg., 1806, 1811-1813, 1815, 1817-1819, 1821-1824.

SPARKS SAMUEL
- 70th Reg., 1809; 105th Reg., 1827.

SPARKS, SOLOMON
- Capt. Talbert's Company, 2nd Batt., 70th Reg., 1811, 1812, 1813, 1815, 1816, 1818, 1819.

SPARKS, WILLIAM
- 105th Reg., 1817.

SPEER (SPEAR, SPEERS), ARTHUR
- 70th Reg., 1833.

SPEER, JAMES
- 105th Reg., 1816.

SPEER, JAMES
- 70th Reg., 1809, 1812.

SPEER, JAMES, JR.
- 105th Reg., 1829, 1833.

SPEER, JOHN
- 1st Batt., 105th Reg., 1810; Rifle Company, 1829.

SPEER, JOHN
- 70th Reg., 1814.

SPEER, JOHN, JR.
- 70th Reg., 1815; 105th Reg., 1828; Rifle Company, 1st Batt., 1829.

SPEER, WILLIAM
- 1st Batt., 105th Reg., 1799; Rifle Company, 1829.

SPENCE, WILLIAM
- 70th Reg., 1822.

SPIRE, JOHN
- 105th Reg., 1822.

SPITZER, DANIEL
- 105th Reg., 1817-1820.

SPITZER, DANIEL, JR.
- 10th REg., 1830.

SPITZER, DAVID
- 105th Reg., 1830, 1831.

SPITZER, JOHN
- Capt. Berry's Company, 1st Batt., 105th Reg., 1806, 1830.

SPITZER, SAMUEL
- 105th Reg., 1828-1830.

SPITZER, STEPHEN
- 105th Reg., 1831.

SPIVEY, DANIEL
- 105th Reg., 1824.

SPOTTS, ADDISON A.
- 105th Reg., 1829.

SPOTTS, EPHRIM
- 70th Reg., 1819, 1820.

SPOTTS, FRANCIS P.
- 105th Reg., 1834.

SPOTTS, GEORGE

****

****

- 105th Reg., 1813, 1818, 1819.

STONE, WASHINGTON
- 105th Reg., 1827.

STONE, WILLIAM
- 1st Batt., 105th Reg., 1804.

STONER, MICHAEL
- Troop of Cavalry, 1st Batt., 105th Reg., 1809.

STOOP, ALEXANDER
- 70th Reg., 1821.

STOUT, DAVID
- 1st Batt., 105th Reg., 1806; Capt. Dixon's Rifle Company, 1808; Capt. Houston's Troop of Cavalry, 1808, 1809, 1811.

STOUT, JAMES
- Rifle Company, 1st Batt., 105th Reg., 1829.

STRONG, WILLIAM
- 2nd Batt., 105th Reg., 1799.

STROUP, PETER
- 105th Reg., 1825.

STURDEVAANT, MILHAM
- 105th Reg., 1835.

STURGEON, JAMES
- 105th Reg., 1831.

STURGEON, JOHN
- 70th Reg., 1810, 1813, 1814, 1820.

SUIT (SOUT), RANSOM (RANSON)
- 70th Reg., 1818, 1819.

SULLIVAN, JAMES
- 70th Reg., 1827; 105th Reg., 1829.

SULLIVAN, JOHN
- 70th Reg., 1824, 1827.

SURBER, ADAM
- Capt. Meek's Company, 1st Batt., 70th Reg., 1806; Capt. Tilson's Company, 1807; Rifle Company, 1807.

SURBER, ALFRED
- 70th Reg., 1833.

SURBER, HENRY
- Rifle Company, 1st Batt., 70th Reg., 1807.

STEWART, WILLIAM
- 70th Reg., 1817.

STICKLEY, GABRIEL
- 105th Reg., 1831, 1834, 1835.

STICKLEY, JOHN
- 105th Reg., 1835.

STIFFY, JOHN
- 70th Reg., 1801.

STILL, JESSE
- Capt. Berry's Company, 1st Batt., 105th Reg., 1808, 1809.

STILL, LEWIS
- 70th Reg., 1813-1815.

St. JOHN, ARTHUR
- 70th Reg., 1825.

St. JOHN, SAMUEL
- 70th Reg., 1814, 1816.

St. JOHN, WILLIAM
- 1st Batt., 70th Reg., 1798, 1801, 1815.

STOCKLEY, ISAM
- 1st Batt., 70th Reg., 1798.

STOFFLE (STUFFLE), ISAAC
- Capt. Goodson's Company, 2nd Batt., 105th Reg., 1806, 1807; ("Sr.") 1819, 1820, 1824.

STOFFLE, JACOB
- Capt. Goodson's Company, 2nd Batt., 105th Reg., 1806, 1807, 1833.

STOFFLE, PHELTY
- 105th Reg., 1814.

STONE, JAMES
- 1st Batt., 70th Reg., 1798, 1802; Capt. Smyth's Company, 2nd Batt., 1803.

STONE, JOHN
- 70th Reg., 1801, 1809; Capt. Miller's Company, 2nd Batt., 1811, 1812, 1813; 105th Reg., 1813.

STONE, JONATHAN
- 70th Reg., 1816.

STONE, LEWIS
- 105th Reg., 1811, 1813.

STONE, SAMUEL

****

****

TABORS, JESSEE
- 70th Reg., 1821.

TALBERT (TOLBERT), CHARLES
- 70th Reg., 1800, 1814.

TALBERT, JOHN
- 70th Reg., 1822, 1824.

TALBERT, JOSIAH
- 70th Reg., 1809, 1816.

TALBERT, MATTHEW
- 70th Reg., 1827.

TALBERT, THOMAS
- 70th Reg., 1815; 105th Reg., 1826; 70th Reg., 1830.

TALBERT, THOMAS S.
- 105th Reg., 1832, 1835.

TALBERT, WILLIAM
- 70th Reg., 1825, 1827.

TANCASTER, FOUNTAIN
- 70th Reg., 1817.

TANKERSLEY, JOHN R.
- Capt. Berry's Company, 1st Batt., 105th Reg., 1806.

TANKERSLEY, WILLIAM
- Troop of Cavalry, 1st Batt., 105th Reg., 1809, 1813, 1814.

TAPLEY, PETERSON
- 105th Reg., 1817.

TAPP, LEWIS
- 70th Reg., 1829.

TARIS, WILLIAM
- 70th Reg., 1801.

TARUS (?), JOHN
- 70th Reg., 1825.

TATE, CHARLES C.
- 105th Reg., 1827-1829.

TATE, GEORGE
- 70th Reg., 1814.

TATE, JOHN
- 70th Reg., 1802.

TATE, JOHN B.
- 70th Reg., 1830.

TATE, JOHN M.
- 70th Reg., 1820, 1821.

TATE, LEONIDAS H.
- 70th Reg., 1830.

TATE, SAMUEL
- 105th Reg., 1814; Artillery Company, 1815.

TATE, THOMAS
- 70th Reg., 1821, 1823.

TATE, WILLIAM C.
- Capt. Tate's Company, 2nd Batt., 70th Reg., 1811, 1812.

TAYLOR, BIRD
- 70th Reg., 1823.

TAYLOR, DAVID
- Capt. Craig's Company, 1st Batt., 70th Reg., 1803.

TAYLOR, HENRY
- 70th Reg., 1824.

TAYLOR, HENRY S.
- 70th Reg., 1830.

TAYLOR, JAMES
- Capt. Tate's Company, 2nd Batt., 70th Reg., 1811.

TAYLOR, JOHN
- 105th Reg., 1827, 1828, 1831.

TAYLOR, MICAJAH
- 70th Reg., 1811, 1831.

TAYLOR, NATHANIEL
- 105th Reg., 1813.

TAYLOR, SIMON (SIMION)
- 70th Reg., 1802; Capt. Talbert's Company, 2nd Batt., 1803.

TAYLOR, STEPHEN
- Capt. Talbert's Company, 2nd Batt., 70th Reg., 1803, 1807, 1811, 1812.

TAYLOR, THOMAS
- 70th Reg., 1809, 1812, 1814-1816; 105th Reg., 1816; 70th Reg., 1818-1820.

TAYLOR, WILLIAM
- 70th Reg., 1809, 1812, 1815-1817, 1820, 1821, 1825; 105th Reg., 1831.

TAYS, ROBERT

****

- Capt. Martin's Company, 105th Reg., 1808

TEATOR (TEETOR), JACOB
- 2nd Batt., 105th Reg., 1802; Capt. Fulkerson's Company, 1808-1810, 1811, 1815, 1818, 1822.

TEATOR, JOHN
- 2nd Batt., 105th Reg., 1802; Capt. Larkey's Company, 1806.

TEATOR, MARTIN
- 2nd Batt., 105th Reg., 1799, 1802, 1804.

TERRENCE, SAMUEL
- Capt. Berry's Company, 1st Batt., 105th Reg., 1810.

TERRY, ROWLAND
- 105th Reg., 1821, 1825.

THACKER, JOEL
- 70th Reg., 1817.

THACKER, JOSEPH
- Capt. Tate's Company, 2nd Batt., 70th Reg., 1811.

THACKER, RANDOLPH
- 70th Reg., 1817.

THARE, THOMPSON
- 105th Reg., 1819, 1820, 1822.

THOMAS, ABIJAH
- 70th Reg., 1812.

THOMAS, BENJAMIN
- 2nd Batt., 70th Reg., 1798.

THOMAS, DANIEL
- 70th Reg., 1820, 1822.

THOMAS, DAVID
- 70th Reg., 1800-1802; Capt. Craig's Company, 1804, 1830.

THOMAS, JACOB
- 70th Reg., 1823.

THOMAS, JOHN
- 2nd Batt., 105th Reg., 1804.

THOMAS, JOHN
- 1st Batt., 70th Reg., 1798, 1802; Capt. James Scott's Company, 2nd Batt., 1811, 1818, 1826.

THOMAS, JOHN B.
- 105th Reg., 1825, 1826.

THOMAS, JONATHAN
- 70th Reg., 1800; Capt. Craig's Company, 1st Batt., 1803, 1805.

THOMAS, LEWIS
- 70th Reg., 1818.

THOMAS, REUBEN
- Rifle Company, 1st Batt., 70th Reg., 1807, 1813.

THOMAS, THOMAS
- 1st Batt., 70th Reg., 1798, 1800, 1801; Capt. Byars' Company, 1st Batt., 1806, 1807.

THOMAS, WILLIAM
- 105th Reg., 1819; 70th Reg., 1835.

THOMPSON, ANDREW
- Capt. Beatie's Company, 70th Reg., 1804.

THOMPSON, EVAN S.
- 70th Reg., 1810; Capt. William Byars' Company, 1st Batt., 1811, 1812, 1813, 1816-1819, 1822-1824, 1830.

THOMPSON, GEORGE W.
- 105th Reg., 1814.

THOMPSON, GRANBERSON
- 70th Reg., 1832.

THOMPSON, JAMES
- Capt. Lyon's Company, 70th Reg., 1804; Capt. James Scott's Company, 2nd Batt., 1811, 1826.

THOMPSON, JAMES G.
- 70th Reg., 1835.

THOMPSON, JAMES P.
- 105th Reg., 1830; 70th Reg., 1833, 1834.

THOMPSON, JOHN
- Capt. George Byars' Company, 1st Batt., 70th Reg., 1811, 1812, 1818, 1826, 1827; 105th Reg., 1833.

THOMPSON, JOHN T.
- 105th Reg., 1834.

THOMPSON, MARK
- 70th Reg., 1802; Capt. Talbert's Company, 2nd Batt., 1803.

THOMPSON, MARTIN
- 70th Reg., 1809.

****

THOMPSON, MOSES
- 70th Reg., 1809, 1817, 1818.

THOMPSON, NICHOLAS
- Capt. Beatie's Company, 70th Reg., 1804, 1813.

THOMPSON, SHELDON
- 105th Reg., 1823-1825.

THOMPSON, WILLIAM
- Capt. Byars' Company, 1st Batt., 70th Reg., 1807.

THOMPSON, WILLIAM P.
- 70th Reg., 1815.

THORNBURGH, THOMAS
- Capt. Talbert's Company, 2nd Batt., 70th Reg., 1803; 1st Batt., 105th Reg., 1806; Light Infantry Company, 1809.

THURMAN, JOHN G. (?)
- 105th Reg., 1835.

TILSON, HELLINS (HILLINS)
- 70th Reg., 1825, 1827, 1829.

TILSON, LEMUEL
- Capt. Tilson's Company, 1st Batt., 70th Reg., 1807.

TILSON, RANSON
- 70th Reg., 1816.

TILSON, SAMUEL
- 70th Reg., 1802.

TILSON, STEPHEN
- 70th Reg., 1814.

TILSON, THOMAS
- 1st Batt., 105th Reg., 1812; 70th Reg., 1825.

TILSON, WILLIAM
- 70th Reg., 1824, 1829.

TIMMERMAN, ABRAM
- 105th Reg., 1817, 1818.

TINSLEY, FRANCIS
- Capt. Byars' Company, 1st Batt., 70th Reg., 1806.

TIPPET, WILLIAM
- 70th Reg., 1801; Capt. Beatie's Company, 1804; Capt. Tilson's Company, 1st Batt., 1806.

TIRRY, DANIEL
- 70th Reg., 1800.

TOBIN, NATHAN
- Capt. Edmondson's Company, 1st Batt., 105th Reg., 1810.

TODD, JOHN N.
- 105th Reg., 1815.

TODD, THOMAS
- Capt. Craig's Company, 1st Batt., 70th Reg., 1803.

TOMASS (?), ISAAC
- Rifle Company, 1st Batt., 70th Reg., 1807.

TOMASS, JOHN
- Rifle Comapny, 1st Batt., 70th Reg., 1807.

TOMBLIN (TUMBLIN), THOMAS
- 70th Reg., 1826; 105th Reg., 1829.

TOMBLESON, ERASTIS
- 70th Reg., 1815, 1816.

TOMBLINSON, JABIAS
- 70th Reg., 1827, 1830.

TOMBLINSON, JAMES
- 105th Reg., 1805; Artillery Company, 1808, 1811.

TOMBLINSON, WILLIAM
- 70th Reg., 1817.

TONCRAY, EZRA
- 1st Batt., 105th Reg., 1803.

TONCRAY, GOODSON
- 105th Reg., 1828.

TONCRAY, JAMES
- 105th Reg., 1821.

TONCRAY, JOHN
- Capt. Bradley's Company, 1st Batt., 105th Reg., 1806, 1811, 1812.

TOOL, ARCHIBALD
- 70th Reg., 1801.

TOOL, ARTHUR
- 70th Reg., 1809.

TOOL, JOHN
- Capt. Logan's Company, 2nd Batt., 70th Reg., 1811, 1812.

****

****

****

WALLIS, WILLIAM
- 70th Reg., 1809, 1812.

WALTON, JOHN
- 105th Reg., 1815.

WALTRIP (WALTRAP), JAMES
- Capt. Tate's Company, 2nd Batt., 70th Reg., 1811, 1813.

WAMPLER, MICHAEL
- 70th Reg., 1826.

WARD, DANIEL
- 105th Reg., 1819.

WARFIELD, JOHN
- Capt. Goodson's Company, 2nd Batt., 105th Reg., 1807.

WARHAM, JOHN
- 70th Reg., 1802.

WARHAM, ROBERT
- Capt. Talbert's Company, 2nd Batt., 70th Reg., 1803.

WARMSLY, THOMAS
- Capt. Hinds' Company, 2nd Batt., 70th Reg., 1806.

WARNER, THOMAS
- 1st Batt., 105th Reg., 1804, 1805.

WARRAN, JOHN
- 105th Reg., 1805; Capt. Berry's Company, 1st Batt., 1809.

WARREN, BAZIL
- Capt. Beatie's Company, 70th Reg., 1804; Capt. Dixon's Rifle Company, 105th Reg., 1808; Capt. James Scott's Company, 2nd Batt., 70th Reg., 1811; 105th Reg., 1818, 1819, 1823, 1828.

WARREN, CLARK
- 70th Reg., 1821.

WARREN, WALTER
- Artillery Company, 105th Reg., 1815; 1822.

WASHAM, JOSEPH
- 1st Batt., 70th Reg., 1798, 1800, 1802; Capt. Smyth's Company, 2nd Batt., 1803, 1814, 1815, 1821.

WASHAM, ROBERT
- 70th Reg., 1802, 1810.

WASHAM, THOMAS
- 70th Reg., 1814, 1815, 1818.

WASHAM, WILLIAM
- 70th Reg., 1812.

WATKINS, BENJAMIN
- Capt. Tilson's Company, 1st Batt., 70th Reg., 1803; Capt. Campbell's Company, 1804.

WATKINS, WALKER
- 105th Reg., 1822.

WATSON, DAVID
- 70th Reg., 1822; Rifle Company, 1st Batt., 105th Reg., 1829.

WATSON, EDWARD S.
- 105th Reg., 1834.

WATSON, JAMES ("Laurel")
- Rifle Company, 1st Batt., 105th Reg., 1829, 1831.

WATSON, JOHN
- 70th Reg., 1825; 105th Reg., 1828.

WATSON, JOHN W. C.
- 105th Reg., 1834, 1835.

WATSON, JOSIAH
- 70th Reg., 1814.

WATSON, ROBERT
- Rifle Company, 1st Batt., 105th Reg., 1829.

WATSON, THOMAS
- 70th Reg., 1801, 1802, 1812.

WATTERS, JOHN
- 105th Reg., 1825.

WAYMIRE, HENRY
- 70th Reg., 1817.

WAYMIRE, VALENTINE
- Capt. Edmiston's Company, 1st Batt., 70th Reg., 1807.

WEACHAM, JOSHUA
- 105th Reg., 1835.

WEARUM (?), DAVID
- 105th Reg., 1834.

WEAVER, JACOB
- Capt. Fulkerson's Company, 2nd Batt., 105th Reg., 1808.

****

WEAVER, JOHN
- Capt. Fulkerson's Company, 2nd Batt., 105th Reg., 1808.

WEAVER, JOHN, JR.
- Capt. Fulkerson's Company, 2nd Batt., 105th Reg., 1808.

WEBB, HENRY
- 70th Reg., 1814, 1815; 105th Reg., 1817.

WEBB, HENRY
- 105th Reg., 1820, 1821.

WEBB, JOHN
- 70th Reg., 1835.

WEDDING, AUGUSTUS
- 70th Reg., 1830-1832, 1834.

WEISE, WILLIAM
- 105th Reg., 1824, 1825.

WELCH, WILLIAM
- 70th Reg., 1800.

WELE, HARRY
- 70th Reg., 1813.

WELLS, ANDREW
- 105th Reg., 1824.

WELLS, JAMES
- 70th Reg., 1826, 1830.

WELLS, JOHN
- 70th Reg., 1800.

WELSH, WILLIAM
- Capt. Bradley's Company, 105th Reg., 1808.

WERT, ADAM
- 70th Reg., 1815, 1816.

WERT, GEORGE
- 70th Reg., 1809, 1810.

WERT, WILLIAM
- 70th Reg., 1809.

WEST, ISAAC
- Capt. Fulkerson's Company, 2nd Batt., 105th Reg., 1809.

WEST, JOEL
- Capt. Hayter's Company, 2nd Batt., 70th Reg., 1807.

WEST, JOHN
- Capt. Berry's Company, 1st Batt., 105th Reg., 1810.

WEST, OBEDIAH
- 105th Reg., 1816.

WHALEY, HERCULES
- 2nd Batt., 70th Reg., 1798.

WHEELER, CHARLES
- 70th Reg., 1815.

WHEELER, DAVID
- Capt. Campbell's Company, 1st Batt., 70th Reg., 1804; Rifle Company, 1807.

WHEELER, FRANCIS
- 70th Reg., 1822.

WHEELER, JAMES, JR.
- Capt. Campbell's Company, 70th Reg., 1804.

WHEELER, JESSE
- 70th Reg., 1799, 1801.

WHEELER, JOHN
- 70th Reg., 1802, 1817, 1819.

WHEELER, OLIVER
- 70th Reg., 1799; Rifle Company, 1st Batt., 1807, 1812, 1820, 1826.

WHEELER, WILLIAM
- 1st Batt., 70th Reg., 1798, 1812.

WHISTENHUNT, PETER
- 2nd Batt., 70th Reg., 1798.

WHITE, ABRAHAM
- 70th Reg., 1800, 1802.

WHITE, ALEXANDER
- 1st Batt., 105th Reg., 1812, 1813-1815.

WHITE, BLOOMER
- 105th Reg., 1835.

WHITE, CLAIBORNE
- 105th Reg., 1815-1817.

WHITE, DAVID
- 1st Batt., 70th Reg., 1798, 1800, 1801.

WHITE, EDWARD
- 70th Reg., 1826.

WHITE, HUGH
- 105th Reg., 1828, 1829, 1834, 1835.

****

WHITE, JAMES
- 1st Batt., 105th Reg., 1800.

WHITE, JAMES
- 70th Reg., 1825, 1827.

WHITE, JAMES L.
- 105th Reg., 1835.

WHITE, JOHN
- 70th Reg., 1800, 1817, 1818.

WHITE, JOHN
- 1st Batt., 105th Reg., 1800, 1817.

WHITE, JOSEPH
- Artillery Company, 105th Reg., 1815; 70th Reg., 1820, 1821, 1826.

WHITE, MOSES
- 70th Reg., 1812, 1817.

WHITE, RICHARD
- 70th Reg., 1826.

WHITE, RICHARD, JR.
- 105th Reg., 1816-1819.

WHITE, ROBERT
- 1st Batt., 105th Reg., 1800; Capt. Beatie's Company, 2nd Batt., 70th Reg., 1807.

WHITE, SAMUEL
- 1st Batt., 105th Reg., 1812, 1813.

WHITE, THOMAS
- 105th Reg., 1835.

WHITE, WILLIAM
- Capt. Hayter's Company, 2nd Batt., 70th Reg., 1806, 1807, 1809.

WHITE, WILLIAM
- 105th Reg., 1813; Artillery Company, 1815, 1817.

WHITE, WILLIAM J.
- 105th Reg., 1811; 70th Reg., 1815.

WHITE, WILLIAM Y. C.
- 105th Reg., 1835.

WHITEHEAD, AARON
- 70th Reg., 1827.

WHTIEHEAD, FRANCIS
- 1st Batt., 70th Reg., 1798.

WHITEHEAD, MOSES
- 70th Reg., 1824.

WHITEHOUSE, GEORGE
- 70th Reg., 1819, 1820.

WHITESIDES, SAMUEL
- 1st Batt., 105th Reg., 1803.

WHITAKER (WHITIKER), AARON
- 70th Reg., 1815, 1818, 1819, 1823.

WHITAKER, BENJAMIN
- 70th Reg., 1815, 1818, 1820.

WHITAKER, ISAAC
- Light Infantry Company, 1st Batt., 105th Reg., 1809.

WHITAKER, JAMES
- 70th Reg., 1809, 1825, 1827, 1830.

WHITAKER, JOHN
- 70th Reg., 1809, 1819, 1820.

WHITLEY, GEORGE
- 70th Reg., 1824, 1827, 1830.

WHITLEY, JOHN
- Capt. Tate's Company, 2nd Batt., 70th Reg., 1811.

WHITLEY, ROBERT
- 1st Batt., 70th Reg., 1798.

WHITLEY, SAMUEL
- 70th Reg., 1820, 1821, 1823-1827, 1830.

WHITESIDE, ABRAM
- 2nd Batt., 70th Reg., 1798.

WICKAM, JOHN
- Troop of Cavalry, 1st Batt., 105th Reg., 1809.

WICKHAM, WILLIAM
- Capt. Rhea's Company, 2nd Batt., 105th Reg., 1809.

WICKLIFF, JOHN
- 70th Reg., 1812.

WIDENER, ABRAM
- 70th Reg., 1826, 1833, 1835.

WIDENER, ISAAC
- Rifle Company, 1st Batt., 105th Reg., 1829.

WIDENER, JACOB

****

- Rifle Company, 1st Batt., 70th Reg., 1807, 1827, 1831, 1833.

WIDENER, JOHN
- Rifle Company, 1st Batt., 70th Reg., 1807.

WILCOX, JOHN
- 2nd Batt., 105th Reg., 1802; Capt. Larkey's Company, 1806; Capt. Fulkerson's Company, 1808.

WILDER, HARDIN
- 105th Reg., 1824, 1826; Rifle Company, 1st Batt., 1829.

WILDER, JAMES
- Capt. Martin's Company, 1st Batt., 105th Reg., 1806; Rifle Company, 1829.

WILDER, LEMUEL
- 105th Reg., 1825; Rifle Company, 1st Batt., 1829, 1830; 70th Reg., 1834.

WILES, BANASTER
- 70th Reg., 1816.

WILES, HAYBURN
- 70th Reg., 1817, 1818.

WILEY, ALFRED
- 105th Reg., 1830.

WILEY, JAMES
- Capt. Tate's Company, 2nd Batt., 70th Reg., 1807.

WILEY, JOHN N.
- 105th Reg., 1833.

WILEY, WILLIAM
- 70th Reg., 1809.

WILKERSON, HENRY
- Capt. Fulkerson's Company, 2nd Batt., 105th Reg., 1808, 1811.

WILKINSON (WILKERSON), THOMAS
- 70th Reg., 1802; Capt. Tate's Company, 2nd Batt., 1803.

WILLIAMS, DAVID
- Light Infantry Company, 1st Batt., 105th Reg., 1807; Artillery Company, 1808-1810, 1811, 1812.

WILLIAMS, ELIAS
- 70th Reg., 1817.

WILLIAMS, ELIJAH
- 70th Reg., (Capt. Craig's Company, 1st Batt.), 1803, 1804, 1812, 1814, 1816, 1817

WILLIAMS, GEORGE
- 70th Reg., 1800; Capt. Hayter's Company, 2nd Batt., 1805; Light Infantry Company, 1st Batt., 105th Reg., 1807, 1808; Troop of Cavalry, 1809.

WILLIAMS, HENRY
- 70th Reg., 1802, 1812.

WILLIAMS, JAMES
- 70th Reg., 1822; 105th Reg., 1822.

WILLIAMS, JOHN
- 2nd Batt., 105th Reg., 1802, 1805; Capt. Larkey's Company, 1806; Capt. Fulkerson's Company, 1808, 1811, 1812.

WILLIAMS, JOHN
- 70th Reg., 1815, 1823, 1824, 1831.

WILLIAMS, JOHN
- 105th Reg., 1834.

WILLIAMS, JOSEPH
- Capt. Campbell's Company, 70th Reg., 1805.

WILLIAMS, LEVI
- 105th Reg., 1834, 1835.

WILLIAMS, PETER
- 70th Reg., 1800, 1802, 1810.

WILLIAMS, RICHARD
- Capt. Campbell's Company, 1st Batt., 70th Reg., 1803-1805, 1809.

WILLIAMS, RUFUS
- 105th Reg., 1834.

WILLIAMS, WILLIAM
- 105th Reg., 1814; 70th Reg., 1815.

WILLIAMS, WILLIAM S.
- 105th Reg., 1815, 1818, 1820.

WILLIAMS, WILLOUGHBY
- 105th Reg., 1818.

WILLIAMSON, GEORGE
- 105th Reg., 1832.

WILLIS, JAMES
- 70th Reg., 1825.

WILLIS, JOHN
- 70th Reg., 1816, 1817, 1819.

****

****

****

****

ZINNINGS, WILLIAM
- Capt. Talbert's Company, 2nd Batt., 70th Reg., 1803.

www.ingramcontent.com/pod-product-compliance
Lightning Source LLC
LaVergne TN
LVHW061246100826
845148LV00008B/1037

9780788477935